D1871763

DECENTRALISATION, PARTICIPATION AND GOVERNANCE

DECENTRALISATION, PARTICIPATION AND GOVERNANCE

PRABHAT DATTA

Publications

KALPAZ PUBLICATIONS
DELHI-110052

Decentralisation, Participation and Governance

Rs. 750

ISBN: 81-7835-394-6

© Prabhat Datta

All rights reserved. No part of this book may be reproduced in any manner without written permission.

Published in 2006 in India by
Kalpaz Publications
C-30, Satyawati Nagar, Delhi-110052
E-mail : kalpaz@hotmail.com

Laser Typesetting at : Master Computers, Delhi
Printed at : Salasar Imaging System, Delhi

To my young Friends

Moinul (Hasan)

&

Abhik (Dutta)

Contents

Introduction

It is a collection of ten articles on the key issues of local good governance in India in general and West Bengal, in particular. Good governance has been viewed from different perspectives. The World Bank which has popularised the concept in recent times, defines good governance as "the manner in which power is exercised in the management of the country's economic and social resources for development". In the perception of World Bank there are four major components namely, public sector management, accountability, legal framework of development, information and transparency. Beyond this narrow technocratic view, there is another perspective developed by the Human Development Report, 2002, where the emphasis is on democratic governance. This broader human development perspective guides the concept of good governance as developed in this book. The first article seeks to explore analytical and methodological issues in the context of local politics and decentralisation for poverty reduction. It attempts to identify and examine the linkages between local political decentralisation and poverty reduction policies and discusses how to study and analyse them. Although there are references to international experiences care has been taken to relate the issues to the situations in our country. This paper was presented at the Conference on Local Politics, Poverty and Decentralisation organised by the Danish Institute of International Studies at Copenhagen in July, 2004.

Democratic decentralisation in India received a new lease of life following two major amendments of the Constitution of India in early 1990s. We have in India today a new crop of panchayat and municipal bodies armed with constituional sanction. As expected in a country of India's size and diversity local self government experience cannot be even and uniform. There are only a few states where the institutions of local self government have been working relatively well. But the over all experience has not been happy. There is a view that decentralisation has been derailed. While such an extreme view needs to be subjected to scrutiny, there is no doubt that there are challenges to democratic decentralisation in India which have been discussed in the article in chapter 2. The article makes a modest attempt to conceptualise the challenges largely under the framework of political will. It examines the gravity of challenges coming from within and without and their impact on the system of democratic decentralisation. All the arguments have been supported by facts and figures collected from both the primary and secondary sources.

The third article in the book reviews the policies and programmes relating to the amelioration of urban poverty in India from historical perspective. Poverty has been understood not in terms of pure economic sense where the emphasis is on income and consumption but in terms of livelihoods, resources, knowledge and rights. The article has touched on the impact of structural adjustment programme in the context of poverty reduction programmes initiated at the instance of the Indian State. It has been argued that diversity and complexity of urban poverty require multi-pronged intervention and at different levels. A case has been made out for development and promotion of people's organisations to deal with poverty issues. The chapter starts with providing a short account of the basic features of urban poverty in India and goes on to discuss the programmes and the processes of involvement of the local bodies and the stakeholders in the reduction of poverty.

West Bengal is one of the very few states where the panchayati raj institutions were given a fresh lease of life by the Left Front Government even before the amendment of Constitution in 1993. Panchayati raj system is guided by the political philosophy of the Left Front Government, although the Act was framed by the Congress government. It is true that quite a few amendments have been made to make the Act conform not only to the needs of the constitutional amendment but also to the ideological and programmatic commitments of the Left Front. The biggest partner of the Left Front is CPI (M) which adheres to political philosophy rooted in Marxism-Leninism. There is a strong view that macro political stability in West Bengal can largely be attributed to the success of the panchayati raj institutions in the state. It has been argued that CPI (M) has carved out a pattern of political organisation in rural West Bengal rare in India, namely, that of involving a penetration in the countryside without depending on the larger landowners. The fourth article attempts a critical appraisal of the working of panchayati raj institutions and the role of the other organisations in the implementation of rural development programmes. One of the objectives of the Left Front Government is to mobilise the masses. In the rural areas panchayats have become major instruments of mass mobilisation. There is elaborate discussion about this role of panchayats and their impact in this regard.

Gram sansad is a new institutional incarnation in West Bengal to mobilise masses formally as well as informally. The Seventy Third Amendment of the Constitution provides for Gram Sabha to ensure participation of the villagers in their governance and development. The West Bengal Panchayat Act was amended in 1992 to set up Gram Sabha at the electoral constituency level. But when the Constitution was amended to create Gram Sabha, the State Government decided to constitute another body called Gram Sansad and the Gram Sabha was reconstituted to exist at the level of the Gram Panchayat in terms of the constitutional mandate. West Bengal is one of the very few states in the country where this kind of institution has been working for some time. Participatory democracy in rural West Bengal examines the working of this body in the state. It also throws some light on the participatory decentralised planning in the state as it started in the form of pilot schemes in selected districts.

Urban governance under the Left Front regime in West Bengal has received a lot of political and administrative attention. The West Bengal Municipal Act has been acclaimed as the best municipal legislation in the country. The Model Municipal Act drafted at the initiative of the Government of India draws heavily on the West Bengal Act and the experiences. The sixth article seeks to present an overview of the perspective and practices in municipal administration in West Bengal. The article explains the backdrop and emergence of new institutional mechanisms in the field of urban governance. Attempt has also been made to capture the functioning of these institutional instruments in the following two articles. The Seventy Fourth Amendment of the Constitution institutionalises citizens' participation through Ward Committees in urban local bodies with three lakh or more population. While there are many states which have not yet formed Ward Committee, Ward Committees in most of the States seem to be units of administrative decentralisation, rather than those of democratic decentralisation. Against this background the West Bengal Government had decided to set up Ward Committee in all urban local bodies irrespective of the size of the population. Chapter 7 analyses the working of Ward Committees in West

Bengal in the light of the empirical study conducted by the author. The study while bringing out the strengths and weaknesses, suggests steps that may be taken to improve the functioning of the Ward Committees. The study was funded by the UNICEF and Institute of Local Government and Urban Studies, Government of West Bengal. West Bengal was the first state in India to introduce cabinet form of Government in municipal administration in 1994 the idea of which was conceived in 1967 at the sixth conference of the Municipal Corporations in Delhi. In 1988 Maharashtra adopted the model in two cities on a trial basis. Madhya Pradesh followed suit in 1998. But Maharashtra has gone back to the original arrangement. In Madhya Pradesh the system is yet to gather adequate momentum. The Mayor-in-Council system has been working in all the Corporations in West Bengal. The experience of working of the Mayor-in-Council System in Kolkata Corporation has been dealt with in Chapter-8. Incidentally, the Left Front had been at the helm of affairs when the system started. Later on, Trinomool Congress captured the seat of power but the Left Front remained in power in Writers Buildings. The interesting experience of these two different phases has been narrated in this chapter.

The idea of metropolitan planning committee in India was conceived by the Seventy Fourth Amendment of the Constitution as an instrument for the preparation of draft development plan for the metropolitan area as a whole. The State Government has been entrusted with the task of framing suitable legislation for this purpose. West Bengal was the first state in India to constitute Kolkata Metropolitan Planning Committee in 2001. Chaired by the Chief Minister this body of 60 members has been working for some time. In order to help the Kolkata Metropolitan Planning Committee prepare the draft development plan, five sectoral committees have also been constituted. Chapter 9 provides an overview of the structure and processes of KMPC.

The last chapter, though a bit different from all other chapters in the book, fits in well with the central theme of the book. Joint forest management is now widely accepted as a new institutional mode for better, efficient and meaningful management of the forests. West Bengal, again, has a pioneering role in this regard. It was awarded international recognition for its performance in this field. The author did a study on the working of the joint forest management programme in West Bengal at the instance of the Forest Department, Government of West Bengal. The findings of the study have been presented in this chapter. Incidentally, the author was invited by the Centre for Development and Environment under the University of Oslo, Norway to make a presentation on this theme on October, 21, 2003. This chapter is an outcome of the presentation.

There are four appendices which seem to be very relevant to the central theme of the book.

While writing these articles I received immense help and support from the members of the academic community and the officials of the concerned government departments. I am indebted to all of them.

I am sure that this book would be useful to a cross-section of readers including policy makers. I am indeed grateful to the management of Kalpaz Publications for kindly agreeing to publish the book.

Prabhat Datta

1

Local Politics, Poverty and Decentralisation

It is now widely acknowledged that decentralised local polity holds great potential for development and poverty alleviation. It can ensure more efficient allocation and utilization of resources, enhance local resource mobilization, facilitate participation of the people, ensure target group orientation in the planning and implementation of development programmes, make monitoring and supervision over the implementation of the development more effective and improve local governance. All these may pave the way for effective poverty reduction strategies. Conceptually, there could be four kinds of linkages between local political decentralisation and poverty reduction policies, namely:

(a) Local political decentralisation can aim to reduce poverty through an empowerment strategy, which creates space for people to effectively participate in the decision-making processes. Where the poor are powerless, as is frequently the case, the reliance on local institutions to allocate relief is problematic, and can end up being at best, indiscriminate and at worst, blatantly iniquitous, as many observers have noted in diverse countries.[1] The local poor need therefore to be empowered. The increase in the access and influence of the local citizens vis-à-vis government offers not just greater effectiveness in promoting economic development but makes institutions of local self-government more responsive to the needs of the poor. Institutional responsiveness has been defined as the achievement of congruence between community preference and public policies. Poverty is now defined as more

> than material deprivation, it is about more than just material outputs ; it is a complex phenomenon involving such issues as lack of choice, voicelessness. Responsiveness of the policies is a matter of the processes through which they are devised, the degree of empowerment and ownership which is felt by those affected by them and therefore, the general legitimacy of the institutions and the procedures by which it allocates resources.

How to measure the degree of responsiveness? Crook and Sverrisson have suggested that it is best measured by direct popular and citizens' assessments through representative surveys.[2] Schick has observed that output measures (expenditures, numbers of schools, clinics etc.) tell us little about actual impact of these outputs on the people's lives nor how their value and quality are perceived.[3] We can study these outputs by undertaking case studies. While doing the surveys it needs to be kept in mind that it is difficult to fit in the responses of the poor people interviewed in our country in the scale such as excellent, very good, good etc. because of the inability of most of the respondents in our case to make such finer distinction.

Responsiveness of decentralised institutions can be assessed by identifying the number of people who participate (e.g. in elections or in public meetings) with special emphasis on the socio-economic background of the people. In post-colonial societies like India's where the poor are divided along caste lines, it is necessary to examine the caste composition also.

In my studies I have seen that a great majority of those who participate in the discussions in the meetings are generally people above the poverty level.[4] Secondly, due the lack of skill and literacy participation of the poor, if it at all takes place, hardly make any effective impact. Thirdly, the poor people are more often than not allowed to raise their voices, as they cannot articulate their problems properly. Fourth, inadequate devolution of powers, functions and resources on the participatory institutions like *gram sansads* in West Bengal often makes participation meaningless. Fifth, there is reluctance and lack of political tolerance on the part of some of the political leaders to often listen to constructive criticisms from the opponents. It is more widely seen in areas where the ruling party is very powerful and without any effective challenge. Participation as an input in poverty reduction strategies has to be understood in the context of how it influences the policy decisions and administrative processes.

The impact of participation is further restrained by the kinds of functions and resources that have been devolved to local government. Local government is still weak in most of the developing countries. There is a general reluctance on the part of the higher level government to devolve adequate functions, funds and functionaries. In India, as per the amendment of the Constitution 29 subjects have to be transferred to the *panchayats*. The actions of the state governments are interesting. Most of the states have devolved functions without corresponding transfer of funds and functionaries. Only one state-Karnataka–has looked into all these three aspects.

There could be three modes of participation—direct at the community or project level, indirect or mobilisation from above. In case of direct participation the main types include turn out in elections, contesting elections and getting elected, taking part in election campaigns, contacting or trying to influence government policies, associational membership.

The forms of participation which engage people between elections, are important. There could be two kinds of participation namely institutional and non-institutional. While the institutional participation refers to participation in the formal structures, non-institutional participation refers to participation in meetings, processions, rallies etc. In our country more particularly in West Bengal the decentralised political institutions organize rallies, demonstrations, meetings where a large number of the poor people get assembled. The 73rd amendment of the Constitution has also institutionalised people's participation in between elections through *gram sabha*. It is the *gram sabha* which is supposed to meet at regular intervals and it is the forum which is supposed to prepare the list of beneficiaries under different poverty alleviation programmes. The problems are as follows: formal meetings are not regularly held. Second, even if held, the attendance is awfully poor. Third, adequate publicity is not given about the meetings. Fourth, there is a lack of political and bureaucratic will to ensure participation of the people at large. Fifth, for many reasons, there is lack of spontaneous interest among the common people. Webster found that in West Bengal the informal meetings before the *gram sabha* meetings are no less important. The decisions are often taken outside the meetings. In states like West Bengal appropriate party structures play crucial role.

In order to assess the impact of decentralisation on poverty it seems necessary to focus on case studies supplemented by periodic revisits for a specific period. The data for the case studies need to be collected through informal interaction and if necessary cross–verification from the neighbouring families may also be undertaken.

The social and economic impact of decentralisation on the levels of poverty can be broken down, as Crook and Sverrisson have suggested, for analytical purposes into four main areas :

- Pro-poor growth or changes in the level of economic activity, wages and or prices which increase the incomes of small farmers, sharecroppers, agricultural labourers and the like.
- Social equity or the extent to which there is redistribution of income or reduction in the levels of inequality.
- Human development, improvements in the quality of life and hence, the life chances of the poor, as reflected in their access to health, education, sanitation or justice.
- Spatial or inter-regional inequality or the extent to which there is redistribution of resources or growth between deprived and economically affluent areas of a country.
- In addition to what they have suggested one may add that there might take place what may be called 'the churning of the submerged humanity' if they find a government at the doorstep with their representatives working for them.

It is also necessary to study the role of the organisations. The poor cannot carry their voices to the policy-making processes because they are not properly heard nor are the properly organised. They cannot organize themselves into pressure groups like the business houses. In West Bengal the poor have been able to influence policy-making to some extent because they have powerful peasant associations backed by the left parties.

(b) Another linkage is in the nature of resource mobilization strategy. The theoretical formulation is that when people are given greater control over local constitutional or statutory structure, they may be motivated to commit more assets to the common good. It has worked well in Kerala through what is known as People's Campaign for Decentralised Planning.

But in West Bengal, the progress is not satisfactory. This theoretical formulation does not appear to hold good in our country. The studies and the data collected by the Eleventh Finance Commission indicate that there is hardly any initiative on the part of the local government institutions to raise resources. Also, there is lack of political will to motivate the people to pay taxes due to narrow electoral calculations.

(c) Local elective political institutions are effective instruments for the delivery of the basic social services. It is widely known that the lack of basic services leading to inhuman living conditions is the primary cause of poverty. In this way many common causes of poverty such as illness, decrepit economic infrastructures and illiteracy can be removed. In West Bengal the *panchayat* bodies have a good track record in this regard. For example, total sanitation programme has been successfully implemented through the *panchayati raj* institutions. *Panchayats* played excellent role in the first phase of the literacy programme called total literacy campaigns. This is an area which needs to be studied. The case study method and focus group interview seem to be useful for this purpose. It would be useful if the case studies are presented in a narrative style.

(d) The local government can be effective instrument for mobilization of masses. This strategy is likely to yield desired results in the implementation of structural reforms programme like land reform. In West Bengal it has been found that the mobilization of the masses has been very useful in implementing structural reforms programme like land reform. Local government in the villages played an important role in conscientising the poor through rallies, campaigns, group meetings etc. It posed a great challenge to the land holding group who could earlier escape law in connivance with the bureaucracy and in the absence of organized and politicized peasantry.

Poverty is rooted in the socio-economic structure. In the developing countries like India land continues to be basic asset in the rural areas. And the landownership is highly skewed. There is alarming concentration of land in the hands of the few, while a large number of people are landless.

The advocates of social capital tend to assume a common collective interest in democratization and to ignore the questions of economic and social inequality and the politics that gives rise to it. In the case of the poor, the socio-economic structure in which their poverty is rooted, is ignored. Poverty in the developing countries like India is essentially power question. The power dimension of poverty is now being admitted by the World Bank. In West Bengal rural poverty would not have reduced had there been no change in the socio-economic structure through land reform and the institutional and emotional support provided to the poor by the local political structures called panchayat institutions. The supporters of social capital neglect the role of the social and cultural practices which reinforce their poverty.

In any analysis of poverty reduction strategies through decentralised local government institutions it is necessary to find out who control or dominate the institutions and thus to find out whose interests are served through the functioning of these institutions. It is therefore important to analyse the socio-economic background of the leaders and the processes of inclusion of the lower classes. The failure to include the people from the lower classes is one of the reasons why poverty alleviation programmes failed to achieve the desired results. In India the grassroots democratic institutions in the villages were captured by the landed gentry and the high caste people who acted as gatekeepers preventing flow of benefits to the target groups. In its relationship with the civil society those in power at the state level may use the institutions of local government both as a vehicle for maintenance of *status quo* through incorporative modes of inclusion or as modes of broadening political base (horizontal inclusion).

As the poor are looked at as actors it is necessary to understand how the activities of the local political organisations interact with the efforts and activities of the poor. The poor face a lot of constraints and develop strategies to counter difficulties. It is necessary to study and analyse the knowledge and experiences of the poor.

The poor in countries like India are divided on the basis of caste, community, religion etc. Some of them have organizations which need to be studied separately.

Incidentally, Mouzelis in his analysis of political inclusion of the lower classes outlines three ideal types:

(a) an integrative mode marked by relatively homogeneous horizontal inclusion of people in the national area.

(b) an incorporative-clientelist mode which brings people into the centre via their insertion into paternalistic, highly particularistic vertical patron-client networks

(c) an incorporative–populist mode where mobilization takes place, e.g., *via* the masses, attachment to a charismatic leader.[5]

Mouzelis says that the incorporative relations of domination tend to prevail in societies where the individual classes are weak in terms of numbers and organizations and where an over all weak civil society is unable to check the state's patrimonial despotic features. The basic effect is the maintenance of the *status quo*.

In West Bengal the State Government has been using the *panchayati raj* institutions to mobilize and politicise the rural poor along class lines horizontally and implement structural reforms programme which benefit them. The State Government also uses these institutions to broaden the support base of the left in rural areas as is evident from the results in the parliamentary and assembly elections since 1978.

Rural politics in West Bengal before June 1978 when elections to the village local self-government were held after more than two decades, revolved around individuals as the institutions were not only moribund but captured by a handful of individuals who were either rich in terms of land holding or food grain dealers or moneylenders. They used to mobilize the people and thus mobilization became vertical. There was a fusion of economic and political power at the local level serving the interests of the particular groups. It leaves democracy weak, something akin to what Gills and Ricamora call "low intensity democracy" in which civil society has little role. Elections were not held at regular intervals.[6] The institutions were devoid of real powers and delinked from the general mass of population. It was a time when rural economy started stagnating. Poverty was widespread but no serious attempts were made to reduce it. In 1976 national rural poverty was 51.2 per cent. In West Bengal it was 58.1 per cent

The rise of the Left Front to power in 1977 and the political-ideological commitment of the Left Front expressed through the Common Minimum Programme brought about a remarkable change in the scenario.

It was weak in rural areas.Immediately after coming to power it decided to hold *panchayati raj* elections. Most of the *panchayat* institutions captured by the left became instruments of political mobilization of the masses.

The elections marked a distinct departure in rural politics in West Bengal as a result of the rise of a new crop of leadership. The elections brought an end to the domination of the landed gentry. The studies of the social background of rural leadership indicated the emergence of the marginalised, the small farmers, landless agricultural labourers and share-croppers. There has been a 'churning of the submerged humanity' as a result of this new rural leadership. The leadership coupled with the churning of the down-and-out has played an important role in reduction of poverty.[7]

In late 1980s the state launched massive literacy campaign known as the Total Literacy Campaign in which the panchayat institutions played key role. West Bengal was awarded an international prize for this purpose.[8] It generated a lot of enthusiasm and took the shape of a movement. The work has taken up by the volunteers recruited by the panchayats. This programme empowered a large mass of population as new consciousness dawned on them.

In 1992 the State Government decided to further strengthen the process of decentralisation through creation of participatory institutions (*Gram Sansad*) at the electoral constituency level in each of the *Gram Panchayats*. The researches about the *Gram Sansad* meeting show that although attendance is still far below the desired level (average attendance being 12 per cent) a good number of the members who attended the meetings are poor (average attendance being 12 per cent).[9] It has implications for poverty reduction because it is the forum for identification of the different poverty alleviation programmes.

The poor do not participate politically only though voting. The other forms of their political participation are collective action, individual contacting, protest actions, stakeholders' associations. In West Bengal while the non-government organisations are very weak, there are no separate stakeholders' associations which do not work under the umbrella of the any political parties. The party-based mass organisations of various types are very active in this state. They act as pressure groups, raise voices of protests organise demonstration, rallies etc. They constitute a dynamic civil society working in close association with the political parties. In West Bengal political parties are actors in the civil society. It does not mean that grassroots movements and non-party actors, as Kothari suggests, cannot be looked at as new forms of organizations and struggle to rejuvenate the local state and to make it instruments for eradication of poverty reduction.[10] They counter administrative inflexibility, the lack of participation resulting from political exclusion and the general elitism characteristic of state-led development strategies of the 1970s and 1980s.

The World Bank has characterised West Bengal as the leader state in poverty reduction. The LF phase has witnessed an improvement in the condition of the poor in the state.[11] One of the most widely noticed signs of this is the decline in migration to cities and reverse migration in some instances because of the greater availability of work in the villages.[12] There had been a steady reduction of rural poverty till 1993-94. In 1983, 55 per cent of the villages in West Bengal lived below the poverty line. It came down to 26 per cent in 1993-94. The latest data released by the National Sample Survey Organisation tend to show a little increase in poverty. Food production has also shown decline in late 1990s. Agricultural wage had tripled between 1977-78 and 1987-88. But it stagnated in 1990s particularly due to low growth in agriculture and large inflow of migrant labour from the neighbouring states.

As result of globalisation agricultural subsidies have been reduced in many countries like India. This has led to a rise in the cost of agricultural inputs like fertilizer. Globalisation has created conditions for import of food grains. Rice is being imported at cheaper prices from Thailand to West Bengal. The cost of local rice is higher. The farmers are getting discouraged to cultivate paddy fields. All these are affecting the farmers who cannot pay higher wages to the agricultural workers whose cost of basic food has increased due to inflationary situation in the economy. In a situation like this the local government is left with little capacity to manoeuvre and has become an onlooker.

References

1. Jean Dreze and Amartya Sen (1996) *Indian Development Regional Development Perspectives*, Oxford University Press, New Delhi.

2. Richard Crook and Alan Sturia Sverrisson (2001) *Decentralisation and Poverty Alleviation in the Developing Countries*, IDS, Sussex, London.

3. A. Schick (1990) "Budgeting for Results" *Public Administration Review*, 50(1).

4. Prabhat Datta (2001) *Panchayats, Rural Development and Local Autonomy*, Das Gupta & Co., Kolkata.

5. Nicos P. Mouzelis (1990) *Post Marxist Alternative Perspective: The Construction of Social Order*, Macmilla, London.

6. B. Gills and J. Rocomora (1992) "Low Intensity Democracy" *Third World Quarterly*, 13(3).

7. G.K. Lieten (1996) *Development, Devolution and Democracy: Village Discourse in West Bengal*, Sage, New Delhi.

8. Prabhat Datta (2004) Literacy, Development and Empowerment : Literacy Programme in West Bengal, *Indian Social Science Review*, Jan-June.

9. M. Ghatak & M. Ghatak (2000) "Recent Reforms in the Panchayat System in West Bengal, *Economic and Political Weekly*, (EPW), January 5.

10. Rajni Kotahari (1998) "The Non-Party Political Processes' *EPW*, February.

11. B. Rogali (1998) Containing Conflicts and Reaping Votes : Management of Rural Labour Relations in West Bengal, *EPW*, October 17-24, S. Sen Gupta and H. Gazdar (1996) "Agrarian Policies and Rural Development in West Bengal" in Jean Dreze and Amartya Sen (ed.) *Indian Development Regional Perspectives*, *op. cit.*

12. See, Neil Webster (1992) *Panchayati Raj and Decentralisation of Development Planning in West Bengal*, K.P. Bagchi, Kolkata and G.K. Lieten (1996) *Development, Devolution and Democracy : Village Discourse in West Bengal*, *op. cit.* Prabhat Datta and Swapan Pramanick (1994) *Panchayats and the People : The West Bengal Experience*, Sanat Book House, Kolkata.

2

Democratic Decentralisation in India The Emerging Challenges

Panchayati raj as the concretised form of democratic decentralisation in modern India is a creation of the colonial rulers. They had taken interest in democratic decentralisation essentially to protect, promote and consolidate the colonial rule. Ripon's attempt, though different from the earlier approach in the sense that he looked at local self-government as the school of democracy and as an instrument of political education of the masses, was also guided by the philosophy of political accommodation of the nationalist leaders who were posing challenges to the colonial rule.

Attempts to introduce local self-governing institutions during the days of the colonial rule started soon after the annexation of India by the British crown. It was a time when the colonial rule was still haunted by the uprising of 1857. It had caused a massive drain on the colonial exchequer. After the uprisings, there were sporadic peasant movements in different parts of the country. The colonial rulers felt the need for developing a network for the purpose of collecting information from the villages. It was also realised by the colonial rulers that the enlightened people who were protesting against the colonial rule, needed to be co-opted into the system of governance to make them act as imperial collaborators in the countryside.

When the country was fighting for freedom under the leadership of the Indian National Congress, Gandhiji and his colleagues promised the nation a vibrant system of village self-government after India became independent. Gandhiji defined his vision of village panchayats thus:

"My idea of village swaraj is that it is a complete republic independent of its neighbours for its own vital wants and yet interdependent for many others in which dependence is a necessity. The Government of the village will be conducted by the panchayat of five persons annually elected by the adult villagers, males and females, possessing minimum prescribed qualifications"[1]

The draft Indian Constitution presented before the Constituent Assembly contained no provision for democratic decentralisation worth the name. Ambedkar remarked in the Constituent Assembly that he was glad to see that the draft Constitution had discarded the village and adopted individual as its unit. He thought that the village was but 'a sink of localism, a den of ignorance, narrow-mindedness and communalism'. In fact, his own experience had given him a negative view of the caste–ridden villages and their panchayats. When Gandhiji learnt that the proposed Constitution did not provide for panchayats, he remarked that this was certainly an omission calling for immediate attention if India's independence was to reflect the voice of the people. The issue was hotly debated in the Assembly. The idea of panchayats as units of self-government in village India was ultimately accepted but it was included in the chapter on Directive Principles of State Policy, which is unenforceable.[2]

The Rise of the Third Generation Panchayats in India

The post-colonial India embarked on rural development through Community Development Programme which failed to evoke people's initiative. This motivated the Indian State to get the state of affairs in the countryside examined by the Balvantrai Mehta Committee. The Committee stressed the need for developing a network of three-tiered elective institutions known as the panchayati raj. The Mehta Committee gave birth to what can be called the first generation panchayati raj in India.[3]

The village self-government in the form of panchayati raj had grown in some parts of the country in the early fifties, although conceptually panchayats were looked upon as instruments of rural development. There is an extreme view that they were 'killed before they were truly born'. The fact, however, remains that the institutions declined. The Asoka Mehta Committee identified three phases in the evolution of panchayati raj in India–the phase of ascendancy, the phase of stagnation and the phase of decline. The first generation panchayats set up on the basis of the recommendations of the Balvantrai Mehta Committee had almost disappeared from the rural scene by the end of 1950s. The Asok Mehta Committee, which examined the issue, prepared a blue print of the second generation panchayats. But the progress was so slow that the Indian State had to amend the Constitution to revitalise the system of panchayati raj. Political exigencies played a major role when Rajiv Gandhi started taking about regeneration of panchayats raj. In 1970s and 1980s the nation witnessed series of movement in different parts of the country (e.g. militant movements in Punjab, Gorkhaland movement in West Bengal, Jharkhand movement) based on primordial loyalties like religion, ethnicity, language. It was difficult for the state governments to handle the issues efficiently. The republic was under stress. It was realised that power had to be shared with local communities. The autonomous local self-government was considered a safety valve for preventing recurrence of such incidents. There is a view that the work of decentralisation was seriously undertaken in 1990s because of the adoption of the policy of liberalization by the Indian State which in effect meant shrinkage of the role of the state. Local government had to be strengthened to ensure that the local functions could be taken care of at the local level through mobilisation of local resources. Incidentally one of the purposes for which local government was taken up by the colonial rulers was to ensure local resource mobilisation for the discharge of the local level functions.

Added to it was the consideration of power politics. In the mid 1980s the Congress was out of power in many major states, even though it was in power at the centre. The opposition parties, which captured power, were mounting pressure for more administrative and fiscal powers for the states. Their opposition to accept centre's decisions affecting the states without obtaining consensus was a cause of concern and irritation to the central government. It is possible that panchayats were sought to be constitutionalised with the hope that it would create similar problems for the ruling parties at the state level as they would demand more powers, functions and funds from the state government. It is argued that this possibility cannot be ruled out for two reasons :

First, even though the Prime Minister, Rajiv Gandhi advocated for decentralisation at the local level, there was no initiative to devolve powers to the state governments. Even the small steps like limiting the numbers of centrally sponsored schemes in the areas constitutionally reserved for the states were not taken. Secondly, the national government tried to establish direct linkage with the district collectors or the panchayati raj bodies bypassing the state government for the implementation of centrally sponsored schemes. D. Bandyopadhaya *et al* suggest "The agenda behind such unusual move was clear–empower the local government institutions and marginalise the states in order to establish hegemony of the centre, as it would be impossible for the numerous grassroots institutions of the vast country to challenge the central authority."[4]

There was resistance to Rajiv Gandhi's attempt to get the Constitution Amendment Bill passed. He failed to master required support in the Parliament. Later on, some of the highly objectionable provisions were removed but the basic structure remained the same. The Constitution was finally amended in 1993.

The Seventy Third Amendment of the Constitution (1993) is a bold step forward in right direction and gave birth to what can be called the third generation panchayats[5]. The Constitutional amendment seeks to give panchayats a new meaning and a fresh lease of life. The basic features of the amendment are as follows:

1. Article 243G defines panchayats as institutions of self-government meaning they have autonomy and power to govern in an exclusive area of jurisdiction

2. The amendment defines the role of panchayats as instruments of economic development and social justice. Incidentally, earlier there was confusion about the role of panchayats. Thus this clarification through constitutional amendment, is significant.

3. The amendment requires the States to hold panchayat elections through the State Election Commission at regular intervals of five years. If State Government dissolves panchayats before the expiry of their full term, it is mandatory on the part of the State Government concerned to hold election within six months from the date of dissolution.

4. The Act provides for reservation of one-third seats and posts of chairpersons for women and weaker sections, i.e., Scheduled Caste (SC) Scheduled Tribe (ST).

5. According to the provisions of the Constitutional amendment the State Government shall constitute State Finance Commission, which will review the financial position and recommend the principles for fund devolution on PRIs and the distribution of funds between the State Government and the PRIs.

The MP Local Area Development Scheme

The actions taken by the Indian State after the amendment of the Constitution did not prove that there was strong political will to strengthen decentralised and participatory local governance in rural India. Mention may be made of the decision of the Indian State to introduce Members of Parliament Local Area Development (MPLAD) Scheme. Under this scheme a sum of Rs. 1,580 crores per year is placed at the disposal of the MPs. The MPs are allowed to spend the money to undertake local area development schemes outside the purview of panchayats and municipalities.[5] In this way the constitutionally mandated local government institutions are bypassed. Under the scheme each MP can suggest to the District Collector works worth up to Rs. 2 crores in a year. The Ministry releases the funds directly to the Collectors who get the works done on the advice of the concerned MP. The funds should be used for creation of durable assets to be vested in government. The Central Government has given an illustrative list of 28 items. There is also a list of works not permissible such as raising of memorials, building of places of worship.

Incidentally, the State Governments are also not lagging behind in undermining the authority of the decentralised constitutional bodies. Some of the State Governments have also introduced similar programme for the MLAs.

The Report of the Comptroller and Auditor General (CAG) (2001) showed inadequate and misuse of the money and diversion of funds. The Report noted that out of Rs. 5018 crores only Rs. 3221 i.e. 64 per cent of the released amount could be spent. In Nagaland, for example, the money was spent for building roads connecting the Church, in Orissa temples were built, in Madhya Pradesh money was spent for building housing complex for the police officials.[6]

In a sample study of audit of 106 constituencies, it was found that out of total expenditure of Rs. 265 crores reported by the Collectors, a sum of Rs. 82 crores, that is, 31 per cent of the total money was, in fact, not spent at all. The guidelines seem to have been observed more in their breach. The CAG report noted that the Ministry often released funds without any co-relation with the end use and it did not insist on the utilization certificates from the implementing agencies.

Some critics feel that most of the schemes being funded and executed form part of the 11th and 12th schedules to the Constitution which define the functional domain of the panchayats and municipalities. The guidelines authorizing the MPs to exercise their personal choice and decision in funding and executing the scheme lead to usurpation of the power and responsibilities of the local bodies. It has been argued that in many instances the choice of schemes and amounts expected can significantly alter or distort local priorities as may be decided or desired by the local bodies.

It has strengthened the hold of the bureaucratic machinery as the money is placed at the disposal of the District Magistrate. It indicates that the Indian State is still more comfortable with the bureaucracy than with the democratically elected local bodies. It reminds us of what Rajiv Gandhi attempted to do to reach the District Magistrates by-passing the Chief Minister in the name of creating conducive conditions for responsive administration. One may find in this attitude of the ruling classes a reflection of the colonial mind in a post-colonial state. Bureaucracy continues to be a more reliable instrument of the Indian ruling classes.

The Substitution of the Word 'Unit' by 'Institutions'

The lack of political will of the Indian State was also evident from the manipulation of the language in the amendment of the Constitution. Article 40 of the Constitution in the Directive Principles of State Policy, conceives of panchayats as units of self-government. The 73rd amendment substituted the word 'unit' by 'institutions'. That the word 'unit' is stronger than institutions needs no explanation. It is wrong to believe that the substitution has no practical significance and has been done without any purpose. The post-Constitution amendment actions or inactions tend to indicate that the Constitutional amendment was not preceded by serious political will of the Indian State.

It may be recalled that an attempt was made through the 87th Constitution Amendment Bill in 1999 to weaken the democratic base of panchayats. It provided for the abolition of elected panchayats at the intermediate level and in some cases, at the zilla parishad level. The bill sought to (a) fill all the seats in the panchayats at intermediate and district level by persons elected as chairpersons of the village panchayats and intermediate level panchayats respectively and (b) to decide the manner in which the chairpersons of the panchayats at the intermediate level or district level have to be elected. The Indian State was compelled to withdraw the controversial Bill under serious pressure from the opposition and tremendous public criticism. But the fact remains that the presentation of such a bill is a clear indication of the approach of the State to decentralised governance.[7]

Devolution in the Conformity Legislations

The 73rd Amendment of the Constitution of India stipulates the transfer of powers and functions to panchayati raj institutions as a part of the decentralisation process. The State Governments were supposed to transfer 29 subjects listed in the Eleventh Schedule of the Constitution. The Working Group on the Decentralised Planning observes, "...... items listed as responsibilities in the states are couched in vague terms. A glance at the variety of these items reveals that they are shopping list of sectors and sub-sectors, broad activities in a sub-sector and activities, sub-activities/specific responsibilities under a broad activity, with no role clarity.... In some states the line departments still exercise the powers of supervision and control over the scheme of subjects transferred to the panchayats"[8] Facts and relevant data tend to show that there has been very little progress with respect to the transfer of funds, functions and functionaries to panchayati raj bodies across the country. The Parliamentary Committee in its 37th report submitted in 2003 has expressed concern at the way the states are working in this regard. The Report of the Task Force on the Devolution of Powers and Functions to the PRIs brought out by the Ministry of Rural Development has admitted that the mandatory provisions of the 73rd Amendment Act are yet to be implemented in letter and spirit by most of the states/UTs even eight years after the said Act brought into force in April, 1993" The conformity legislations of most of the States have not significantly altered the functional domain of gram panchayats as is shown in the table 1.

Table-1 Status of Devolution of Departments/Subjects with Funds, Functions and Functionaries

Sl. No.	*States/UTs*	*No. of Departments/subjects transferred to Panchayats with*		
		Funds	*Functions*	*Functionaries*
1.	Andhra Pradesh	05	17	02
2.	Arunachal Pradesh	-	-	-
3.	Assam	-	29	-
4.	Bihar	-	20	-
5.	Jharkhand	-	-	-
6.	Goa	6	6	-
7.	Gujarat	15	15	15
8.	Haryana	-	Almost all the 29 subjects	-
9.	Himachal Pradesh	02	26 Subjects	No functionary has been transferred. However, GPs and IPs have been made the appointing authorities with regard to 9 functions on contract basis.
10.	Karnataka	29	29	29
11.	Kerala	15	26	15
12.	Madhya Pradesh	10	23	09
13.	Chhattisgarh	10	29	09
14.	Maharashtra	18	18	18
15.	Manipur	-	22	04
16.	Orissa	05	25	21
17.	Punjab	-	07	-
18.	Rajasthan	-	16	-
19.	Sikkim	24	24	24
20.	Tamil Nadu	-	29	-
21.	Tripura	-	12	-
22.	Uttar Pradesh	12	13	09
23.	Uttranchal	-	11	11
24.	West Bengal	12	29	12
25.	A&N Islands	06	06	06
26.	Chandigarh	-	-	-
27.	D&N Haveli	-	03	03
28.	Daman & Diu	05	09	03
29.	NCT of Delhi	Panchayati Raj System is yet to be revived.		
30.	Pondicherry	-	-	-
31.	Lakshadweep	-	06	-

Note:-The provisions of the Constitution (73rd Amendment) Act, 1992 are not applicable to the States of J&K, Meghalaya, Mizoram and Nagaland.

Source:-Goverment of India.

Transfer of Funds

The transfer of functions without corresponding transfer of funds does not make sense. But this has happened. Mahi Pal rightly says that before listing the functions to be performed by the panchayats, the states have introduced certain qualifying clauses.[9] In Andhra Pradesh, Haryana and Tamil Nadu it is "within the limits of its funds". In Punjab "it is to the extent its funds allow to perform". In Madhya Pradesh and Himachal Pradesh, it is "as far as the gram panachayat funds at its disposal".

The Constitution provides for setting up of the State Finance Commission (SFCs). By mid–1990s the first SFCs had submitted their reports. Referring to the role of the SFCs the mid-term appraisal of the Ninth Plan pointed out, "more buoyant taxes like sales tax and excise are kept out of the purview of the PRIs. All SFCs have put great emphasis on internal revenue mobilisation but none has suggested any effective mechanism for PRIs to generate their revenue. The SFC reports have paid less attention to issues of autonomy, financial management and auditing proceedings. The main deficiency of the report lies in the fact that the recommendations are not based on a clear statement of the spending responsibilities of local bodies. Indeed, the absence of attention to the elementary principle, that expenditure assignment must precede any tax or revenue assignment, has made most of the SFC's recommendations suspect".[10] The State Governments have also been slow and hesitant in accepting the recommendations where they are useful in terms of improving the revenue generation capacity of the local bodies. Only two states–Karnataka and Sikkim–have devolved funds to the panchayats for the 29 subjects.

The contribution of PRIs through tax and non-tax is a matter of concern as is amply evident from the figures below:

PRIs own Revenue–GDP Ratios

	Tax	*Non-tax*
1997-1998	0.025	0.020
2002-2003	0.023	0.019
2006-2007	0.021	0.018

Source : Government of India (2002) Report of the Working Group on State Resources.

The own revenue of panchayats (tax and non-tax) as GDP ratios has been declining. The decline is sharper in the case of revenue from tax in comparison with non-tax. Some of the important factors for this unhappy state of affairs are reluctance to mobilise, lack of role clarity as between tier, lack of staff support, unviable administrative area, creation of parallel channels of flow of funds like MP funds, state sponsored schemes independent of PRIs like *Janmabhoomi.*

Transfer of Functionaries

Only two states–Karnataka and Sikkim–have transferred functionaries pertaining to all 29 subjects Arunachal Pradesh, Assam, Bihar, Jharkhand, Goa, Gujarat, Haryana, Punjab, Rajasthan, Tamil Nadu, Tripura, Andaman and Nicobar Islands, Chhatisgarh and Pondicherry have not transferred any functions. Nilkant Rath has pointed out that this has complicated the role of the Twelfth Finance Commission which has been asked to recommend measures for the augmentation of the resources of the local bodies in the light of the recommendations of the SFCs.[11] However, in most of the states the key functionaries of the panchayat–secretaries and executive officers at all levels–are State Government employees who are reluctant to work under the administrative control of the elected panchayats.

A study of 15 select states, namely, Andhra Pradesh, Gujarat, Kerala, Madhya Pradesh, Maharashtra, Tamil Nadu, Orissa, Punjab, Haryana, Assam, Goa reveals that where middle or top tiers have been constituted, states have not endowed them with adequate functional responsibility. Most states have granted a plethora of functional responsibilities but no executive follow up of granting adequate powers, staff and financial resources. Except for four major states where the intermediate and apex bodies have adequate staff, in most other states, either the staff is not directly relevant or inadequate. A study of panchayats in 15 states done by National Institute of Rural Development, Hyderabad shows that the political parties are reluctant to devolve powers. Jean Dreeze has shown that in most States the main responsibility of a *sarpanch* is to oversee the implementation of development programmes[12].

Only the GPs are endowed with taxing powers. The number of taxes assigned to the GPs range from 2 in Tamil Nadu to 12 in Andhra Pradesh and Gujarat. By and large tax base covers property, persons and business. The taxes are inelastic. Even when taxes are assigned the autonomy of the PRIs in this regard is restricted by rules and regulations.

The Conformity Acts recognise the possibility of borrowing by the PRIs. There is a view that the PRIs should be given access to market borrowing. If it is done with state guarantees, the hope is bleak because the state finances are in a bad shape.

Unitary British colonial governance provided the background for centripetal Indian State. Today the system is perceptively moving towards incremental decentralisation. Political decentralisation process is impaired at various stages. For example, MLAs are unwilling to concede powers for fear of being unable to dispense favours to supporters at the grassroots level. In UP, for example, the MLAs refused to approve an ordinance, which provided for functional decentralisation at the GP level without any provision for the accommodation of the MLAs in the committees[13].

Centrally Sponsored Schemes

The creation of a large number of programmes (more than 200 schemes currently) called centrally sponsored schemes (CSS) has posed a challenge to democratic decentralisation.[14] Some of the subjects are included in the 11 and 12th schedules. The share of the CSSs in the plan budget of the federal government has shot up to 70 per cent against less than 30 per cent in 1980s.The schemes are framed at the centre and implemented at the local level. The association of local bodies with the processes does not really serve the purpose because the implementing bodies only implement according to the rules laid down elsewhere. The local government has to accept because the centre has financial clout.

The Seventy Third Amendment of the Constitution conceptualises panchayats as institutions of self-government. A study of tax assignments tends to show that the old tradition continues unabated. There is no serious thought about the needs of decentralised governance. The intermediate and district tiers have not been given substantial taxing power. There is excessive state government control over even the functional domain of PRIs. There is very little autonomy because functional assignments are permissive. Andhra Pradesh, Assam, Bihar, Gujarat, Haryana, Orissa, Punjab and Uttar Pradesh are prominent examples. Even in West Bengal the general criticism is that panchayat functions more as agents of the State Government than as autonomous institutions. Bihar's Panchayat Act 1993 assigns several functions to PRIs but 'subject to such conditions as may be prescribed from time to time". Again, the Bihar Act defines Zilla Parishad as a superior body over the GPs empowered to suspend the executive orders of the GPs. There are states like Haryana where the MPs and MLAs continue to dominate PRIs.

In some states several of the basic services which traditionally belonged to the panchayats like street lighting, provision of drinking water supply, sanitation and drainage, primary health care etc. have not been entrusted to the GPs. For example, in Haryana, GPs practically deal with only drinking water and construction and maintenance of roads to the exclusion of all other basic services.

Panchayat finances are fragile in most states where the total receipts of tax revenue is only 3.5 per cent from 1997-98 in the 15 select states. It is about 5 per cent in Orissa, Punjab, Andhra Pradesh, Madhya Pradesh, Gujarat and Haryana and between 10 per cent and 20 per cent in Assam, Goa and Kerala[15]. The financial devolution to PRIs in different states is reflected in the number of fiscal devolution ratios. The revenue decentralisation ratio (ratio of total local government revenue to total state government revenue) of some of the major states is as follows: 17.65 per cent for AP, 8.9 per cent for Haryana, 30.5 per cent for Kerala, 9.1 per cent for Maharashtra, 9.2 per cent for Rajasthan, 6.3 for UP. Similarly, expenditure decentralisation ratios (ratio of the local government spending to total state government spending) are 16.68 for AP, 7.5 for Haryana, 27.7 for Kerala 7.3 for Maharashtra, 7.1 for Rajasthan, and 5.8 for UP. Except in MP, in most of the states, the middle tier of the panchayat system does not have any taxation powers. PRIs across the states do not have any control over their own physical and human resources. The SFCs have recommended the transfer of those powers, which are less effective, although there has been emphasis on internal resource mobilisation. This is a matter of concern because embedded in the question of financial viability is the issue of self-reliance. The financial autonomy ratio (FAR) for the selected Gram Panchayats (GPs) is below 1 per cent indicating almost total dependence on the grants from the higher-level governments. Even in the states like Andhra

Pradesh, Gujarat, Kerala, Karnataka and Maharashtra, the FAR of the selected GPs is not more than 50 per cent. In Kerala perhaps the best performing state in terms devolution to local bodies, the own revenue of an average GP is only 33 per cent.

The Gram Sabhas

The Gram Sabhas are yet to take off in almost all the states.[16] Reports from the states indicate that the Gram Sabha meetings are not being held regularly. The Institute of Social Sciences team had found in a village in Madhya Pradesh that by December 1995, three meetings were held as against the legal requirement of six meetings.

The MP study done by Participatory Research in Asia (PRIA) group of researchers shows that majority of them did not attend meetings because the people felt that nothing happened at such meetings[17]. The villagers point out that the Gram Sabha had passed a resolution to construct the school building replacing the one-roomed tin-roofed structure. But it did not come up. The sarpanch replied that he had no money for this purpose. The study had further shown that the attendance was thin because the villagers did not know about the dates of the meetings fixed by the Government. Even the sarpanch did not know when the next meeting was due.

Nirmala Buch conducted a study of 11 Gram Panchayats in MP in December 1997 and found that far from an adequate number of Gram Sabha members attending the meetings even all the *panchs* were not present[18]. To cap it all, there was no quorum in more than 50 per cent of the Gram Sabha meetings. There is a provision for mandatory attendance of one-tenth members in the Gram Sabha. Women find it difficult to attend as the timing is sometime in the forenoon, i.e., between 11 a.m. and 1 p.m. Most of the women are not aware even of the rudiments of the Gram Sabha. The issues discussed do not seem to interest a large number of the villagers and hence, except careful and knowledgeable stakeholders, others shy away from the Gram Sabha.

A study conducted in two panchayats in Kerala has shown that the people are in favour of expanding the role of the Gram Sabhas[19]. They want the Gram Sabhas to give the final seal of approval to the activities of the Gram Panchayat. The people interviewed, have suggested that the

Gram Sabha will perform its duties in time provided people are made aware of its role in development activities. Once their felt needs are taken into consideration, they will automatically attend the meetings in large numbers and participate effectively in the activities of the Gram Panchayats.

In some of the States Gram Sabha meetings are generating a new atmosphere in the countryside. Social auditing at the Gram Sabha meetings has also started yielding desirable results. The Gram Sabha meeting in Karnataka successfully combated the time-honoured Devdasi system, which prevailed in 167 villages of Belgaun district[20]. The UMA Research team of Bangalore had witnessed a Gram Sabha meeting at Indore Gram Panchayat in Uttar Kanada district[21]. The Sabha witnessed uproarious scene when the people demanded an explanation from the secretary about the activities. Only a handful of members were familiar with the Act. The presence of the women members was very insignificant. Those who came, were passive observers. Many were hesitant to confront the elected representatives. Most of the questions were raised by the youth. The elders had hardly opened their lips.

The Participatory Research in Asia team studied the working of the Gram Sabhas in Gujarat, Haryana, Himachal Pradesh, Kerala and Uttar Pradesh[22]. The team has noticed that although meetings are being held almost regularly, quorum is hardly achieved. And surprisingly, despite the lack of quorum, the proceedings are prepared. The team is generally of the opinion that there is lack of awareness on the part of the members not only about the time and venue of the meetings but also about the usefulness of such meetings. While talking to the members present in the meeting, the researchers felt that many of them were confused about the role of the Gram Sabha. Some of them perceive the Gram Sabha meetings as the political meetings and the only function of the Gram Sabha is to prepare the list of beneficiaries under the different anti-poverty programmes. They have observed that where the heads of the panchayats or the members have interacted with the people occasionally, the results have been encouraging.

The team points out that except in Kerala and Madhya Pradesh, the advice and the suggestions of the Gram Sabha are not even binding on the Gram Panchayat. In reality, Gram Sabha meetings do not really serve the purpose of either establishing village priorities and overall policy framework for Gram Panchayat or regular monitoring and accountability of the resources and the decisions of the Gram Panchayats.

The scholars observe that most of the heads of the panchayats lack skills in conducting meetings in a manner that could promote wider participation and discussion of the issues affecting the village. Issues of social justice and internal dynamics of the village have rarely been on the agenda items in the Gram Sabha meetings.

The PRIA made an attempt to mobilise Gram Sabhas in the four villages in Andhra Pradesh through what they call Panchayat Resource Centre (PRC). The main activities of the PRC included information dissemination on PRIs, capacity building of elected representatives, Gram Sabha mobilisation, micro-planning support, and networking of *dalit* and women elected representatives. The important methods used were wall writings about the significance of the Gram Sabha, folk threatres and songs, distribution of pamphlets on Gram Sabha and individual communication with the *sarpanches* and ward members. The study brought out that there who attended the Gram Sabha meetings did so not to discuss the issues of development but to receive coupons for ration cards. Those who did not attend the meetings said that as the village secretary was never present in the meetings, their problems remained unattended. They have therefore lost interest. One ward member argued that they did not encourage the people to attend because they would not be able to meet the demands of the people. The study stressed the need for work on both sides of the equation–to make the *sarpanch* accountable and to make people aware of their rights and duties.[23]

An authoritative survey of panchayati raj by NIRD reports as follows: almost all the State Acts have provided for Gram Sabha but its functions have not been spelt out in detail. Consequently, these institutions by and large continue to function ineffectively, though the meetings are generally held as prescribed. The purpose is hardly served in the absence of clear and direct mandate. More often, there is a tendency to conduct the meetings in a formal manner and finalize the proceedings in haste. The prescribed quorum is also not given due importance. The absence of women folk in the meetings has been a common feature. The participation of the people belonging to the weaker section has been marginal.

In West Bengal Gram Sabha created by the amendment of the West Bengal Panchayat Act in 1992, had started working well. Webster's research demonstrated that apart from the compulsory meetings of the Gram Sabha, the informal mighty discussions in some localities, regular public meetings were other forms of participation[24]. Lieten remarked that although the *boktrita* culture was not altogether absent in the Gram Sabha meetings, participation used to take place[25]. Around one fourth of the males he spoke to, stated that they participated in the meeting.

In West Bengal, there is another body called Gram Sansad the geographical location of which is the electoral constituency of the members of the GP. According to the available information and the findings of the studies the Gram Sansad meetings are attended by the people of all age groups. In most of the meetings, the Gram Panchayats publish the reports. There had been many occasions when the meetings generated lot of heat. The formation of the beneficiary committee has been more often than not an issue of debate and discussion. The author himself witnessed a situation where a group of members walked out when the *Pradhan* refused to concede their demand.

There is still a lack of awareness on the part of the *Pradhan* and the members about the legal provisions relating to the Gram Sansad and Gram Sabha meetings. This has been the finding of another study done in Gujarat[26]. The officials present in the meeting have to correct them.

The study done by the author reveals that more than one third of the villagers are not aware of the Gram Sansad[27]. The reactions of the respondents tend to show that there are three reasons for the low attendance of the members in the meetings, namely, lack of time, the general impression that the decisions are not taken in the meetings and the reluctance on the part of a section of the Gram Panchayat members to listen to the suggestions of the meetings. The studies done by the author indicate that the meetings have been more successful in places where the GPs and the parties have taken initiative in synchronising them with the cultural programmes in tune with the local traditions. The modern institutional assemblies need to be tuned with the natural rhythm of the rural life.

A study on the functioning of Gram Sansad in a cross-section of 20 villages in May 1999 bring out certain important issues[28]. The study shows while analysing the occupational category of the voters who attended the meetings that the largest single category was agricultural labourers followed by farmers with less than two acres of land. Those with more lands or had non-farming sources of income constituted about 16 per cent of those present. The analysis of the findings of the study tends to show that the meetings were centered around very practical and concrete problems within the village or cluster of villages: proposals for road repair, where should a tube well be installed, who should receive loan as opposed to broader issues which political parties, trade unions or peasant organizations in West Bengal are concerned with, such as, economic liberalisation, privatisation of public sector. In quite a few meetings, though not in all, the accounts of the previous year and the budgets for the next year for the entire Gram Sansad area were also placed. The study observed, to quote, "Also, while the deliberations are often characterised by lively debates, winners and losers, participants find reasons that they can accept in collective actions, even though it does not coincide with their most preferred choice". The researchers have noticed that the participants actively voice demands for new projects, suggest how allocated funds should be spent and debate how projects should be designed. The *Pradhans* and the local representatives are not spared. They have to answer a lot of questions and often face allegations about the misuse of funds and selection of beneficiaries. The responses of the panchayat leaders to the criticisms indicate that they could not take the voters present in the meetings for granted. There had been occasions when they had to make frank admission about their errors.

Thorlind's study presents a different picture. Gram Sabha and Gram Sansads do not function effectively[29]. Gram Sansad is still in a process of learning and adoption, but they may become important instruments for democratic accountability and participation in the future. It requires awareness among the disadvantaged classes, and practical learning of democratic procedures from their own work as panchayat members.

The District Planning Committees

Another important area where the State Governments have shown scant regard for constitutional provision is the area of district planning. The Constitutional Amendment requires the State Governments to constitute the District Planning Committees (DPCs) to facilitate decentralised planning. A decade has passed.The progress is alarmingly slow as is evident from the table 2.

Table-2

Sl. No.	State/UTs.	Whether DPCs have been constituted	If yes, who is the Chairperson of DPC
1.	Andhra Pradesh	Not constituted	
2.	Arunachal Pradesh	Not constituted	
3.	Assam	Not constituted	
4.	Bihar	Not constituted	
5.	Chhattisgarh	Constituted	Minister
6.	Goa	Not constituted	
7.	Gujarat	Not constituted	
8.	Haryana	Only in 16 Districts. (No. of Districts : 19)	Deputy Commissioner
9.	Himachal Pradesh	Constituted Only in 6 Districts. (No. of Districts-12)	Minister
10.	Jammu & Kashmir	Yet to adopt the provision of 73rd Amendment Act.	
11.	Jharkhand	Not constituted	
12.	Karnataka	Constituted	Zilla panchayat president
13.	Kerala	Constituted	Zilla panchayat president
14.	Madhya Pradesh	Constituted	Minister-in-charge of district
15.	Maharashtra	Not constituted	
16.	Manipur	Constituted only in 2 districts (No. of districts : 4)	Zilla parishad, president
17.	Meghalaya	73rd and 74th Amendments	
18.	Mizoram	73rd and 74th Amendments	not applicable
19.	Nagtaland	73rd and 74th Amendments	
20.	Orissa	constituted	Minister
21.	Punjab	Not constituted	
22.	Rajasthan	constituted	Zilla panchayat president
23.	Sikkim	constituted	Zilla panchayat president
24.	Tamil Nadu	constituted	Zilla panchayat president
25.	Tripura	Not constituted	
26.	Uttar Pradesh	constituted	Minister-in-charge of districts
27.	Uttaranchal	constituted	Minister
28.	West Bengal	constituted No DPC in Darjeeling district. Metro Planning committee in Kolkata District.	Zilla parishad president
29.	A & N Islands	constituted	Zilla parishad president
30.	Chandigarh		Government has decided not to constitute DPCs as 90% of population is covered by municipalities
31.	D & N Haveli	constituted	Zilla panchayat president
32.	Daman & Diu	constituted	Zilla parishad president
33.	NCT of Delhi		
34.	Lakshadweep	constituted	Development Commissioner
35.	Pondichery	Not constituted	

Source: Panchayat Update, July, 2003.

In some states, the DPCs are chaired by the minister of the State Government as in Madhya Pradesh, where as in some other states, the officials head the DPC, as in Tamil Nadu where the collector is the chairman. All these practices seem to be inconsistent with the very spirit of the constitutional amendments on democratic decentralisation. The practice of appointing the Minister as the chairperson was criticised by the Standing Committee on Rural and Urban Local Government in 2002. But nothing has happened. Even the Ministry of Rural Development took 6 months to write to the State Governments for taking necessary actions. The table below shows the composition of the DPCs in different states:

Table-3
Composition of District Planning Committees in various States

State	*Total Members*	*Elected Members*	*Nominated Members*	*Chairperson*	*Secretary*
Kerala	15	12	03	President of the Zilla Parishad	District Collector
Madhya Pradesh	15-25	Four-fifths	One-fifth	Minister nominated by the State Govt.	District Collector
Maharashtra	30-50	Four-fifths	One-fifth	Minister nominated by the State Govt.	District Collector
West Bengal	10-100 depending on size of the district	Four-fifths	One-fifth	President of the Zilla Parishad	District Magistrate
Rajasthan	25	20	5	President of the Zilla Parishad	Chief Planning Officer of ZP
Uttar Pradesh	20-40	Four-fifths	One-fifth	Minister nominated by the State Govt.	Chief Development Officer of the District
Karnataka		Four-fifths	One-fifth	President of the Zilla Parishad Mayor/ Municipal President of District Hq. Vice Chairman	CEO of ZP
Tamil Nadu		Four-fifths	One-fifth	Chairman- ZP President, Vice Chairman– Collector.	CEO of District Panchayat

Chart–4

No	*State*	*Parallel Body*	*Areas of overlap/substitution*	*Institutional Linkage with PRIs.*
1.	Uttar Pradesh	Water User Group (WUG)/Site Implementation Committee (SIC)	• Formulating, developing and approving plans of the area covered by the WUG • Selection of beneficiaries (farmers) • Construction, maintenance and management of link and main drains • Policy decisions like decision on rates of water charges.	Village Pradhan may be the ex-officio chairperson of the SIC.
2.	Haryana	Gram Vikas Samity	Supervision of construction of work out of the funds released by HRDF Board, decentralised planning or any other state government scheme.	The samity consist of 4 members of gram panchayat Chairperson–Sarpanch Elected Members–one panch each from SC community, BC community and a woman panch
3.	Andhra Pradesh	Janmabhoomi	Planning and implementation of development programmes at the local level	Sarpanch and the concerned ward member finds representation in the Habitation Level Committee of Janmabhoomi.
4.	Gujarat	Joint Forest Management	• Cultivation, collection and sale of minor forest produce • Conservation and maintenance of common property resources	• A representative of village panchayat will serve as one of the members of the mandal or committee • Village panchayat itself may become a mandal or committee for the purpose of JFM.
5.	Rajasthan	Watershed	Minor Irrigation	Panchayats can become Project Implementing Agency (PIA) for watershed projects on priority basis.
6.	Himachal Pradesh	Vigilance Committee	Supervision of gram panchayat works/schemes costing upto Rs. 50,000/-	Supervisory body within gram panchayat of the works, schemes and other activities of Gram Panchayat.
7.	West Bengal	District Primary Education Council	Overlapping with Standing Committee on Education at District and Intermediate level.	

Source: Participatory Research in Asia (2002) Parallel Bodies and Panchayate Raj Institutions : Experiences from the States.

The DRDAs Untamed

The District Rural Development Agencies (DRDAs), which handle crores of rupees, should have disappeared from the scene following the 73rd amendment of the Constitution. But no such signs are visible. The battle is going on in some states. The DRDAs have been constituted as late as in 2002. Some State Governments have refused to comply with the Central Government guidelines to ensure that the DRDAs get merged with the ZPs and the Central Government has failed to enforce it. The para-statal bodies have become anachronistic, and have no right to exist after the amendments of the Constitution. The Central Government is duty-bound to enforce the provisions of the Constitution. The inability on the part of the Indian State to ensure it raises questions about the real political will at the top.

The Rise of Parallel Bodies

Added to it is the emergence of a series of parallel bodies in different states as shown in the chart-4.

Broadly speaking, the functions performed by the parallel bodies can be classified as ensuring user\beneficiary participation, convergence of programmes and promoting\ensuring efficiency. While these are the basic functions of the PRIs, the matters like irrigation, watershed management and development and minor forest produce come under the purview of the Eleventh Schedule which lays down the functions of the PRIs.The Gram Vikas Samity in Haryana and the Vigilance Committee in Himachal Pradesh encroach upon the statutory functions of the panchayat bodies as spelt out in the Panchayat Acts of the respective states. The Task Force on PRIs has argued that the Village Development Committee set up by the Government of Haryana negate the provisions of the 73rd Amendment Act regarding reservation of SC, woman and seems to replace the elected Gram Panchayats. The *Janmabhoomi* (JB) programme tends to mobilize local people, the entire state administrative machinery and draws upon all the existing central and state government schemes as resource for development work and thus substitute the functions of the Gram Panchayat. Although the Sarpanch is to preside over the JB, the real player is the officer.It has created another problem. The Gram Sabha meetings convened by the Gram Panchayat have become less important because of the realization on the part of the people that fewer benefits are available through panchayats. The Task Force on PRIs observes that it has a content of people's participation and social mobilisation, but it bypasses PRIs.

There is another set of parallel bodies in states like Maharashtra where exist traditional panchayats with different legitimising sources. In Maharashtra, for example, there exists village "collectives" called "gavki". The "gavki" is constituted by the elite upper castes, the rich and undoubtedly, only the patriachs of the village, women excluded. Before the amendment of the constitution these bodies functioned alongside the elected panchayats. Unfortunately, they continue even today. Lele narrates an interesting case of how a 'gavki' defied the panchayat. The gavki decided to auction the sand from the riverbed and the money earned was to be a contribution to its own fund. The GP raised objection to it. A conflict arose. The persons who raised objection to this issue, were the more informed active villagers, some *dalits* and women, associated with a local NGO who were in favour of the panchayats However, they do not have strength to go against the 'gavki'. The 'gavki' has been found to be more effective in areas where women or *dalits* are in power. Thus, as Lele rightly observes "reservations which intended to empower both these marginalised sections in rural governance are being made ineffective by the established powers in the rural areas"[30].

Caste panchayats in some states have outgrown their functions as local dispensers of justice. Recently a caste panchayat in Nauranjabad village in UP's Meerut district ruled that a young woman pregnant with the child of her second husband, return to her first husband who had reappeared after five years. The argument was that he first husband, though assumed dead, had never divorced her. Married off at just 14 years to soldier Mohammed Arif Gudiya had barely spent a week with him when Arif was called to duty at Kargil War. After four years 'widowed' Gudiya's parents with the consent of the Community, married her off to her cousin Toutiq. Gudiya became pregnant. Now the caste panchayat declared her second marriage illegal. The constitutional panchayat has nothing to do.[31]

Muscled by a medieval morality these caste collectives are known to punish by ostracising, publicly disgracing, making the guilty chew excreta, stripping, parading woman maked, presiding over torture, prescribing rape as retribution. In July, 2003 the upper caste Goli Panchayat in Bamtolar village in Seoni district in Madhya Pradesh delivered retributive rape as justice. Three *dalit* women from the Mahar caste were gang raped by eight upper caste men because an upper caste boy had eloped with a boy from their family.

Around the same time 60 villages from Jhapa Udan, 17 Kilometres from Muzzaffarpur stripped Sumitra Dai as a penalty for filing a complaint with the judicial magistrate against *Mukhia* and his men accusing them of filching the money alloted to her under the Indira Awas Yojana. 19 *dalit* families of Munda village in Madhya Pradesh were ostracized because they protested when cattle of the upper caste here herded into the land allotted to them by the government

The general reaction against the parallel bodies is that they represent processes external to the constitutionally mandated role of panchayats and enable bureaucracies to override democratic bodies. Thus they pose serious threats to the effective functioning of local self-governing institutions.

Transparency: Right to Information

One of the objectives of democratic decentralisation is to make the governance transparent. And for that purpose a few state governments like Rajasthan, Madhya Pradesh have taken some legal initiatives, such as, granting the right to information. What is happening in the field is a matter of really grave concern. The Majdoor Kisan Shakti Sanghatan (MKSS) in Rajasthan led by Ms. Aruna Roy sought all records pertaining to the five year development activities in the Janpad Panchayat in February, 2002[32]. The Gram Sevak refused to give information for 10 months. Later on, the Gram Sabha passed a resolution that the information asked for could not be provided because it would create tension in the area. The district officials took the plea of the resolution and expressed their helplessness. It was argued that the panchayat is a constitutional body. It is,therefore, not possible for the officials to intervene in order to compel the panchayat to furnish the information The MKSS met the Chief Minister and the Panchayati Raj Minister without any effective results.

Undermining Elections

Attempt to undermine elections is still on. The record of some of the State Governments with regard to the holding of elections is less said, the better. Some of the states have taken years to hold elections. Postponing elections under one pretext or another has become a routine matter. The elections to panchayats have been completed in almost all the states after a series of legal battles and interventions by the civil society organisations. Gujarat has recently set a unique example. The State Government announced incentives to the extent of Rs. 1 lakh to those panchayats, which would be able to hold elections on the basis of consensus. In a divided society like ours, spontaneous consensus in the interest of a large section of people is a myth. If there is at all any consensus, it is that of caste, religion etc. and basically class. It is a veiled attempt to guide local democracy from the top and in the interest of the ruling classes. Incidentally, the Santhanam Committee (1963) examined the scope of unanimity in panchayat elections. The Committee came across villages where the anxiety for unanimity and consensus meant the continuation of the traditional authorities and suppression of the new spirit of the youth. It was felt that the securing of unanimity through cash incentives was not desirable. The silver lining is that the people of Gujarat seem to have rejected the idea as is evident from the contests that characterised the elections in more than 90 per cent of the GPs.

Interestingly, what is happening in some states in the name of achieving unanimity is a cause of serious concern. During the panchayat elections in Karnataka in 2000 some of the seats were auctioned. The Election Commission could not interfere on the ground that if the voters made an arrangement among themselves to ensure unanimous election it was beyond the legal competence of the Commission to intervene.In order to augment the resources some of the seats were put to bidding in Andhra Pradesh in 2001. Even the reserved seats were not spared. The highest amount for the post of the *Sarpanch* in Velpur village under Guntur district was 10.10 lakh[33].

The electoral processes have been criminalized in some of the states like Uttar Pradesh (UP) Bihar. In the intermediate panchayat elections in UP there was blood bath, which resulted in the killing of 200 persons. *Dalits* were threatened with dire consequences. The Election Commission had to ban the entry of two ministers into their native blocks wherefrom their wives were contesting. One contestant for the ZP Presidentship had 42 criminal cases against him.

It is interesting to note that the holding of elections at regular intervals can bring about significant change in the socio-political profile of rural India[34].The study has shown that the caste system in Tamil Nadu weakens following the elections.

Actions of some of the State Governments

Legislative actions and decisions of some of the State Governments are undermining the process of democratic decentralisation. For example, the Chattishgarh government has passed an order prescribing basic literacy as the minimum educational qualification for contesting a panchayat seat. This provision has dangerous implication as it will reduce the democratic space for the poor people particularly poor women, minorities and the *dalits* many of whom do not have basic literacy. It seems repugnant to the spirit of the constitutional mandate of panchayats as instruments of planning for economic development and social justice. It will thus impede the process of empowerment of a large mass of population in view of the fact there is still a large chunk of population without basic literacy.

Another interesting case of similar nature is the constitution of the Third State Finance Commission by the present Government of Kerala under the chairmanship of a retired IAS officer who was chief secretary earlier and is currently involved with the work of the Government of Kerala. The other two members are serving officers–secretary, expenditure and secretary, local administration.

The SFCs are modelled on the Union Finance Commission and it is intended to take an objective, enlightened and independent view in making recommendations in order to enable the local government institutions as institutions of self government as envisaged in the 73rd and 74th Amendments of the constitution. The SFCs are required to fix the size of the divisible pool and to design the methods for inter se distribution of the share of the local bodies on an equitable and efficient basis. It has also to evaluate the critical gap at various levels taking into account the tax assignment, on the one hand and financial responsibilities, on the other.

Doubts have been expressed about whether it would be possible on the part of the retired or serving officials associated with the work of the government to play their roles properly. Interestingly, the Eleventh Finance Commission observed that appointment of the serving officers as chairman or members put a limitation on the SFC to act as an autonomous body to make recommendations in a free and independent manner.

Mention may also be made about another legislative actions in some of the states like Haryana, Delhi, Himachal Pradesh, Maharashtra, Madhya Pradesh, Rajasthan where it has been mandatory for all the elected members to follow two-child norm. Nobody who have more than two children, would be able to contest local elections. It may be recalled that the Task Force on Panchayati Raj set up by the Rajiv Gandhi Foundation has rejected the restrictive provision as violative of human rights. It also leads to malpractices like desertion of women, sex selection test, female feticide, neglect of girl child. The empirical studies indicate that the *dalits* and women have been disqualified on this ground. It is discouraging young women and the disadvantaged sections from entering local politics.

Women Empowerment

In order to add a new dimension to the process of democratic decentralisation, namely, gender justice, the 73rd amendment of the Constitution provides for reservation of seats and the posts of chairpersons for the women. All the state Acts have incorporated this provision and elections are being held accordingly. But the studies indicate that women elected to PRIs are yet to play their roles properly[35]. While this may be attributed to number of factors, it has been found that the women members have failed to perceive their role properly particularly due to the inadequate and ill-conceived training, lack of time and required literacy. Even when some of them are able to perceive their role, they cannot perform due to multiplicity of constraints. The social conditions are not conducive. The domestic load and commitment continue to remain the same. The party or the social leaders who have motivated them to contest elections, do not extend necessary help and support. On the contrary, they want them to work as per their dictation and any attempt on their part to develop independence causes displeasure of their leaders. As a good number of them belong the family of the leaders it generates problems in the family. Added to it is the lurking feeling that they have been elected for one term only because the seats are reserved for the women. They think that they would be replaced by the male members in the next elections. The officials do not attach importance to them[35]. There have been cases in states like UP where the officers have refused to talk to them. For the women coming from the poor families the problem gets compounded. They have to spend much of their time to meet both ends. Even when they can manage some time they cannot attend meeting because they do not have conveyance expenses for traveling to the office. The meagre meeting allowance is not paid timely.

It should however be pointed out that the political space provided to women in panchayats has started bringing about change, though slowly. The findings of a study on the working of panchayats in six states conducted by PRIA reveals that ".......... 25 per cent woman notice change in their status within their family after they have been elected........... about 60 per cent of women said that they would encourage women to stand for election. The same percentage (60 per cent) is contemplating to contest PRI election again".[37]

The Gradual Withdrawal of the State from the Social Sector

Decentralisation is not an end in itself. It is a means for the achievement of specific ends. In Indian case, the ends have been identified by the relevant amendment of Constitution, namely, economic development and social justice. Following the adoption of the policy of liberalisation the Indian State has allowed market to have a free play and the State is gradually withdrawing itself from the domain of social development. Take, for example, the case of education. The share of expenditure from all the Central Government departments devoted to education was 4.1 per cent in 1990-91. It came down to 3.8 per cent in 1998-99. India, taken together the expenditures of the Central and State Governments, spent 6 to 8 per cent of its Gross Domestic Product on the social sector in 1990s–lower than that in 1980s. It was low compared to other developing countries and certainly compared to East Asian countries. It was low compared to the ratios recommended by the United Nations Development Programme.[38]

In 2000-01, the Central Government discontinued a number of development programmes from 256 to 117. The Planning Commission has transferred 21 programmes to the State Government and discontinued

36 programmes. The details are as follows: Agri-sector from 41 to 5, Animal Resource Development Sector from 24 to 12 high schools and primary education sector from 45 to 10.

There has been a sharp decline in the real per capita social sector expenditure by the Government of India. It was Rs. 98.21 in 1996-97. It came down to Rs. 53.58 in 1997-98. Interestingly the Central and State Governments spent during 1997-98 a sum of Rs. 12,000 crores on the police sector. It was little less than the budgetary provision for agriculture and allied sectors.

SOME CASE STUDIES OF NEW EXPERIMENTS

The MP Experiments

The MP Government has launched what is called Gram Swaraj. In the words of James Manor, "this experiment is a leap into the unknown"[39]. Gram Swaraj as a system of local self-governance at the village level, moves from indirect to direct democracy. It seeks to empower the people and not their representatives and thus to bring an end to *sarpanch raj*. To operationalise the system in the field it has been decided that Gram Sabhas have to be strengthened in order to enable them to exercise all the powers exercised by the panchayats. It calls for devolution of more powers to the Gram Sabhas. Thus the Gram Sabhas will become decision-making bodies. And for the purpose of implementing decisions the Gram Sabhas will constitute eight standing committees. These committees shall be accountable and responsible to the Gram Sabhas. There shall be a separate finance committee with a treasurer. In this way the Gram Sabhas will turn into institutions of self-government.

But the Gram Sabha meetings as we have discussed above, are not held regularly in any part of the state. Quorum has become meaningless in Gram Sabha meetings because the attendance register is taken from house-to-house for securing signatures of the absent members. The Gram Sabhas have turned out to be places for approving beneficiary lists for the government schemes. There is, in fact, a lack of devolution of significant powers to Gram Sabhas. The standing committees are not generally formed through elections, as the regular Gram Sabha meetings do not provide opportunity for holding elections. In most of the villages they have been formed by government fiats with the help of the government functionary. The so-called 'elected' members of the Gram Sabha are not aware of their role and responsibilities.

The parallel committees have been formed by the State Government for implementing programmes of the line departments like forests, education, and health. They dilute the authority of the committees and weaken panachayat as the government channels its developmental resources through such parallel committees.

Initially there was sharp reaction from the *sarpanchas*. There was mobilisation of the *sarpanch* as a community against the introduction of Gram Swaraj Act leading to a filing of a case questioning the constitutional validity of the new system. The Government retreated and brought them back in the panchayati raj system by making them co-signatories for operating the Gram Swaraj account.

The idea of Gram Swaraj has not been institutionalised because of the absence of effective communication strategies. It has resulted in a lack of awareness about the new concept. There is a view that the hidden agendum has been not to empower people but to contain the new emerging leadership from the panchayats of women, *dalits* and tribals. Second, the government apparatus has not responded favourably. The bureaucracy is resistant to change. Even the panchayat secretary refuses to give access to information, as it would dilute his authority. Third, the capacities of the Gram Sabhas in most of the villages are inadequate to operationalise the institution.

The concept of district government now being developed in Madhya Pradesh with a lot of fanfare undermines the authority of democratic and decentralised governance. It infringes upon the autonomy of local self-government, which is a constitutionally ordained feature of panchayats in India. Even after the assurance of the State Government that it will continue to devolve powers and authority to these bodies, there is strong doubt. Some scholars refer to the possibilities of conflict in case both these bodies are empowered. The concept of local self-government loses its significance when a minister who represents the State Government, heads the District Planning Committee.

The fiscal and political decentralisation has been very limited. It has not led to any fundamental change in the countryside. The powers granted to the panchayats are narrow in scope. In fact, they amount only to deciding how employment generation funds would be spent, how pragramme beneficiaries would be identified. The control of the panchayat over the state functionaries is illusory because salaries are paid by the Block Development Officer. Since the state controls the flow of funds to panchayats and planning and implementation of all major projects, there is little scope for independent initiative, which, according to Amartya Sen is one of the major pillars of local self-government. The problems of land reform, education and primary health have not been addressed by the PRIs. "Digvijoy Singh's real intention has been the transplanting of the West Bengal and Kerala model of political decentralisation into Madhya Pradesh while emptying it of genuine transformational potential"[40].

People's Campaign in Kerala

Kerala under the rule of the Left Democratic Front initiated a unique model of planning popularly known as people's campaign for decentralised planning. Its programme of involving people in all activities, from identification of development issues and resources at the local level through project formulation, implementation and monitoring to social auditing for transparency has few parallels. A distinguishable feature of the decentralisation experiment in Kerala has been the devolution of 35 to 40 per cent of the state's plan fund to local self–government institutions (LSGIs) along with the transfererence to them of officials of line departments. The data available for the year 1999-2000 indicated that the campaign succeeded in translating into reality the expectations about the investment outlay by making credit accessible to the poor and mobilising small savings in the form of beneficiary contribution. With mass involvement in the planning process innovative ideas were put forward to resolve the problems of development. About 250 models have evolved within a span of three years for various sectors. Examples include vegetable cultivation at Kunjikuzhi GP in Alapuzha district, intervention in primary education at Kayoor-Chemeni GP in Kasargode district. The exercise negated the notion that planning is a highly technical job to be done only by the specialised technocrats[41].

There was a change of government in 2001 from the Communist of India (Marxist)–led Left Democratic Front to the Indian National Congress-led United Democratic Front. The budget for 2001-02 showed that the new Government revised the fund allotment to LSGIs downward by 16.43 per cent. The Government had also revised the guidelines for people's campaign. Earlier, the task force was the most important instrument for decentralised planning. Each task force included, *inter alia*, an activist, a technical expert, a government official and an elected representative of the LSGI and functioned with a chairman (elected representative to the LSGI). In the new guidelines the officials have been given prominence. The secretary, GP has been made the convener. In order to ensure that the interests of the vulnerable sections of the society, such as, women are protected, it was laid down that one third of the task force members would be women. Further, sectors other than women development had to co-opt one member for other sectoral committees. The new guidelines have dropped all these clauses.

Concluding Observations

Thus democratic decentralisation is today facing a lot of challenges from within and without. There is lack of political will and bureaucratic support apart from conceptual confusion and iniquitous social structure characterised by hierarchically structured caste system and highly unequal ownership of land (the bottom 39 per cent of the rural households own only 5 per cent of all assets while the top 5 per cent own 46 per cent). It has been noticed that the change of regime adversely affects the working of PRIs What is no less important is the support base of the party or coalition of parties in power. There is lack of people's initiative, which is considered as one of the important pre-conditions for the successful working of the panchayati raj system. A great majority of the elected functionaries is not capable of handling the bureaucrats. The service conditions of the civil servants deputed to the PR bodies are such that it is difficult to make them accountable to the PR functionaries. Another problem with the political functionaries is their lack of competence to manage complex projects.

The first generation panchayats had also started with a lot of euphoria in 1950s but things started changing within a few years. In fact, there are strong threats to panchayati raj even today, coming from, namely, the Central Government and the Union Parliament the State Government and the legislature, the bureaucracy and the social structure[42]. One constitutional amendment cannot cure all the ills. One has reasons to express doubts about the future of constitutionally ordained PR bodies as institutions of self-government and instruments of economic development and social justice.

Notwithstanding the fact that there are very powerful impediments to the successful growth of the panchayati raj in India, there are certain silver linings. It has been realized by the Indian State that another round of Constitutional amendment is necessary to strengthen the PRIs and for this purpose a high-powered committee consisting of some of the Chief Ministers has already been constituted. Second, there has been increasing interest of the people and the press about the panchayati raj. Third, the NGOs are very active in this field.

References

1. M.K. Gandhi (1942) 'My Idea of Village Swaraj', *Harijan* July 26.

2. Prabhat Datta (1992) *The Second Generation Panchayats in India,* Kolkata Book House, Kolkata, p. 2.

3. Prabhat Datta (1998) *Major Issues in the Development Debate*, Kanishka, New Delhi, pp. 14-19.

4. D. Bandyopadhaya *et. al (2003)* 'Dependency Versus Autonomy: Identity Crisis of India's Panchayats' *Economic and Political Weekly*, September 20.

5. Prabhat Datta (2001) *Panchayats, Rural Development and Local Autonomy : The West Bengal Experience,* Das Gupta & Co. Kolkata, pp.19-20. George Mathew (2002) 'Enemies of Panchyati Raj', *The Hindu*, January 11.

6. Era Sezhiyan (2002) Development Directions, *Frontline,* March, 15. Purnima S.Tripathi (2004), "The Case Against MPLADS" *Frontline,* November 5.

7. George Mathew (2002) 'Threat to Grassroots Democracy', *The Hindu*, Feb16. D. Bandyopadhaya (1999) 'Constitution Eighty Seventh Amendment Bill, *Economic and Political Weekly*, (EPW), 9 April.

8. Government of India (2002) *The Report of the Working Group on Decentralised Planning and Panchayati Raj Institutions for the Tenth Five Year Plan* (2002-2007) Planning Commission, New Delhi, p. 9.
9. Mahi Pal (2004) Panchayati Raj and Rural Governance, *EPW*, January 10.
10. Government of India (2000) *Planning Commission*, New Delhi, pp. 175-76.
11. Nilkanta Rath (2004) 'Twelfth Finance Commission and Minimum Needs', *EPW*, June 4.
12. Cited by Richard Mahapatra (2003) 'Toothless at 10', *Down to Earth*, January.
13. *The Telegraph* (1999), June 24.
14. M.A. Oommen, (2002) 'Decentralisation and the Tenth Plan' *The Hindu*, Jan. 1.
15. PRIA (1999) *The Status of P.R. Finances in India, New Delhi.*
16. Prabhat Datta (2003), *Towards Good Governance and Sustainable Development*, Das Gupta & Co. Kolkata.
17. Participatory Research in Asia (PRIA) 1997. *Strengthening PRIs in India* (unpublished).
18. Cited by K. Jayalakshi in her paper 'Role of Gram Sabhas in Betul district in MP' presented at the national conference on Gram Sabha held at NIRD, Hyderabad during July 28-29, 1999.
19. John Oommen, "Gram Sabhas : The Live Wire in the Planning Process in Kerala" *Journal of Rural Development*, Vol. 18, No. 2.
20. P. Menon (1996) "Sex Slaves no more : Devdasis of Belgaum District break free", *Frontline*, February, 9.
21. See, *Uma Prachar* (1997) Janurary-March.

22. PRIA, *ibid.*

23. Anil Kumar Vaddiraju and Shagun Mehrotra (2004) 'Making Panchayats Work', *EPW*, September 11.

24. N. Webster (1992) *Panchayati Raj and Decentralisation of Development Planning in West Bengal*, Calcutta : K.P. Bagchi p. 99.

25. G.K.Lieten (1998), 'Rural Development in West Bengal : Views From Below', *Journal of Contemporary Asia* Vol. 24, No. 4, p. 328. See his book *Development, Devolution and Democracy : Village Discourse in West Bengal* 1998, Sage, India.

26. See Dr. Kartar Singh "The Role of the Gram Sabha in Village Development", *Kurukshetra,* October, 1999.

27. Prabhat Datta (19996) 'Politicising Rural Development : Lessons from India's West Bengal', *Asia–Pacific Journal for Rural Development*, December, 1997 and (1997) 'Politics at Blade and Grassroot', *The Telegraph, July, 10.* Prabhat Datta (2000) *Panchayats, Rural Development and Local Autonomy: the West Bengal Experience*, Dasgupta & Co., Kolkata.

28. M. Ghatak and M. Ghatak (2000) 'Recent Reforms in the Panchayat System in West Bengal' *EPW*, January 5.

29. Robert Thorlind (2000), *Development, Decentralisation and Democracy,* NIAS : Sweden.

30. Medha Kotwal Lele (2001) 'Local Government: Conflict of Interests and Issues of Legitimisation', *EPW*, December 22.

31. *Outlook,* October 11, 2004.

32. *Panchayat Update* (2001), March.

33. *Panchayat Update* (2001) August.

34. S.K.Gupta (2001) "*New Panchayats and Subaltoen Resurgence*", *EPW*, July 21.

35. Prabhat Datta (2003) *Empowerment of Women Through Panchayats in West Bengal : An Exploratory Study*, Dasgupta & Co., Kolkata.

36. R. Srivastava (1999), 'Two Steps Forward, One Step Back', *Seminar*, January.

37. PRIA, *op.cit.*

38. S. Mahendra Dev & Jos. Mooij (2002) 'Social Sector Spending in the 1990s' *The Hindu*, February 1.

39. James Manor (2001) 'Madhya Pradesh Experiment with Democracy', *EPW*, March 3.

40. Amitabh Behar (2003) 'Madhya Pradesh : Experiment with Direct Democracy', *EPW*, May 17.

41. S. Mohankumar (2002), 'From People's Plan to Plan sans Plan', *EPW* April.

42. G. Mathew (2000) 'Threats to Grassroots Democracy', *The Hindu* ; Feb. 17.

3

Decentralisation and Urban Poverty Reforms in India

Of the problems to be ameliorated in the 21st century poverty is perhaps the most basic. Despite the differences surrounding the idea of development there is a general agreement except from the post-development school that it must include tackling poverty. The World Bank has identified reducing poverty as the fundamental objective of economic development.

Poverty is a concept that aggregates the situation of a number of people in a community or involves an abstract description of insufficiencies rendering a decent life impossible. As such poverty cannot be defined in universal terms because the community differs and because a decent life has different meanings to different people in different countries. Still, there is scope to discuss poverty in general terms because some aspects of life such as starvation and lack of shelter come within the concept regardless of the context.

Recent Trend in Poverty Studies

The recent trend in poverty studies has been to move beyond an approach rooted in narrow conceptualization of poverty based upon income or consumption towards one that captures some of the diversity and complexity of poverty. The result of the conventional approach is the headcount measure expressing the number of people below the poverty line. Participatory approaches have been introduced to capture how poverty is perceived by the poverty group. At the same time attention has been broadened out form a focus on the poverty condition to one that includes the processes and dynamics of poverty and a discussion on the relation between them[1]. The European study of poverty reduction has recently developed a four-dimensional conceptualization of poverty, which includes livelihoods, resources, knowledge and right[2]. Livelihood covers the condition of a household and the means by which it reproduces itself and includes income and asset ownership. Resources covers household access to credit, education, health, drinking water etc. Knowledge covers information and education that shape the cognitive world of the poor. Finally, rights embrace formal and traditional rights possessed by the individuals and their households, land, tenancy, women's rights etc.

Unique Features of Urban Poverty

Poverty in urban areas has some unique features. In the light of studies on urban poverty one can identify some distinctive elements as follows :

(a) urban livelihood systems are different from those pursued in the countryside.

(b) urban labour markets and the position of poor within them provide the single most important determinant of poverty in urban areas.

(c) the poorest are found among the unemployed and casually employed.

(d) the urban poor may pay more for their goods and services and are often more vulnerable than the rural poor to changes in market conditions, price increases because they live in an almost entirely monetised economy.

(e) the operation of the urban land market is a particular feature of urban areas which adversely affects the poor, who are squeezed out of valuable land and are compelled to live in peripheral or marginal locations.

(f) what distinguishes the day-to-day life of the poor urban dwellers from their rural counterparts is the relationship with the built-in environment characterized by appalling overcrowding, contaminated water, poor or absent sanitation, lack of basic services etc. Thus urban poor are more exposed to severe environmental health risks.

Urbanisation of Poverty

Urbanisation of poverty is now a global trend. Half of the world's poor live in urban areas. It is estimated that 60 per cent of the urban population in the developing countries is poor There is a serious debate about the exact numbers of the poor and how to measure poverty. In urban areas estimates range from 200 billion to at least 600 billion. The fact, however, remains that there has been an increase in the number of urban dwellers living below poverty line since1980s and 90s throughout the world.

Conceptualising Poverty in the Indian Context

In the Indian context poverty is measured primarily in terms of consumption expenditure data following the recommendation of the Lakdawala Committee. The Government of United Kingdom's Department for International Development (DFID) Report associates urban poverty in India with unsanitary living conditions, limited or no access to service, complex social relationship and high levels of vulnerability. It is also associated with specific categories of people and with particular individuals. In peri-urban areas poverty is associated with the process of deagrarianisation where farmland is being developed for urban areas. This affects patterns of labour force participation, social change, changing demands of infrastructure (e.g. for solid waste) and pressure on natural resource systems[3].

The organizer of Urban Basic Services in Alappuzha town in Kerala identified nine factors. Families with four of them were listed as poor. The factors include:

1. *kantcha* houses;
2. lack of access to safe drinking water;
3. lack of sanitary latrine;
4. one or more illiterate adults in the family;
5. one or no one employed;

6. the family eating two or fewer meals a day;
7. children of five years in the family;
8. alchoholics or drug addicts in the family;
9. belonging to SC or ST.

Coming to urban poverty it needs to be stressed that modernization theorists and neo-classical economists believe that urban poverty is a temporary phenomenon. It will disappear over time as urban consumption matches production and migrants become integrated into city life. However, the experience in India from 1970s suggests otherwise. Since 1970s onwards the squatter settlements had grown along with an expending informal sector indicating very little impact of the trickle down economy reaching the vast majority of the urban population. Studies in 1980s showed that the incidence of poverty rose in urban areas. This has been confirmed by studies on the urban impact of structural adjustment programme. Referring to Maharashtra, Karnataka, Tamil Nadu and even Andhra Pradesh, Kundu says that it could be due to the nature of development itself. Casualisation and marginalisation of the workforce might contribute to the rise of poverty.

Estimating India's Urban Poverty

The first attempt to estimate poverty in India was made in 1962 by a Working Group of Experts after taking into account the recommendations of the National Advisory Committee of the Indian Council of Medical Research. The Working Group proposed to define poverty in money terms.

In 1977 the Planning Commission constituted the Task Force on Projections of Minimum Needs and Effective Consumption Demand. It defined poverty line as per capita consumptions level, which meets average per capita daily calories requirement of 2400 calories in rural areas and 2100 for urban areas along with a minimum of non-food expenditure.

The method devised by the Task Force generated controversy. It was argued that the incidence of poverty was not properly reflected. The Planning Commission constituted another Expert Group in 1989. It did not redefine poverty line but estimated separate poverty line for each state by disaggregating national level poverty line. The Planning

Commission has accepted the Expert Group method for its official poverty estimate since 1996. A recent sample survey (5th round-2000) shows that there has been a decline in urban poverty from 30.37 in 1993 to 28.76 in 1999-2000. The poverty in 1993-94 was measured in terms of per capita income per month, which stood at 274.88. It rose to Rs. 451.19 in 1999-2000.

The data collected by the National Sample Survey Organization tend to indicate that poverty level n small and medium towns is higher than the metro or other large towns. In fact, in the towns with less than 20,000 population, poverty is as high as that in rural areas.

Who the Urban Poor are in India

In the early years of planning exercise urban poverty in India was viewed as a fall-out of rural poverty. This was partly true and applicable to the first generation urban poor. After more than five decades of development planning we have now second and third generation of urban poor who have inherited poverty. The urban poverty group population can broadly be classified into four categories[4].

(a) poor who have inherited poverty;

(b) new migrants from rural to urban areas;

(c) new generation of poverty group population who have descended into poverty due to a number of factors;

(d) Scheduled Castes (SC), Scheduled Tribes (ST) and other disadvantaged sections of the population.

A study by National Institute of Urban Affairs (1987) found that 68 per cent of their samples of urban poor were women and children. A good chunk of them belong to the members of SC, ST and minorities. A study for the Planning Commission by the National Center for Human Settlement and Environment brought out that 18 occupational categories account for the bulk of the workers belonging to the poor households and 50 occupational categories account for 90 per cent of the total number of workers. They are engaged in transport (cycle-rickshaw, auto-rickshaw, head loaders) construction business (bricklayers, painters, carpenters, casual workers etc.) and manufacturing in micro units.

Role of the Poverty Group in Urban Life

The urban poor should not be looked at as the 'unfortunate tumour' in the urban life. Looking at the history of urbanization in India one can easily find out how they have, through their labour, contributed positively toward the construction of every aspects of city and thus become an inalienable part of the urban life processes in a number of ways[5]. They provide the market for many industrial products; they keep the huge informal sector running first by providing cheap labour and then as consumers. Their labour power plays immense role in the rise and growth of the urban sector. The welfare state has, therefore, responsibility to take care of the urban poor.

It has also to be admitted that the most demanding of the urban challenges in India is the challenge of poverty. It poses a great threat to the social fabric and economic well being of Indian urban life.

Poverty Group Perception of Poverty

A series of impact assessment studies done at the instance of DFID India in 1997 demonstrate that poor urban people highlight employment, assets, savings and income as the key determinants of their well being. This is heavily related to the security of assets. The studies bring out that poor people's needs can be broadly categorized under three headings- survival, security and quality of life[6].

Manifestations of Urban Poverty

The National Commission on Urbanization (1989) has shown that urban poverty manifests itself in various forms, namely :

(a) proliferation of slums;

(b) fast growth of the informal sector;

(c) increasing casualization and underdevelopment of labour and

(d) crushing pressure on civic services.

The Commission feels and quite correctly that poverty cannot be classified adequately in terms of income, expenditure or consumption patterns alone. "Poverty is complex in context, texture, characteristics, impact and implications. The focus should be on human degradation resulting from poverty not only on numbers. What is required is a multidimensional concept inclusive of the environment, access to services and social psychological supports".

Classification of Poverty Alleviation Programmes

Alleviation of poverty, if not complete eradication, has been the declared goal of the post-colonial Indian State. One of the important agenda items of India's development planning is the formulation of policies to tackle the poverty, both urban and rural. In fact, there has been a sustained effort through the five year plans to provide some relief to the urban poor. Such an effort was also necessitated to tame the teeming millions living in urban pockets. However, the National Commission on Urbanization has attempted a classification of poverty alleviation programmes as implemented in India. They are as follows:

(a) shelter and physical environment related programmes;

(b) nutrition supplement programmes including public distribution;

(c) employment generation programmes and

(d) programme for the development of citizens' participation and development of institutional capacities of the service agencies.

Slum Clearance and Slum Development

In the first and second five year plans slum clearance constituted the core of shelter related programmes. This led to the birth of the Central Slum Areas (Improvement and Clearance) Act. It resulted in clearance of slums from the prime areas of the major city. People were relocated at the low areas of the city outskirts. Unfortunately, the basic purpose was defeated. The recovered prime land in the central areas of the city was put to highly profitable use both by the public and private sectors. Many of the allottees in the resettlement colonies had to sell off their land to the rich people in the face of hike in land prices. The State failed to live up to the expectations of the slum dwellers who were derived of the basic urban services.

Environment Improvement Programme

In order to set things right the Government of India initiated a new scheme in 1972-Environmnet Improvement of Slum Areas (EIUS). The scheme was designed to provide minimum civic facilities in the slum areas. The scheme has been transferred to the State sector in the seventh plan. The scheme includes provisions like one tap water for every 100 persons, construction of sewer-open drains with normal outflow, construction of storm water drains, community bath and community latrines, widening of existing lanes and provision of street lighting.

It is necessary to note that this approach to equate the urban poor with slum dwellers is devoid of reality. The poor people can often be found distributed throughout a city; living in servants' quarters, *chawls*, small squatters settlements and pavements. Very often they are found in middle class and affluent areas where they perform the needed services for the rich as domestic aid, drivers, sweepers, *dhobis* etc.

Community Participation

In the 50's community participation in development programmes became a national slogan following the recommendations of the Ford Foundation team. In the urban sector it was introduced in 1958, the purpose being to improve the quality of life of the poor in urban areas. The scheme known as the Urban Community Development (UCD) covered provisions like (a) regularisation of slum dwellers on the existing slums by granting them house site *pattas* (b) convincing people for a planned outlay by mutual adjustment and taking up housing programme on self-help basis by the beneficiaries themselves (c) improvement of environment by providing basic amenities.

The first pilot project was taken up in Delhi with the assistance of the Ford Foundation. It was designed to function as a part of the local body and was reviewed as a link between the people and the ULBs. The basic objective was to strengthen local voluntary organisations and establish bustee level bodies.

The Fifth Plan: A New Approach

The Fifth Plan (1974-79) was the first to recognize the existence of large-scale poverty in India without making any distinction between rural and urban poverty. Apart from stressing the need to enable the poverty group to have access to the minimum private consumption of at least Rs. 40.6 and to raise the share of the bottom 30 per cent in total private consumption to about 21.98 per cent, it proposed no national poverty alleviation programme. It sought to reduce the incidence via economic growth processes and general national level programmes such as minimum needs programmes, public procurement and distribution of essential goods and reservations for the SC, ST and other backward classes.

The Sixth Plan Approach

The Sixth Plan (1980-85) was a step further as it sought to develop an approach to poverty issues. The plan document attempted to address the problem in three stages: (a) identification and measurement (b) developing realistic targets and (c) formulation of specific programmes. Thus there was no concerted, planned move to attack urban poverty. The document stressed the need for lifting 6 million urban poor above the poverty level essentially through the provision of additional consumption benefits and better and more equitable distribution of health, sanitation, housing etc.

The Sixth Plan recognized the limitations of the income growth approach. To quote "specific policy measures will be needed to influence the composition of output in favour of mass consumption goods but also to ensure a more even regional and class distribution of output"[7].

Integrated Development of Small and Medium Towns

In an effort to check inflow of people to the large cities the Central Government launched a community participation-based scheme-Integrated Development of Small and Medium Towns (IDSMT) during the Sixth Plan period. The primary purpose was to create infrastructural facilities and employment opportunities in a large number of selected towns with less than one lakh population so that the city-bound migrants could be attracted. The scheme covered programmes such as Central assistance for residential land developments, development of commercial and industrial estates, improvement and construction of roads, bus and taxi stands, construction of slaughterhouses and provision of low cost sanitation. The programme is now facing a setback following low investment of the Central Government on this account.

The Seventh Plan Perspective

The urban poverty issue was given serious consideration during the Seventh Plan period (1985-90). The document reflected concern of the development planners to address poverty question more directly and in a focused manner. In the first place, the document noted the growing incidence of urban poverty and pointed out that on the one hand, the uninterrupted migration from rural areas led to the rapid growth of slums in many cities and towns, and one the other hand, to overcrowding in relatively unskilled and other low paid jobs in the informal sector. The Seventh Plan emphasised the need for improving the living conditions of the slum dwellers. Secondly, it was further felt that the effective tackling of urban poverty called for a major thrust on employment generation and creation of productive assets. The strategy suggested in the plan document included provision of gainful employment to the unemployed particularly women and youth, raising the earning of those in law paid jobs, stepping up productivity and learning of the self employed workers and improving the access of the urban poor to basic amenities such as education, health care, sanitation, safe drinking water.

The Seventh Plan recognized the economic problems of the urban poor. It was felt that the credit has to be given to the poor to enable them to start their own ventures. An income-generating programme known as the Self-Employment Programme for the Urban Poor (SEPUP) was launched in 1986.

People's Participation

The need for people's participation in solving their own problems was given importance in 1980s. This led to the launching of urban basic services programme (UBSP) in 1985. The programme aimed to improve and upgrade quality of life of the urban poor, especially the women and children. The programme included provisions like (a) extension of child care and health services, water and sanitation facilities and income generation activities of mothers (b) improvement of the provision of basic services with special emphasis on learning opportunities in early childhood (c) extension of health and community education services, awareness and consciousness-raising programmes such as film shows.

The ULBs were given the overall responsibility for implementation of the programme. The UPA cell was created under the ULB to generate local municipal contributions, promoting linkages and convergence with all the sectoral departments[8].

Employment Generation Programmes: NRY

In 1989 came the Nehru Rozgar Yojana (NRY). The major objectives of the programme were: (a) to create employment opportunities for the unemployed and underemployed urban poor and to arrange for skill/ training, credit and subsidy facilities, input and marketing support and so on; (b) to create opportunities for the unskilled and semi-skilled labour force living below poverty line through such small labour intensive schemes as would create public assets and (c) to provide financial support, both loan and subsidy, for the improvement of the shelter conditions of the households of the poor. The NRY consisted of three schemes-micro enterprises (SUME), urban wage employment (SUWE) and housing and shelter upgradation (SHASU). One of the important objectives of NRY was to involve the ULBs in the implementation of the programmes. They were supposed to play key role in the selection of employment-oriented activities, identification of beneficiaries, provision of land and space for employment activities etc.

In 1988 the National Commission of Urbanisation (NCU) critically reflected on the urban poverty. The Commission noted with great concern that urban development continues to remain isolated from the national planning process. It sounds a word of warning couched in strong terms: "…..unless the question of urban poverty is tackled, the energies of the poor utilized for productive activity, and an environment created in which the informal sector becomes profitable, we cannot save our country"[9].

The Eighth Plan Approach

The Eighth Plan (1990-95) appeared to have taken care of the serious criticisms leveled by NCU about he concept of urban development being divorced form the national planning process. The approach paper contained a section entitled urban planning and unemployment putting the thrust on poverty alleviation.

During the Eighth Plan period there had been a planned endeavour to ensure convergence of the programmes under the name of Urban Basic Services for the Poor (UBSP). In line with that there came into being Prime Minister's Integrated Urban Poverty Eradication Programme (PMIUPEP) in November 1995. It was conceived as a programme under which all sectoral programmes will converge. The National Slum Development Programme launched in 1996 aims at upgrading urban slums b making provision for physical and social amenities, community infrastructures, shelter etc. The scheme is implemented by the grassroots bodies like the Neighbourhood Committees and the Community Development Societies under the overall responsibility of the ULBs. Every ULB is required to create a separate budget sub-head for slum development and urban poverty reduction. They are also expected to form Slum Development Committees with co-opted members from NGOs/ community based-organizations etc. to oversee implementation of all slum development programmes.

The PMIUPEP was launched after the 74th amendment of the Constitution. The programme spelt out the role of ULBs in the processes of planning, implementation, monitoring and evaluation. Apart from creating a separate UPE Cell in each town being covered under the programme, there was also provision for the establishment of a separate Town Urban Poverty Eradication Fund (TUPEF) under the ULB in each town by pooling resources from the Centre, State and ULBs. The responsibility of the ULBs was extended to identification, preparation of town action plan, project formulation and execution, coordination with non-government and other stakeholders, monitoring and reviewing the programme.

The Convergence under SJSRY

In 1997 NRY, UBSP and PMIUPEP were withdrawn and merged to form a new consolidated scheme known as Swarna Jayanti Sahari Rozgar Yojana. This programme was launched in pursuance of the recommendations of the Hashim Committee appointed by the Planning Commission. The Committee recommended that:

(a) the self-employment component of all poverty alleviation programmes be combined into a single programme valid for all urban areas all over the country.

(b) Wage employment and physical infrastructure development component of all these programmes be merged and be made applicable to all urban areas having population up to one lakh.

(c) Shelter component of all programmes to be retained either as a separate scheme or merged with the National Slum Development Scheme (NSDP).

The programme formally launched in 1998 seeks to provide gainful employment to the urban unemployed in two ways, namely, encouraging the setting up of self-employment ventures or provision of wage employment. It consists of two schemes-urban self-employment programme (USEP) and urban wage employment programme (UWEP).

The USEP has three distinct parts, namely, (a) assistance to individual urban beneficiaries for setting up gainful self employment ventures, (b) assistance to groups of urban poor women for setting up gainful employment ventures under the scheme of Development of Women and Children in Urban Areas (DWCUA), (c) training of beneficiaries, potential beneficiaries and other persons associated with the urban employment programme for upgradation and acquisition of entrepreneurial skills. The UWEP is founded on the principle of utilization of labour for construction of socially and economically useful public assets. It is based on the creation of suitable community structures on the UBSP pattern.

The Uniqueness of SJSRY

The uniqueness of SJSRY lies n the guidelines where women have been given key role in the implementation of the programme. The ULBs are the designated nodal agencies for implementing the programme through a three-tiered committee comprising women members belonging to below-the-poverty line families. The community based organizations include Neighbourhood Groups (NHGs); Neighbourhood Committees (NHCs) and Community Development Society (CDS).

Neighbourhood Group (NHG)

This is an informal association of women living in Mohalla or *basti* or neighbourhood group of manageable size (preferably to 10 to 40 to represent urban poor or slum families), geographic contiguity and homogeneity being the basis to carve out the boundaries of the NHGs. At least one women resident among them who is willing to serve as a volunteer, should be selected as a Resident Community Volunteer (RCV) through community consensus or election or any other democratic process. There should be change of rotation (if need be) of such volunteers at periodical intervals. The responsibilities of the RCVs include:

(i) to serve as a channel of information and communication among the families in the cluster;

(ii) to represent the views of the groups in the Neighbourhood Committees and Community Development Societies and other forums;

(iii) to support planning, implementation and monitoring of activities at the neighbourhood level;

(iv) to foster and encourage participation in community improvement; and

(v) to motivate the community for being members of thrift and credit society; and to contribute to community development fund.

Neighbourhood Committes (NHCs)

A Neighbourhood Committee (NHC) is a more formal association of women from the above Neighbourhood Groups located in close proximity and as far as feasible within the same electoral ward. The Committee should consist of all the RCVs from the neighbourhood groups one executive committee member (with voting right) of NHG as well as one female member (without voting right) from each family which falls under the jurisdiction of NHC concerned. There can also be provision for honorary membership without a voting right for Community Organizers (COs), representatives from other sectoral programmes in the community like ICDS supervisor, school teacher, etc. The Convenor/ President of the NHC will be selected/elected by the executive members of the NHC. The convenor will ensure that the meetings are convened on regular basis. The NHC's functions are as follows:

(i) to identify local problems and priorities;

(ii) to provide suggestion for groups involvement in meeting community needs and goals (mini-plans);

(iii) to support local action with partnership of responsible agencies including community contracts;

(iv) to provide feedback to agencies of programme effectiveness and out-reach especially for children and women;

(v) to develop community capacity through training in association with COs, NGOs and other sectoral departments;

(vi) to develop community based thrift and credit system as well as neighbourhood development fund;

(vii) to facilitate the recovery of loans from the beneficiaries in time; and

(viii) to assist/carry out community surveys in accordance with the guidelines.

The NHC may be registered under the Societies Registration Act, or other appropriate Acts if so desired. If registered the NHC may also apply for grants-in-aid under various schemes.

Community Development Society (CDS)

The CDS is a formal association of all the Neighbourhood Committees at the town level based on common goals and objectives. The CDS may consist of elected/selected representative of NHCs as executive members (with voting right) as well as one female member from each family (without voting right) which falls under the jurisdiction of CDS; and other members with honorary membership (with no voting right) which may include community organizers, representatives of NGOs, sectoral department, leading citizens, elected representatives of the area and other resource persons. The Community Development Society (CDS) should be registered under the Societies Registration Act or other appropriate Acts to provide access to grant-in-aid under various schemes and for a wider financial and credit base. A CDS is required to perform the following functions:

(i) to represent needs of all the communities, especially women and children;

(ii) liaise and link up with agencies and departments to promote action in the community towards fulfillment of their needs;

(iii) to identify specific training and arrange for their organization;

(iv) to facilitate community surveys to be carried out to identify the genuine beneficiaries for economic and shelter benefits;

(v) to prepare community plans and proposals, mobilizing resources from the community, town or other sectoral departments;

(vi) to extend help to Bank in coordination with UPE Cell, for ensuring repayment of loans by the beneficiaries in time; and

(vii) to create small community assets in low income areas in consultation with town UPE Cell and Urban Local Body (ULB).

The association of women with the implementation of poverty alleviation programmes is likely to bring about desired results in two ways. It will empower women and enable them to play the role of planners and achievers within their own surroundings.

Special Central Assistance for Slum Upgradation

There is also another scheme for upgradation of slums known as the Special Central Assistance to States for slum upgradation. This scheme has many components which include provision of physical amenities like water supply, storm water drains, community bath, community infrastructures to be used for pre-school education, non-formal education, adult education, community primary health care buildings, provision for shelter etc. The scheme is implemented by the community structures set up under SJSRY programme.

As we find form the above discussion the SJSRY is a two-pronged programme and seeks to attack poverty through generation of self-employment and wage employment opportunities. If the SJSRY succeeds in generating regular wage employment, poverty may take downward trend; this is less likely if such employment is in the casual sector. Throughout the urban sector poverty is highest among households supported by casual labour and self-employment. The attack on poverty through self-employment depends on the poor taking out commercial loans from the official banking system on the recommendations of the local governments. Again, it implies more than simply providing credit as it includes access to markets and reasonably priced raw material and favourable terms of trade for the products. The SJSRY has failed to address these issues.

The Empowerment of Local Bodies

The 74th amendment of the Constitution has created opportunities for decentralised management system. The ULBs have become empowered local institutions with elected representatives responsible for identifying, formulating and implementing development programmes aimed at fostering economic development and social justice. It is, however, true that many states are yet to use the opportunities afforded by the amendment of the Constitution. The Planning Commission has noted that although most states have conducted elections, only a few states have initiated new ways of involving local communities in the planning process, undertaken capacity building programmes for elected members, or created effective functional and financial decentralisation. The conformity laws tend to show that only a few states such as, Kerala, West Bengal and Tamil Nadu have made comprehensive law devolving functions to municipalities.

Ninth Plan Perspective

The Ninth Plan emphasizes on social protection. To quote "Sustainability of the growth process demands that they (the disadvantaged) should be viewed as active participants and indeed partners in the process of development and not as passive beneficiaries of public largesse. The need, therefore, is to create the conditions by which the disadvantaged are not only empowered to take advantage of the opportunities created by the growth process but also to contribute actively in the process of wealth and well being. For this purpose the individual capabilities of the people have to be enhanced through education, information and access to appropriate technology". The Ninth Plan has a new commitment to prepare a National Charter for Social Justice to ensure all round development of the disadvantaged through a three-fold strategy:

(a) empowering those with disabilities making as many disabled people as possible self-reliant and economically productive.

(b) reforming social deviants-restricting the production of alcohol and distribution of drugs in India along with supporting rehabilitation centres,

(c) caring for other disadvantaged people, enforcement of legislation against prostitution and beggary, development of girl child, expanding services for street children.

Issues in UP Strategies

The above discussion brings out that urban poverty alleviation strategies have focused on five things, namely :

(a) enhancing productive employment and income for the poor;

(b) improving general health and other welfare services in the slums;

(c) building infrastructures and creating better environmental facilities including shelter in the slums;

(d) developing and upgrading skills and imparting vocational training to the poor;

(e) encouraging self-help concept among the slum dwellers;

(f) extending safety net or providing for social protection.

The Changing Approach to Urban Poverty

Evidently, there has been a discernible change in the approach of the Government of India to poverty. Initially all efforts at tackling urban poverty had concentrated on slums. Shelter improvement coupled with environmental improvement of slums got the top most priority. The Sixth Plan focused on small and medium towns. The Seventh Plan witnessed a sharp break by recognizing the economic problems of the poor. People's participation began to gather momentum. The Eighth and Ninth Plan targeted convergence of the poverty alleviation programmes and focused on access to productive employment, shelter and services. The present attempt is to encourage self-help programmes and involvement of non-government organizations and civil society sectors. The Ninth Plan places emphasis on social protection and empowerment.

The changing focus reflects the change in the concept of role and responsibility of the State towards the poor and the State's perception about the poverty group population. There is again a lack of holistic approach. It is to be realized that the roots of the poverty are deep-seated and calls for a concerted approach and political will. The study of the evolution of policies indicates that the State has frequently preferred to change the names of the programmes without a basic change in the approach. The change of names of the programmes calls for new guidelines. The implementing agencies find it difficult to keep pace with this frequent, meaningless change of names. The recent emphasis on the participation of private agencies, banks, non-government organizations is a corollary of the adoption of the structural adjustment programme.

Economic Reforms and Poverty Reduction

The importance of social sector expenditure in reducing poverty is well-known. Throughout the 1990s, social sector expenditure as a percentage of GDP, was lower than that in 1990s. The data collected from the Economic Surveys, Government of India tend to show that while in 1989-90 the real per capita social sector expenditure by the Government of India was Rs. 61.72, it came down to Rs. 53.58 in 1997-98. Social sector expenditure in the 1990s was low. It was low compared to what India spent in 1980s; it was low compared to other developing countries, and certainly compared to East Asian countries, and it was low compared to the ratios recommended by the United Nations Development Programme.

Anti-Poverty Strategy: the Basic Elements

In our country the poor are not only unorganized but also ignorant and illiterate. They cannot assert their rights. The first basic element in any poverty alleviation programme should, therefore, be to assist and facilitate the poverty group to organize themselves. They need to be empowered to articulate their demands, assert their rights and put up resistance against exploitation. Care has to be taken to ensure participation of the poor in the implementation of the programmes meant form them. It will give the programme self-sustaining strength. The opportunity has been provided through community structures in the slums. But there is no formal linkage between these structures and the ULBs, which are nodal agencies for poverty alleviation programmes. It is necessary to formalise their relationship.

The formation of elective ULBs by itself cannot take care of the poverty problem. The more fundamental question is the social background of the leadership. There should be adequate representation of the down-and-out.

The employment generation programmes need to be coupled with massive training activity for formation and upgradation of technical skill.

It cannot be doubted that the poorest of the poor are mostly casual workers without any assets. The vocational training has to be imparted to the poor so that they can earn on their own. Of late, the concept of self-help groups has gained considerable currency. It is working well in many developing countries.

Credit and Micro-credit

Micro-credit is now being projected as a panacea for alleviation of urban poverty. The success of Grameen Bank in Bangladesh has led to similar experiments in India. It may succeed in replacing the monelender but its impact on poverty alleviation is not well established. According to a study only 5 per cent of the borrowers have been able to lift themselves from the poverty line.

Social Protection

Of late, the scholars refer to social protection as an important instrumentality for reducing poverty. It has been defined "as public actions taken in response to levels of vulnerability, risk and deprivation which are deemed socially unacceptable within a given polity or society". The World Department Report (2000) lays stress on three types of action to reduce poverty-opportunity, empowerment and security.

The problem with poverty alleviation programmes is that the benefits do not reach out to the target group. The NIUA study (1987) found that 40.4% of the sample household drawn from the urban poor in 20 cities felt that they did not receive any benefit out of a dozen programmes listed. A majority of those who reported benefits derived them from the activity of the local government such as water connection, sanitary connection and electricity. The reasons identified by the study include corruption, lack of proper publicity, lack of administrative commitment, poor implementation, political interference, lack of funds, improper and inadequate definition of beneficiary.

The Current National Thinking

The Current national thinking on poverty alleviation is that it is possible to alleviate poverty through decentralised governance and participatory planning. The scholars believe that one might expect to find four kinds of linkages between decentralisation and poverty reduction as follows:

Political devolution can aim at poverty reduction through an *empowerment strategy* that creates 'space' for people to effectively participate in decision-making processes. An attempt to increase the assess and influence of local citizens vis-à-vis government may be driven by the belief that institutions of the State will thus become more responsive to the needs of the poor.

Poverty reduction might also be linked through a resource *mobilisation strategy*. When people are given greater control over local statutory structures, they may be motivated to commit more assets to the common good.

Decentralised government may also be seen as a more effective means to deliver basic social services, thus alleviating many of the common causes of poverty such as illness, economic infrastructure and illiteracy.

A fourth possible linkage is an *incorporation strategy* where Central Government may promote the 'participation' of local population in political structures that have no real control over development resources. This strategy may be motivated by a desire to maintain contact with grassroots sentiments in order to anticipate and contain the negative political consequences of poverty while not expending resources toward improving the likelihoods of the poor.[11]

Most of the current poverty alleviation programmes envisages involvement of local bodies, private agencies, banks, non-government organizations and local communities. The Government funds constitute only a part of the total resources-the remaining is expected to come from the institutional sources, private entrepreneurs and local residents. This is in consonance with the structural adjustment programme. Within this framework, as *Kundu* has shown, the fund-providing agencies enjoy greater authority in designing the project, its location. They may dictate terms which may undermine and affect the project objectives. The poor who can, at best, contribute their labour, would have very little to say in working out the details of the project. This poses a new challenge to the urban poverty alleviation programmes.[10]

The inequality in the provision of infrastructure and basic services across the states and size categories of settlements has increased consequent upon the adoption of structural adjustment programme and slow withdrawal of the state from the domain of development. This is because the less developed states with weak and uncertain economic base have been able to make very little capital investment. Also, they have very little capacity to attract private entrepreneurs or institutional finance.

The diversity and complexity of urban poverty requires interventions by different types of institutions and at different levels. Poverty rooted in illiteracy, lack of clean drinking water, insecurity of tenancy or lack of basic health provision are of such a general nature that state-level programmes, albeit implemented through local government or local non-government organization (NGOs) are the most direct and effective way to pursue poverty reduction. At the local level, however, there are also groups of the poor constituted by a number of over lapping dimensions of poverty. Factors of gender, ethnicity, relationship to land, geographic locality and relation to labour market can combine to produce a local socio-economic constellation of the poor. National institutions and programmes have difficulty in identifying and reaching such groups. Poverty reduction requires local people's organizations that are responsive to the specific interests of such groups, promoting their interest, establishing their rights in conflict with the practices and interests of government departments, local politicians, and local cultural and social values. In the ultimate analysis, poverty is rooted in the class character of the society. The capitalist state in the developing countries guided by the philosophy of structural adjustment programme in the given world situation, cannot alleviate poverty, not to speak of its comnplete eradication. The eradication of poverty calls for structural change, not the so-called cosmetic change in the policy. The experiences in our country tend to show that the change of regime ideologically committed to the poor can give some relief to the poor people and can reduce poverty to some extent despite the constraints noted above.

References

1. B. Baluch (1996) 'Neglected Trade-offs in Poverty Measurement' IDS Bulletin 27(1). pp. 36-42, L. Engberg-Pederson (1998) 'Studying Poverty: Concepts and Approach' in N. Webster (ed.) *In Search of Alternatives: Poverty, the*

Poor and Local Organizations, CDR working Paper, Copenhagen.

2. A Cox et al, (2000) *European poverty Reduction and the Poor*, Macmillan, London.
3. DFID (2001) *Urban Poverty and Vulnerability in India*, New Delhi.
4. Kiran Wadhava (2000) 'Urban Poverty Alleviation Strategy', *Human Settlement*, Vol. III, No. 2, April.
5. Sanjay K. Ray (1993) 'State, ideologies and Urban Poor in the Third World', *Economic and Political Weekly*, December 4.
6. Cited in the DFID Report, *op. cit.*
7. Planning Commission (1980) *Sixth Five Year Plan* (1980-85) p. 51.
8. Akshaya Kumar Sen (2000) 'Role of Urban Local Bodies in Poverty Alleviation Programmes' *Human Settlement*, Vol. III, No. 2, April.
9. *Report of the National Commission on Urbanization* (1987), Government of India, Ministry of Urban Development, New Delhi.
10. Amitabh Kundu (2000) Poverty and Employment in Urban India: A Perspective for Formulating Development Stretegy, *Human Settlement*, Vol. III, No. 2.
11. J. Bossuyt and J. Gould (2000) *Decentralisation and Poverty Reduction: Elaborating the Linkages*, Institute of Development Studies, Maastrict; ECDPM.

4

Rural Development through Panchayats in West Bengal

Post-colonial India embarked on rural development through the community development programme in 1950s. It was a multipurpose open-ended programme. It was based on the philosophy that rural life was an organic whole, and no improvement in any sector was possible unless an attack was made on all sectors simultaneously.

As an officially sponsored programme imposed from the top this programme was not designed to evoke people's initiative. The Balvantray Mehta Committee while examining rural development and the allied issues, recommended the introduction of the three-tiered elective structures known as panchayats for ensuring people's participation leaving scope for structural variations at the state level.

But the institutions of panchayats did not strike firm roots. The lack of political attention coupled with bureaucratic neglect crippled the institutions. Funds and functions were not given to them. Jain argues," the institutions were killed before they were truly born".[1]

The grim food situation in the 1960s triggered a search for directly production-oriented programmes, as for example, the intensive agricultural district programme. These programmes aimed at accelerating agricultural growth in selected regions that were naturally endowed with good soil and irrigation facilities. Faster growth was achieved but it resulted in regional imbalances and further miseries for the poor who did not receive the benefits of growth.

In the 1970s the development thrust shifted to the target group, namely, small and marginal farmers as reflected in the creation of such bodies as the small farmers development agency, and the marginal farmers and agricultural development agency. Productivity movement was sought to be balanced by an egalitarian concern. Attempts were also made to offset regional imbalance by undertaking special programmes for the underdeveloped regions, such as, the drought prone area programme and the command area programme.

The implementation of these programmes reinforced the role of the bureaucracy. In 1970s the rural development bureaucracy had crossed the figure of 80,000. Funds were given directly to the bureaucratic agencies bypassing the panchayats wherever they existed in some form or the other. Narain observes, "Nothing has done greater harm to panchayats than the effort to bypass them institutionally in launching target-oriented development programmes and in this effort, international funding agencies have contributed to a great extent".[2]

Thus the target groups became the recipients rather than active participants in the development process. The potential beneficiaries came to be viewed "as patients rather than as agents of development".

This approach continued in subsequent plan documents, although there was a shift in the emphasis. While earlier plans reiterated a concern for reducing economic disparities and for equality of opportunity, a programmatic approach to poverty alleviation evolved only with the Sixth Plan, and has been continuing. It provided a target, a time frame, a package of programmes and a separate allocation of resources. The Sixth Plan devised the Integrated Rural Development Programme (IRDP) as an instrument of intervention in the problem of target groups.

The administration of the programme was entrusted to a new body called District Rural Development Agency (DRDA) which became the channel for flowing central funds. The panchayat institutions were, thus, bypassed. The mushroom growth of government registered societies and corporations for the implementation of specific centrally sponsored schemes bureaucratized the rural development process.

The question of revitalization of participative institutions for rural development began to merit serious attention of policy makers since the mid-1980s. The culmination of the process was the amendment of the constitution in 1993. Panchayat institutions today form a part of India's constitutional system.

The Rise of the Panchayat Institutions in West Bengal

West Bengal was late starter in respect of panchayats. The political instability in the state during late 60s and early 70s further complicated the situation. During the days of the Congress rule panchayats were almost non-existent in functional terms. The villagers became dependent on the bureaucracy. The Congress government enacted the West Bengal Panchayat Act, 1973 but did not implement it. It was the Left Front Government (LFG) installed in 1977 which took up the matter.

The Left Front Government in West Bengal

The Left Front, a coalition of 10 leftist parties, was constituted in the basis of a common programme consisting of as many as 36 items. It is committed, *inter alia*, to decentralisation of power protecting the interests of the poor, public participation in administration and, thus to clip the wings of the bureaucracy and radical social change. It is 'a Marxist government with a difference'. It is a coalition of democratic and progressive forces, not all of whom are Marxists (Communist Party of India (Marxist)). It may be recalled that the biggest partner of the L.F. is the Communist Party of India (Marxist) which is ideologically committed to lead the struggle for the establishment of the people's democratic state, has participated in the State Government to use it "as an instrument of struggle to win more and more people and more allies for the proletariat and in their struggle for the cause of people's democracy and at a later stage, for socialism".[3] It has been held that the L.F. ministries are the instruments of people's mobilization and struggles and not of solving basic problems. The immediate political objectives which the party has been trying to achieve through its participation in the government, has been identified as isolating the main party of the ruling classes, advancing the ideology of the party, liberating the working class and the people, especially the peasantry from the grip of bourgeois ideology, increasing the confidence of the people in themselves and against the bourgeois-landlord government led by the big bourgeoisie and so on.

The L.F. has not captured state power. It has, what may be called, political power. As a result, it has been operating within the framework of a number of constraints, namely, social-structural, economic and constitutional. The L.F. has captured power through parliamentary democratic method. The social structure characterized by capitalism and feudalism remains unchanged. This structure retards the process of pro-poor capitalist development.

The Constitution is not designed to protect and promote the interests of the poor. It was framed by a handful of persons belonging to the upper echelons of the society. Bethlehem found that there were different types of members in the Constituent Assembly, namely, landlords, members of the royal families, highly placed professionals, big bourgeoisie.....". Ghanashyam Shah had shown that the Hindus constituted 83 per cent of the total members out of whom 45 per cent were zaminders, rich peasants, and retired government servants.[5]

The constitution that emerged after the Independence, is essentially unitary with some federal features. It clothed the federal government with more powers at the expense of the autonomy of the federating units. Added to it have been the persistent efforts on the part of the Central Government to encroach upon the limited domain of the State Government. The more important powers of revenue-raising are so concentrated in the hands of the centre that out of the total tax and non-tax revenue raised in the country, about two-thirds get raised in the hands of the centre and remaining only one third in all the states taken together. Jyoti Basu comments, "The State Governments under the present set up have neither real autonomy nor radical powers to undertake any radical and really effective measures of relief and reform".[6] The point has been succinctly re-affirmed by Amartya Sen thus "Given the constitutional and real political division of powers between the centre and the states in India, there are obvious limits to what the Government of West Bengal can do in pursuit of its political and economic objectives".[7]

The Immediate Tasks of the Government on the Rural Front

The L.F. when it was voted to power in 1977, was faced with three tasks on the rural front. In the first place, it was required to regenerate the stagnant rural economy and to promote economic equality through land reforms. The growth in the agricultural sector during the first two plans was only 11.9 per cent as against the national average of 32.3 per cent. The second task was to democratize the rural governing processes dominated by the bureaucracy and the village influential. The rural people had participated in panchayat elections only in 1958-59. The institutions were thereafter either superseded or left in the moribund condition. The third task was to undermine 'rock departmentalism'.

Apart from the politico-ideological imperative, the LFG had political compulsion to concentrate on rural West Bengal. The data of the Assembly elections held in 1977 showed that its support base in the rural areas was weaker than that in urban areas. The L. F. secured 49.1 per cent votes in urban districts (Calcutta, Howrah, 24-Parganas, Hooghly, Darjeeling, Nadia, Burdwan) but in rural districts (Murshidabad, Midnapore, Coochbehar, Jalpaiguri, Bankura, Purulia, Birbhum, West Dinajpur, Malda) it was 41.3 per cent.

Atul Kohli is of the opinion that the L.F.G. had two options-rapid expansion of the party and restructuring of local government. The L.F.G. opted for the latter. The leaders might have felt that the rapid expansion of the party would destroy the party as the well-knit and disciplined organisation. Secondly, it intends to accomplish its political goals by building its power base primarily on the lower middle class and lower classes.[8]

Incidentally it is wrong to say that democratic decentralisation is antagonistic to the ideological foundation of the communist parties. Democratic centralism is the organizational principle of the party. But democratic decentralisation is the principle of governance. It is argued that decentralisation helps revolutionary process and strengthens class struggle. E.M.S. Namoodiripad says, ".............. My faith in democratic decentralisation................ arises from the fact that it helps the working people in their day-to-day struggles against their oppressors and exploiters".[9]

The Approach of the Left Front Government to Panchayats

In its election manifesto the Left Front promised to hold elections to the panchayat institutions. It was further emphasized that all development activities of the government in rural areas in the state would be handed over to panchayats. The elections were held in 1978 with the active participation of the political parties. Sengupta (1979) comments, "For the first time in this republic's history there was a keen contest for roots of power. In an open democratic and peaceful context.———never in the history of India's politics did a political party penetrate so deeply and methodologically the ancient fairness of the village.[10]

The electoral slogan of the Left Front in 1978 elections was 'destroy the centres of vested interests'. The Left Front spelt out its intention to use panchayats as platforms for fighting against rural vested interests and raising the hopes of the rural people hereby. The then Left Front chairperson characterized the election as a struggle for establishing the rights of the poor peasants, agricultural labourers, village craftsmen etc. against the vested interests and exploiting classes in the village.[11] It was further held that through panchayat elections the power will be decentralised and only with the organized force of the village poor and middle class the task of establishing the power of the people curbing that of the administrative officers, could be carried out.

It was an election in which the parties, for the first time in the history panchayat elections in India, participated with their flags, banners and festoons. The idea of party-based panchayats is in tune with the leftist approach to panchayats. Arguing the case for it Namboodiripad, a veteran leader of the CPI(M), says that in the name of non-partisanship the Sarvodaya approach seeks to disarm the poor in their fight against local gentry who are interested in transforming the panchayats into their instruments.

The biggest partner of the L.F.G is CPI (M). It is clear from the party documents that the party has a long-term political objective, which it calls 'political organisational perspective'. At each level of the panchayats the party has sub-committee which guides the panchayat bodies. This committee is a very powerful one. It has, however, been stated in the party document that the political leadership of the party is established 'only when people in their own experience accept the political perspective of the party as their own'. There are three directions in the party document :

(a) We must involve the people irrespective of all classes and creed in the activities of the panchayats. The people of the area must be made aware of the fact that it is their money and work. They will decide the priority of expenditure and implementation of development works.

(b) If everything is concentrated in the hands of a few and people are kept in the dark, even the honest operation will arouse suspicion. Our aim is not to do mercy to the people but to intensify class struggle.

(c) The process of decision-making must start from the people.

New Rural Leadership

The elections generated a completely new type of rural leadership in West Bengal unheard of in modern India's panchayat tradition. The ground was, however, prepared in 1969-70 during the days of the United Front government when a massive drive had been undertaken to detect and vest lands that had been clandestinely retained by landowners beyond their legal entitlement. This had weakened the hold of the big landlords on village society. The panchayats in West Bengal or in most parts of India, "have seldom been free of domination by landlords or rich peasants. This is beginning to change in West Bengal. The CPM is carving out a pattern of political organization in rural West Bengal rare in India, namely, that of involving a penetration in the countryside without depending on the larger landowners".[12]

A large number of macro and micro studies suggest that panchayats are free from the domination of the big landlords. Several studies suggest that the panchayats at the village level are controlled mainly by the middle farmers who already have significant resources under their control with a large percentage being teachers and other professionals.

The representation of the rural poor on village panchayats has been fair, and there has been an increasing representation of Scheduled Tribe and Caste members. The significant presence of poor peasants, bargadars, (agricultural) labourers, school teachers etc. in panchayats has been proved in many research studies. All these have brought about a change in the co-relation of class forces in the countryside and "churning of the submerged humanity".

The social background of the members of the gram panchayats proves that the Left Front has been reasonably successful in mobilizing different sections of the rural people. The new leaders now carry on the task of mobilization of masses in rural areas. This change in the balance of power has made it possible to implement a number of far-reaching social programmes that are often considered politically infeasible in many other states.

There was a view that although the low caste and the poor people had been elected in large numbers, the real powers remained in the hands of the *Bhadralok*. Things did change, as Lieten has established from his study, after 1993. The once dominating Brahmins and other upper castes have been replaced in more than proportionate numbers from among the poor classes belonging, namely, to the SC/ST communities. This policy wagering on the poor and the middle has made it possible for LFG to achieve two objectives at one go-a fair degree of development and more equitable distribution of fruits of development.[13]

The transformational potential of the panchayats has been documented by Echeverri Gent. This study views panchayats as an institutional system that allows for the possibility that subaltern groups may exercise their agency to accumulate political and economic resources and reduce social inequities.

Rural Development Policy of the Government

In rural development policy, there could be three kinds of choice :

(a) the market oriented approach which expects development to be extended from the pioneering upper layers to the less-enterprising and less-endowed villages,

(b) the revolutionary radicalism which aims at taking assets from the rich and re-building the production basis through reliance on the poor. It involves sharp class struggle with a chaotic impact on the social and political order and economic activities. Its success depends on the control over the organs of the state powers.

(c) the third choice is one where the emphasis is on the poor and the many, but the policy is one which benefits the middle class, and is not very strongly against a section of the rich peasants. Referring to this option Lieten says, "the class struggle remains but within the accepted procedures".

The rural development policy of the Left Front government is guided by the philosophy of what may be called redistribution before growth to ensure growth with social justice. The policy has three broad objectives. In the first place, it aims at involving the people not only in the process of implementation of development programmes but also in the processes of preparation, implementation and monitoring of development plans by building up decentralised structures at the grassroots level. Secondly, it seeks to bring about a change in the co-relation of class forces in favour of the poor and working people by involving them in an organized manner in the process of development. Thirdly, it attempts to raise class consciousness of the people through radicalization of political processes and politicization of development.

Two important features characterize the rural development process in West Bengal, namely, curbing the power of the bureaucracy as far as possible within the framework of the Indian constitution and horizontal mobilization of the masses.

The three-tiered panchayats constitute the foundation on which stands the entire edifice of rural development in West Bengal. The Gram Panchayats (GPs) which function at the grassroots level, and are in direct touch with the people, carry the responsibility of implementing various development programmes, projects and schemes at the village level in terms of identification of beneficiaries, location of project sites etc. They are informally, though significantly, associated with the peasant organizations. The Panchayat Samitis (PSs) and Zilla Parishad (ZPs) are responsible for the adoption and implementation of schemes and measures for the development of agriculture, cottage industries, water supply, irrigation, execution of any function assigned by the State Government, and co-ordination and implementation of development plans, schemes, projects and programmes relating to the development policy of the State Government at the block and districts respectively and through various standing committees.

There are two kinds of programmees-village-centred, general programmes namely, improved health conditions, drinking water supply, school environment, literacy classes, all weather roads etc. and class-centred programmes such as land reforms, increasing agricultural wages.

Land Reforms

The core of rural development policy is land reforms. The LFG lays stress on two aspects of land reforms, namely, recording of names of sharecroppers and redistribution of surplus lands among the landless. Added to it is the policy of the government to extend institutional credit cover to the land reforms beneficiaries.

In the field of land reforms numerous studies have documented that the bureaucracy has colluded with the land-holding classes to stall the implementation of the programmes. The Government of India's (1973) report of the Task Force on Agrarian Relations in India has cited bureaucracy as an important factor responsible for the failure of the land reform. It has indicated that the members of the civil service are closely aligned with the landed gentry in the rural areas who want to stifle the reforms. At the lowest levels, the bureaucratic functionaries are petty landlords, and cannot otherwise survive without the support of the richer peasants.

Thus the successful implementation of land reforms calls for limiting the bureaucracy and political mobilization of the prospective beneficiaries. In fact, at one point of time it was felt by the Task Force on Agrarian Relations and quite rightly that a certain degree of politicization of the peasantry was the *sine qua non* for the implementation of the land reforms programme. Consequently the Committee on Tenancy Reforms recommended that the panchayats be associated with the task of implementation of land reforms as the official agencies would require more experience.

Incidentally, West Bengal has a tradition of mobilising the rural poor since the mid-1970s. The cultivators organised canal tax movement in 1920s. The Tebhaga movement of 1940s and early 1950s led to the legislation in 1953. The food movement of 1950s and 1960 had drawn in poor peasants, sharecroppers and agricultural labourers and artisans. There were movements during the days of undivided Bengal also. During the days of the colonial rule movement was organised by the rural poor in the face of landlords' high rents; in 1950s Santhali tribals rose in rebellion against oppressive whites and other outsiders.

The panchayats and peasant organizations play the most effective role in implementing these programmes. In fact, "West Bengal", as Baruah (1990) argues, "provides one of the rare instances of land reform programmes initiated by radical rural political mobilization with significant participation by the agrarian underclass."[14] The programme of recording of names of sharecroppers popularly known as the operation barga (OB) programme was formerly undertaken by the bureaucracy. The traditional method has been supplemented by the establishment of functional linkages between the bureaucracy and the panchayats while the gram panchayats play the most crucial role in the OB programme.

The programme was implemented through two innovative strategies:

(a) There were legal changes supportive of sharecroppers' claims. Among the changes in the land laws the onus of proving that he does not have sharecropping rights, was placed on the landowners. The eviction of sharecroppers for the ostensible purpose of self-cultivation was made more difficult by defining self-cultivation more rigorously to mean participation by the land-owners and/or the person's family as manual labour related to cultivation.

(b) The Left Front Government utilized the mobilization of the rural poor in this task. The strategy was to rely on "group action on the part of the beneficiaries to enable them to overcome the fear psychosis by creating a mutual support system."

Meetings were held in the villages attended by the sharecroppers and the officials. While doing a study on the processes of implementation the author had noticed that the OB camp started with an address by the panchayat chief. He promised wide ranging support to the beneficiaries. While interviewing the sharecroppers it was gathered that this was preceded by a meeting in every locality organized under the auspices of the Krishak Samity.[15]

It should be mentioned here that the State Government had organized earlier what was called conscientization camps which helped the bureaucracy to think afresh of their role as change agents. "It sets in a process of change of mind at least among a few functionaries at the cutting edge of administration".[15a]

However, after such meetings a tentative list is prepared. The landowners were allowed objections which were also heard and verified in public. This was followed by the issue of certificates.

The recorded sharecroppers are not afraid of confronting their landowners for getting their dues. The study by this author had shown that in case of disputes regarding the share of crops between them and their landowners they would not submit to the former. They would like to take the matter up with the panchayats and peasant organizations. While panchayats provide them support from within the political sub-system, the peasant organizations provide support from outside.

The panchayats are entrusted with the task of carrying out the land redistribution programme. At the Panchayat Samity level there is a standing committee on land reforms which performs this task. It is this committee which, with the help of the Gram (village) Panchayats, prepares the list of persons to whom the vested lands would be redistributed. The success has been commendable. It is claimed that with the association of village panchayats the average rate of recording increased by about 300 per cent. Of the total agricultural land redistributed through land reforms in India nearly 20 per cent has been contributed by West Bengal, although in the total agricultural land in India the state's share is less than four per cent. And 50 per cent of the beneficiaries come from SC and ST.

Land redistribution has affected more than 21 per cent of the rural families and eight per cent of the total cultivated area in the state. There has been a shrinkage at the top categories of the land-owning classes in the state. According to the NSS data 70 per cent of the agricultural land in West Bengal is in the hands of the small and marginal farmers. The national average is 34.30 per cent. The study done by State Institute of Panchayats and Rural Development tends to show that 87.20 per cent assignees of the vested land have been able to hold land in their possession, 83.82 per cent of them have re-paid bank loans, 63 per cent send their children to school. The two measures together have resulted in a structural situation considerably different from that in most other states in India. These steps have tilted the power balance in rural areas in favour of the small and poor producers and have thus created conditions conducive to the empowerment of the poor.

Lieten's study has shown that the impact of OB and land ceiling polices on the relations of productions has been negligible but "in the wake of collective empowerment, labour-employing land owners have learned to placate the agricultural labourers and have learned to live with an equilibrium. Such an equilibrium may appear as a non-antagonistic capitulation to the land owners, but it may also be regarded as a controlled class struggle aimed at the common good of all concerned...........".

Non-land input support

In order to make land reforms measures effective it is essential to support these measures with the provision of non-land inputs, such as irrigation, agricultural implements, manures and fertilizers and infrastructural facilities, particularly credit and marketing. Otherwise, the beneficiaries would be left to the mercy of the market. In the provision of all these non-land inputs there is, again, the question of choice of technology. In West Bengal this has been done keeping in view the interests of the poor farmers. The quote a government document, "the working farmers are endowed with labour power, and there is in rural areas often a relative abundance of local resources. The socially appropriate choice of technology regarding the non-land inputs in this alternative approach should, therefore, be one which should be modern and at the same time, make efficient and improved use of labour and local resources. The philosophy has prompted the State Government to extend minor irrigation facilities.

This support has far reaching consequences on the beneficiaries. It has instilled in them a sense of self-confidence and dignity'. More than 70 per cent respondents for the study done by the author on land reforms has reported their ability to cultivate land without any support from the landowners. The International Labour Organisation (1979) commented favourably on the government's decisive action for peasants, sharecroppers and agricultural labours against landlords and big farmers and on the direct communication in a way that instilled confidence in the poor.

Implementation of the Centrally Sponsored Programme

The panchayats in West Bengal did remarkably well in respect of implementation of the centrally sponsored beneficiary-oriented and employment generating anti-poverty programmes like National Rural Employment Programme (NREP), Rural Landless Employment Guarantee Programme, Integrated Rural Development Programme

(IRDP), Jawahar Rozger Yogana (JRY) etc. For the implementation of IRDP there was a sub-committee at the block level with the *Sabhapati* as the chairman. The list of beneficiaries was prepared by the Gram Panchayats. Although the concurrent evaluation had brought out that all the beneficiaries were selected by the Gram Panchayats, the actual work was done by the peasant organizations and branch committees of the party at the village level. The list prepared by them was given formal sanction by the IRDP sub-committee.

The findings of the concurrent evaluation of 1987-88 show that in terms of felt needs, maintenance and after-care of assets in generating additional income for the beneficiaries as well as crossing over the poverty line, West Bengal has performed relatively better. The evaluation done in 1989 found that West Bengal performed better than the average in terms of the proportion of people crossing the poverty line of Rs. 3500 ; maintenance and quality of assets created, inclusion of working capital in costs and sufficiency of help. The selection process is 100 per cent controlled by the Gram Panchayat compared with 65.41 per cent average for the country as a whole.[16]

Westergaard's study (1986) suggests that NREP has had considerable success in providing employment for the rural poor. Chaudhuri's (1980) and Kohil's (1989) studies of the food for work programme accord the programme some success. Dreze (1990) also found that IRDP overwhelmingly benefited the landless labourers. Swaminathan (1990) has also noticed similar success while comparing the state's performance in implementing IRDP in West Bengal and the southern state of Tamil Nadu. Webster (1992) found that the benefits under the employment generation programme and IRDP had gone to the poor and improved their living conditions.

There has, of late, been a change of situation. Panchayats do not seem to be as active as they were earlier. Many panchayats fail to make use of the money given to them. It is true that the panchayats are overburdened. But this cannot be an excuse for their inability to spend money for alleviation of rural poverty when, as per the latest data, 31 per cent of the rural people live below the poverty line.

The implementation of rural development programmes through panchayats and land reforms constituting the core, have produced desired results. During the 1980s production of food grains in West Bengal grew more rapidly than in any other Indian state. The growth of food grain production in West Bengal averaged 6.7 per cent during the period 1983-84 to 1994-95 compared with 2.7 per cent for the country as a whole. West Bengal became the highest food grain-producing state leaving Punjab and Haryana behind during 1990s. During 1980s and 1990s West Bengal's agriculture sector grew at about 6 per cent outperforming all other major states in this respect. The state also registered the highest rate of growth of per capita cereal consumption while there had been a decline for the country as a whole.

The employment generation programmes have benefited the local people by creating some useful assets and tackling poverty. The State Government's commitment to decentralisation through panchayats has meant that the Gram Panchayats have been able to play an important role in the planning and execution of programmes. The study suggests that funds allotted to JRY should be made available to the panchayats well in advance as late disbursement has led in the past to the underutilization of resources. It has been observed that in order to make more qualitative improvements in the programme attention should be concentrated in fewer projects in any particular year with more emphasis on long term asset durability.[17]

The rural economic scenario has undergone a remarkable change. Rural employment has increased by about 63 per cent from 2.2 million in 1980 to 36.473.6 million in 1991. The total number of enterprises has increased by over 71 per cent from 10.44 lakh to 18.88 lakh during the second period. As a result the share of agricultural labourers in the total main workers in the state declined from 25.2 per cent in 1981 to 24.5 per cent in 1991. During the same period the share of the agricultural labourers in the total work-force in the country has increased from 24.9 per cent to 26.2 per cent. The average daily rate of the agricultural labourers in the state has increased by more than 71 per cent from Rs. 13.78 in 1986-87 to 1990-91.[18]

Compared to other states West Bengal has a significantly low rate of debt to private money lenders in rural areas. Admitting this in a report the union labour ministry attributes this to land reforms. Private money lenders exist in a much reduced number in the state. While in 1977-78 less than 26 per cent of the total outstanding rural debt was with the private money lending system, the same source can be accounted for about 12 per cent of the total outstanding rural debt in 1993.[19]

The National Sample Survey (NSS) data show that the poverty rate declined more rapidly in West Bengal during the 1980s than in any of the other 18 largest states in India. C.P. Chandrasekhar and Abhijit Sen had shown that among the fifteen most populous states the decline in the proportion of rural population under poverty line between 1977-78 and 1993-94 was the highest in West Bengal. The World Bank (2000) identified West Bengal and Kerala as two states where poverty rate has remarkably declined. The World Bank categorised West Bengal as a leader state in this regard in 2001.

The change of socio-economic profile of the countryside has been made possible through political participation of the poor. The latter has been achieved, as Webster suggests, on the basis of the panchayati raj programme of decentralised government together with the programme of agrarian reforms that have facilitated the political participation of the poor.

He further argues that it has been achieved through a different kind of discourse on poverty, a discourse articulated by sharecroppers, agricultural labourers, scheduled castes, tribes and women. They spoke of their right to improved life, their right to the change in the reform being introduced, and not least their right to elect, without interference, the local panachyat.

Another factor which has made political participation of the poor possible is the fact that the poor are organised. It is not simply political organisation but organisation around different types of productive activities such as fish, irrigation, molasses manufacture, around market activities such as fish, milk, bidi, rice, around poverty relief activities such as grain stores, education, club and around social and religions activities.[19]

Elsewhere Webster says that the presence or coming together of these three dimensions-local institutional channels, a discourse on poverty, and political organising practices-created political space in 1980s and 1990s that the poor have gained from. It has led to a process of democratisation at the local level that has helped to secure pro-poor development path in this period.[20]

Apart from the improvement in the living condition of the rural people, the human development scenario has also improved. There has been a decrease in infant mortality rate in rural West Bengal from 91 per thousand to 56 per thousand in 1999 while the national average was 75 per thousand. It has further came down to 53 in 2003.

There has been a decline in mortality rate in the rural areas. In 1999 it was 7.2 per thousand while the national average was 8.7 per thousand. In Kerala it was 6.4. West Bengal was the second best. West Bengal's success in the implementation of rural sanitation programme through active participation of panchayats has been widely acclaimed. West Bengal has bagged the best performance award from the UNICEF according to which it can be a model for the developing countries.

There has been an increase in the per capita calorie intake of the rural people between 1983 and 1994 in four states, namely, Kerala, West Bengal, Orissa and Maharashtra. The largest absolute increase was in Kerala followed by West Bengal, Orissa and Maharashtra.

Rural Development through People's Participation

The Left Front government also has taken participative institutions to the doorsteps of the people to establish direct contact between the leaders and the people, that is, to transform representative democracy into participatory democracy, as an effective method of mass mobilization not only at the time of elections but also at regular intervals, at least twice in a year. Mass mobilisation is necessary not only for electoral gains but also for ensuring benefits to the poor, the weaker sections of the community. A comprehensive amendment of the West Bengal Panchayat Act in 1992 provided for a new tier called Gram Sabha to be constituted at each electoral constitutency. The Gram Sabha was to meet at least twice a year. It was required to hold discussion on the report to be submitted to it by the Gram Panchayat. The Gram Panchayats were required to carefully consider the comments, observations and recommendations of the members in the meeting. The steps taken were to be reported in the next meeting.

The West Bengal Panchayat Act, 1973 has been amended again to make it conform to the requirements of the 73rd amendment of the constitution. The institution called Gram Sabha has been substituted by Gram Sansad, while the Gram Sabha continued as a body of direct democracy at the level of the Gram Panchayat. Gram Sansad is an institutional innovation for ensuring the mobilization of the people and their participation in the planning and implementation of the programmes meant for them.

Stakeholders' Participation in the Programme Implementation

One of the functions of the Gram Sansads is to encourage stakeholders' participation in programme implementation for which it is required to constitute beneficiary committees comprising not more than nine members who are not members of the Gram Panchayats. This committee has to work for ensuring active participation of the people in implementation, maintenance and equitable distribution of benefits of one or more schemes in the area. The study indicates that the committees have started working. There was confusion at the initial stage about the role of the beneficiary committee vis-a-vis that of the elected members. Significantly, the highly polarised political scene in West Bengal has not been reflected in the working of the committees. It speaks of a high degree of development consciousness of the rural people of West Bengal.[21] It is necessary to mention that the amendment of the West Bengal Panchayat Act, 2003 had abolished beneficiary committee. There is now at the level of the Gram Sansad Village Development Society which will be formed by the Sansad in terms of the provision of the Act.

Participatory Decentralised Planning

Decentralised development planning with active participation of the people has been on the agenda of the LFG for long. A three-tier local planning structure was by and large in position by the time decentralised planning was introduced in 1985. At the district level there are two tiers : District Planning and Co-ordination Committee (DPCC), more of a deliberative body; the District Planning Committee (DPC), its executive arm and the Block Planning Committee as the planning agency at the block level. Each of the planning bodies is headed by the political heads of the concerned panchayats, the top most body being headed by the Minister hailing from the district. This arrangement worked effectively in two districts, namely, Medinipur and Bardhaman. The experience indicates that each GP prepared a statement of their most acutely felt needs and submitted to the P.S. Taking into account the felt needs of the people and the resources of the block, the P.S. prepared schemes to be implemented. The ceiling for schemes was Rs. 1 crore. The district planning machinery integrated the block plans, municipal plans, area/ notified are authority plans and other inter-block and district level schemes into a draft district plan.

In 1999 an attempt was made to accelerate the decentralisation process. The planning process has been decentralised. All the subjects under the 11th schedule have been transferred to panchayats. The line departments have been given instruction to identify and transfer the district sector schemes. The panchayats have been given powers to exercise functional control over the district and field level staff of the respective departments. In 1999-2000, 17 departments allotted Rs. 4239.99 to the ZPs for the execution of the departmental schemes. As per recommendation of the State Finance Commission the State government released a sum of Rs. 100 crores untied funds to the panchayat bodies.

In order to strengthen the process decentralised participatory planning Convergent Community Action was launched in 4 blocks on pilot basis. The CCA focuses on two things (1) convergence of the services of the various sectors and (2) participation of the community in planning, implementation and monitoring of services that have bearing upon its well being.

The pilot studies have brought out that the villages had misgivings at the initial stage when the data about the households were collected. Some of them felt that the government would take away their lands. A few others found no meaning in this kind of exercise.

The field workers played important role in removing the misgivings. After long hours of meeting they could make most of them realise that the data were needed for the effective implementation of the development programmes.

There was anti-pathy among a section of the government officials who felt that they could do the work themselves. They thought that the participation of the people would not make much difference. But as the programme took off, the attitude of the bureaucracy changed.

It was also noticed that the gram panchayats were not adequately motivated. They looked upon CCA programme as another programme for which money would come from the higher level government and their task would be to implement the programme.

This programme was implemented throughout the district in Jalpaiguri during 1999-2000. It was found that it gave a boost to people's participation. Apart from the increase in the numbers of the meetings held, participation was better. People forgot their political differences and tried to arrive at consensus. It helped reduce political tensions in some of the villages.

The Government is now working on a project for further decentralisation to be supported by the Department of International Development, Government of UK. The project is expected to take off shortly.

Engendering Development

Of late, gender empowerment has become an important concern in development discourse. The Seventy Third Amendment of the Constitution is an important milestone on the road to women's political empowerment as it has made it mandatory to reserve one-third seats for women. It has worked wonder even in states like West Bengal where women's participation in panchayat was not more than 4 per cent before the reservation of seats for them was made in 1992. The next election held in 1993 witnessed more than one-third women members in panchayats. In 1998 the figure rose to 36 per cent.

The studies indicate that despite social structural constraints and dominance of patriarchal values women have started taking active interest in panchayats work. They are trying their best to perceive their roles and perform as far as possible. The Kultikari study where there is all-women panachyat, brings out that women have done remarkably well in joint *patta* and literacy programme. According to the study done by Jayati Gupta West Bengal's peformance in the joint patta programme is the best in the country.

There are a few other studies dealing with the empowerment of women through panchayats. The findings of some of the studies bring out that women are yet to play their roles properly. The traditional outlook in the villages, lack of education and awareness, inadequate family and political support, non-cooperation from the male counterparts have been identified as some of the important reasons leading to the peripheral participation of women. The researches done have, however, shown that despite limitation women have been exposed to bigger world. Their status in the society has to some extent, increased. It is also true that women except without compulsion are not given important assignment. But the fact remains that many of them have started evincing interest. Some of the studies have highlighted the commendable performance of women who belong to the SC/ST Community.

In order to empower women in general there is a programme called Development of Women and Children in Rural Areas (DWCRA). Those who are familiar with the field situation, would agree that in some districts this programme has been very successfully implemented. Currently, the emphasis is on the formation of the self help groups. This programme has started gaining momentum in West Bengal. Midnapore, for example, has taken up the programme very seriously. A team of panchayat pradhans was taken to Andhra Pradesh to see for themselves how this programme brought about a change in the life of poor women in Krishna district. In Midnapur 16,000 self help groups have been formed during the last two years. The amount of money collected comes to approximately 11 crores. Added to is another 12 crores received in the form of bank loans and from the government's scheme. Each of the group gets about Rs. 25,000 from the banks and government programmes; if they can save money properly for six months. This has reduced dependence on the moneylenders. There has developed immense interest in small scale industries throughout the district. The self-help group members have started making ropes, collecting sal leaves, manufacturing incense sticks and the like. They are selling these items in the local *hats*. All these have generated self-confidence and awareness. Panchayats are playing important roles in motivating the poor women to form groups and providing support to them as far as possible.

Concluding Observations

It is clear from the foregoing discussion, as Lieten says, in its rural development policy the LFG has focused on three inter-related types of intervention-modification of the relations of production, re-constitution of the political power structure through the revival of the panchayat bodies elected along party lines and playing its political cards so as to maintain a stable and orderly regime for a period unsurpassed in Indian history. One of the most important features of rural development through panchayats in West Bengal is horizontal mass mobilisation by politicised panchayats.

The panchayats and mass organizations like peasant's organizations are utilized for political mobilization of the masses. The Congress which the Left Front had defeated in 1977, mobilized the masses vertically. The landlords, rich and middle peasants, moneylenders and dealers in foodgrains had acted as instruments of mobilization. The political machine described as 'the Ghosh machine' strengthened the system of spoil distribution manned exclusively by the rural gentry. Heavy reliance on them led to dependence on a select number of individuals, the local notables for distributing favours to the masses on behalf of the party. The strategy, thus, overruled any role of the local institutions and mobilization of cadres to penetrate into the rural areas, which could have been done by keeping close contact with the inhabitants there. And thus the general mass of people become alienated.

In its total dependence on the goodwill of the rural gentry, the party set before itself the unattainable objective of the welfare of the rural poor by the rural gentry. One need not necessarily have to be a Marxist to realise the antagonistic interests of the rural gentry, on the one hand and the rural poor-the small and marginal peasants, landless tenants, agricultural labourers and village craftsmen, on the other.

The above analysis has repeatedly stressed that the Left Front has broken new grounds in mobilizing the rural poor through panchayats and peasant organizations for the implementation of the rural development programmes. It has paid rich political dividends. Rural West Bengal has been a stable source of support for the Left Front, as indicated from the results of elections after grassroots mobilization through panchayats and peasant organizations began.

One may argue that politicization of development through mass mobilization, unless carefully monitored, has the possibility of the means (political mobilization of masses) overshadowing the ends (rural development). In the space-capturing politics this possibility cannot be underestimated. The Left Front government has before it the classic case of the government of Karnataka under the Chief Ministership of Devaraj

Urs in the seventies. Urs had chalked out a strategy of political mobilization of weaker sections of the people to pose a decisive challenge to the political influence exercised by the two dominant castes-the Lingayats and the Vokkaligas. Urs met with remarkable success in implementing the strategy during his lifetime. However, in the long run Karnataka could not benefit from the strategy because political mobilization of weaker sections-most of whom were the rural poor-failed to have any durable effect. The strategy remained excessively political in overemphasizing the mobilization of masses and failed to produce sustainable improvement in their social and economic status.

Horizontal mobilisation has in some cases produced disastrous results. There have been occasions when horizontal mobilisation has so wrongly empowered the poor as to create an opportunity for him to take personal revenge on those who belong to his class. This results in alienation of the poor from the party and joining the other party. Clearly, care has to be taken to ensure that politicisation does not unnecessarily take aggressive turn.

Horizontal mobilisation has resulted in reduction of the influence of the rural rich in all spheres of rural life. It has helped in removing the sense of alienation of the poor in the countryside. Their power over village has increased. The institutional development of panchayats in terms of the creation of new bodies such as the gram sabha in 1992 and the gram sansad in 1994 helps in developing among the poor a sense of participation in governance apart from enhancing the transparency in the functioning of panchayats. The Mukarji-Bandyopadhaya Committee (1993) has mentioned that panchayats have brought about 'a churning of the submerged humanity in the rural areas'.

Herring's (1991) study of Kerala shows that there are limits to the mobilization strategy if it is excessively pre-occupied with re-distribution. He finds that while mobilization of the rural poor in Kerala has contributed to distinctly high levels of social welfare among the poor it has led to legislation and contentious labour relations which has reduced growth. West Bengal has also started experiencing this difficulty in some areas. It has also incited farmers to put their lands in less labour intensive crops thereby adversely affecting employment generation. Attempts should be made to strike a balance between re-distribution and accumulation.

A group of critics feel that the politicization of development has an inherent limitation as it helps institutionalize the spoil system which includes the grant of favours in cash and kind to party workers, supporters and sympathizers. Although one finds some such cases here and there it is wrong to suggest that it has spread through all the panchayats. Had it been so the Left Front would have lost its political clout significantly in the villages. In grassroots institutions there is a direct and regular contact between the people and their leaders, which has recently been strengthened through the formation of Gram Sabha and Gram Sansad and Village Development Society.

The relatively successful working of the panchayati raj in West Bengal has created an undesirable situation of ever-increasing dependence of the villagers on the panchayats.It is a matter of concern because it is hampering people's initiative which is one of the most important requirements for the healthy growth of all grassroots democratic institutions. It was this lack of initiative which led to the failure of the community development programme in 1950s. It was argued that the elected democratic bodies would unleash people's initiative. And it was this initiative which acted as fuel for the commendable success of the second generation panchayats in West Bengal. If the present situation continues unabated then the panchayat system in the state will be facing a severe crisis.

There is a view held by Ruud and Bhattacharya that CPM has failed to transform local politics but proved itself to be an elite that has used the government at both local and national levels as a way to generate the clients central to government based patronage. This point has been contested by Webster from his village studies. He started the study in 1977 before the LFG was installed and continued during 1978 followed by revisits in 1987-88 and 1998. His studies indicate that the reforms have been implemented by the local government in a pro-poor way and suggest that bias has not occurred systematically in the implementation of government programmes. He says "At a more general level, the fact of West Bengal's economic growth and the fact that it has been achieved without a radical restructuring of the socio-economic structures, leaves the charge of new elitism-seriously weakened. If there is elitism, it is not one that seeks to monopolise the gains at the expense of the poor".

Finally, some scholars have raised a theoretical point, namely, the induction of the poor peasants into the institutions takes away their militancy and thus stands in the way of the achievement of the ultimate objective, namely, the destruction of the capitalist system. It has been said that the project to revolutionize the poor has given way to that of 'manufacturing consent for the regime through co-option'. Neil Webster says that there has been a toning down of revolutionary politics for further consolidation of political power. This has been achieved by a shift away from structural reform and re-distribution of resources towards an efficient delivery of external resources under various programmes. He however admits that the system has delivered the good and contributed to the welfare and involvement of the socially and economically disadvantaged groups. This is a point which deserves serious consideration because it helps system maintenance values getting developed. It is detrimental to the declared political objective of the left parties. A serious observer of the village scene in West Bengal also notes receding interest among the poor in rallies, processions etc. because the opportunities in the agricultural sector make them busy in the field. Consumerism is also touching their minds slowly. Added to it is the changing cultural profile of the villages characterized by the apparently attractive television and video-programmes and a feeling of fearlessness generated by the uninterrupted rule of the Left Front. As the election results indicate they vote for the Left Front, but do not seem to be as serious and keen as they were earlier, in participating in programmes organised by the Left Front. This speaks of the failure of the Left Front in conscientizing the people and raising their level of political consciousness.

The Left Front, despite its skills of popular mobilization, as Dreze and Sen (1995) feel, has not been to able "to achieve a real transformation in the fields of education and health" which have a significant bearing on the living conditions of the rural poor.Paramesh Acharya has shown the failure of the panchayat bodies to promote and improve the quality of the primary education in the villages.[22] It is unfortunate that the panchayats are not playing important role in the post-Total Literacy Programme. It has in fact, turned out to be a bureaucratic programme. It is unexpected of left-dominated panchayats because literacy is very important to generate consciousness, which is necessary to bring about social change.

Politicization of rural development in West Bengal is based on strong political will, radical ideological back up, disbanding of the traditional power structure and continuous vigil and supervision by the well-grilled and well-knit cadre-based party machinery. It has resulted in some amount of social homogenization, improvement of living conditions of the rural poor and augmentation of awareness of the general mass of population about their rights and place in the society and secularization of the political processes in the countryside. All these have created conditions for the release of collective and individual efforts for radical socio-economic change. People in their turn have positively responded to the government. This people-centered and party-inspired development model may well be a path-setter and a good example for the third world. But the fact remains that this kind of unique convergence is very rare indeed.

The West Bengal model of rural development does not appear to be replicable elsewhere without bringing about a change in the ideology and class character of the regime and creating pro-poor bias in the grassroots democratic institutions. The experience suggests that it is possible to effect improvement in the living conditions of the rural poor in a state within a federal system in a liberal democratic set up in the post-colonial developing countries. And as development question is essentially a power question any attempt to replicate the West Bengal system has to be preceded by a change in the co-relation of class forces in the countryside. Given the socio-economic structure in the post-colonial countries land reform has to be given top most priority in the rural development programme.

Land reform is the key to rural development for the post-colonial developing countries. Land reform can alone create some degree of socio-economic equality in an otherwise unequal rural social situation. And successful implementation of land reform calls for politicisation of the peasantry and active participation of the pro-poor grassroots democratic bodies. This can alone ensure mobilisation of the masses along horizontal lines without which transformative rural development programme cannot be implemented. All these require party based grassroots democracy.

There is need for strong political will backed by politico-ideological compulsion. The party should be so structured as to carry command from the top. There should be top-bottom interaction through structured interactive channels. The party with pro-poor ideology and commitment to decentralised development should be active watchdog. There should be political surveillance from the top so that the recalcitrant members cannot escape punishment.

The wings of the bureaucracy have to be clipped to the maximum possible extent particularly because of the colonial tradition of the bureaucracy. But care has to be taken to ensure that the bureaucracy does not become hostile to the political bosses. The growing conflicts between the bureaucratic and political elements will result in retardation of development. Each one of the administrative partners has to develop respect for the other. Neither the overdeveloped bureaucracy nor the overenthuastic politicians unaware of the rules of the game of the liberal democracy, can yield desired results.

Political stability has to be ensured so that the programmes can be implemented on a continuous basis. This continuity is necessary to ensure that the fruits of development reach out to the target groups. The target group has to be involved in the processes of development as active actors, but not as passive recipients of the benefit of the programme. Their participation will not only ensure that the benefits reach out to the target group but also help improve the quality of the benefits. It will help preserving public assets created as a part of the rural development programme. It will unleash their initiative to strengthen the system which promotes their interest.

There is need for carrying on conscientisation campaign on a sustained basis without which they may get co-opted into the system which it is supposed to wreck the from within. Radical politicisation of the poor cannot be done without raising their literacy status. Literacy programme has to be taken up as a part of the rural development programmes.

Support to facilitate a political space from the perspective of the poor might well facilitate poverty reduction. It calls for presence or coming together of three dimensions-local institutional channel, a discourse on poverty and political organising practices which created political space in 1980s and 1990s that the poor have gained from.

In the efforts to improve the living conditions of the rural poor the support of the middle class has to be won. Aggressive politicisation of the poor may alienate the middle class leading to unnecessary antagonism which will halt the process of development.

The participatory forums like Gram Sansads can be useful places for intensifying class struggle. Class-consciousness of the people can be sharpened in these kinds of meetings. It calls for a crop of leaders whose consciousness is very high and who can motivate the people.

References

1. L.C. Jain, (1987), *Grass Without Roots*, New Delhi : Sage (India).
2. I. Narain, 1987. 'Revival of Panchayati Raj' *Indian Council of Social Science Research Newsletter*, July-September, p. 6.
3. M. Basavapunniah, (1985) 'On para 112 of our Party Programme' *The Marxist*, January-March, p. 35.
4. C. Bettleheim, 1968 *India Independent*, London, p. 106.
5. Ghanashyam, Shah, 1990 'Caste, Class and the State', *Seminar*, March, p. 31-32.
6. Jyoti, Basu, 1991, *Jyoti Basu Speaks*, Information and Cultural Affairs Dpartment, Government of West Bengal.
7. Amartya Sen (1998) 'Issues of Development in the LF's Success and Failure', *The Statesman*, January 1.
8. A. Kohli, 1989, *The State and Poverty in India : Politics of Reform*, New York : Cambridge University Press, pp. 112-113.
9. E.M.S. Namboodripad, 1962. 'Political Parties and Panchayati Raj', *Indian Journal of Public Administration*, October-December, p. 621.
10. B. Sengupta, 1979, CPI(M) *Promises, Prospects and Problems*, New Delhi : Young Asia Publications, p. 118.
11. P. Dasgupta, 1978 : *Desh Hitaishi* (in Bengali) April 7.
12. Atul Kohli *'The State and Poverty in India : The Politics of Reform, op. cit.*

13. G.K. Lieten, 1996 *Development, Devolution and Democracy : Village Discourse in West Bengal*, Sage, New Delhi p. 61.

14. S. Baruah, 1990. 'The End of the Road in Land Reform, Limits to Redistribution in West Bengal', *Development and Change*, Vol. 21, p. 122.

15. P. Datta, 1988 *Land Reforms Administration in West Bengal*, New Delhi : Daya Publishing House, p. 48.

15a. D. Bandyopadhaya, 1978. *Land Reforms in West Bengal* Calcutta : Government of West Bengal, p. 11.

16. B. Dasgupta, 1995. Institutional Reforms and Poverty Alleviation in West Bengal, *EPW*, October 14-21.

17. R.P. Slater, et al (ed.) 1991. *Participation and Development*, Hyderabad : National Institute of Rural Development, p. 63.

18. Tushar Mohanti, 1994 'Bengal Farm Labour Gains Little', Calcutta, *Economic Times*, July 12.

19. N. Webster, (1992) Panchayati Raj and Decentralisation of Development Planning in West Bengal, Calcutta K.P. Bagchi, pp. 78-90, 99.

20. N. Webster, (2000) 'Democracy, Development and the Institutionalised Participation of the Poor for Poverty Reduction' in Paul Collins (ed.) *Applying Public Administration in Development : Guideposts to the Future*, John Wiley and Sons Ltd, London.

21. Prabhat Datta, (2003) *Towards Good Governance and Sustainable Development*, Dasgupta & Co. Kolkata, p. 192.

22. Paramesh Acharya, 2002 'Education Panchayat and Decentralisation : Myth and Reality *Economic & Political Weekly*, Feb. 23.

5

Participatory Democracy in Rural West Bengal

Participation has, for the last 20 years, been widely used in the discourse of development. For much of this period the concept has referred to participation in the social arena, in the community, in the development projects. This led to the rise to the concept of participatory development as a means of strengthening the relevance, quality and sustainability of the development projects. Of late, participation is viewed in the context of good governance which is generally understood as "both a broad reform strategy, and a particular set of initiatives to strengthen the institutions of civil society with the objective of making government more accountable, more open and transparent and more democratic".[1]

Local governance calls for an increased participation of the civil society in activities that traditionally formed part of the public sphere. It is argued that it will improve the efficiency of public services, make local government more accountable and transparent, and deepen democracy complementing representative forums with participatory forums.

One of the most popular state forms that has opened spaces for a wider and deeper participation of citizens at the local level, is the decentralisation process which has got unprecedented momentum in the 1990s. All but 12 of the 75 developing countries five million people have implemented some form of decentralisation with more than varying degrees of financial and political power. Parallel to these developments, enabling legal frameworks and institutional channels for citizens' participation at the local level have been developed in many of these countries.

Legal Enabling Environment for People's Participation

Philippines	: Local Government Code (1990)
India	: 73rd and 74th Constitutional Amendments (1993-94)
Honduras	: Municipal Law (1990)
Bolivia	: Popular Participation Law (1992)
Namibia	: Local Authority Act (1992)
Uganda	: Local Government Act (1997)
Tanzania	: Local Authorities Act (1992)

Selected Examples of Institutional Channels for Peoples' Participation

Tanzania	: Ward Development Committee
Zimbabwe	: Village Development Committee
Uganda	: Resistance Councils and Committee
Nepal	: Village Development Council
Colombia	: Overseeing Committee
Bolivia	: Village Committees
China	: Villagers' Committees
India	: Gram Sabhas and Ward Committees

The Seventy Third Amendment of the Constitution

The 73rd Amendment has thrown up many new challenges to the rural local government one of which is grassroot participation.[2] The amendment has attempted to institutionalize people's participation through a body called Gram Sabha which had earlier existed in some states more in name than in action. While Gram Sabha has found a place in all conformity legislations, the state like West Bengal has taken a step forward by creating a new body called Gram Sansad at each electoral constituency level, and thus having two sets of participatory bodies Gram Sabha and Gram Sansad. This paper seeks to examine the workings of the Gram Sabha and the Gram Sansd in West Bengal. It also offers suggestions about how to improve the working of these institutions.

Panchayati Raj in West Bengal

Before we discuss the concept and practice of participatory governance in West Bengal, let us start with a brief backdrop of the panchayat system in the state. While India embarked on the first generation panchayats following the recommendations of the Balvantray Mehta Committee in early 1950s, West Bengal started late in early 1960s when the institutions started stagnating in other parts of the country. Although the West Bengal Panchayat Act was passed in 1956, the implementation of the Act was phased. By 1963 only 50 percent of the villages and 60 percent of the rural population were covered by the panchayat system. In 1963 came the second Act on panchayati Raj–the West Bengal Zilla Parishad Act. The delayed birth of panchayats received further setback because of political violence and upheavals which engulfed the state after the ceremonial inauguration of panchayati raj on October 2, 1964. In 1973 the Congress Government attempted to make a consolidated piece of legislation which became the starting point of the second generation panchayats initiated by the Left Front Government in 1978.[3] The beginning was made by holding elections to all the three tiers in June 1978 after a long gap.

The table below provides a view of the various tiers and their areas of the operation.

Table 1

Tier	*Geographical Area*	*Average population*	*Average number of voters at the Tier level (1998)*	*Average number of Voters per seat*
Gram Panchayat	Cluster of 10-12 villages	16902	10339	678
Panchayat Samitit	Community Block	165736	101387	3917
Zilla Parishad	District	3407945	1962154	4587

The lowest level of electoral unit in the panchayat system in West Bengal is the Gram Panchayat which covers about 10-12 villages totaling around 10,600 residents. It has 15-20 seats of representatives elected every five years. In 1998, there were 3,226 Gram Panchayats with 49,199 members. An electorate composed of around 700 voters elected each member.

The Gram Panchayat (GP) is headed by the *Pradhan* and *Upapradhan*. They are elected from amongst themselves by the Gram Panchayat members. It is a powerful body wielding powers, authority and resources. Above the Gram Panchayat there is Panchayat Samiti (PS) at the block level each of which covers on an average 115 villages and eligible voters of about 1,01,387. In 1998 there were 329 Panchayat Samitis in West Bengal with a total of 8515 members, all elected by the people. It is headed by the Sabhapati. At the district level there is a Zilla Parishad (ZP) headed by the Sabhadhipati. He enjoys the ramk of the Minister of State. The PS and ZP function through a number of sector specific subject committees.[4]

The Unique Features

Unlike in most of the other states panchayats in West Bengal are party-based. The election to all the three-tiers is held on the basis of open party competition. The party plays important role in the running of panchayats. The idea of party-based panchayats is in tune with the Leftist perspective on panchayats. Arguing the case for it, E.M.S. Namboodiripad says that in the name of non-partisanship, the Sarvodaya approach seeks to disarm the poor in their fight against landed gentry who are interested in transforming the panchayats into their instruments.[5] The panchayats, in the perception of the Left Front Government (LFG), are not simply instruments of planning for economic and social development, they are political institutions to bring about a change in the co-relation of class forces in the countryside. People's participation is not understood merely for the purpose of ensuring better governance and more effective implementation of development programmes. It has radical connotation. The LFG, as the Minister-in Charge of Panchayats and Rural Development says, is inclined to ensure that "the people do not suffer from any illusion that their basic needs could be achieved with a radical structural change of the existing production relations...... people learn from their experience of participation in organized manner about the limitations inherent in the existing socio-economic structure and thereafter, they can unleash struggles for implementation of an alternative developmental strategy in an nation-wide scale to overcome these limitations."[6]

Another unique feature of the Panchayati Raj in West Bengal lies in the social background of panchayat leadership.[7] The representation of the rural poor has been fair and there has been increasing representation of the disadvantaged sections, namely SC/ST in all panchayat bodies which started even before the reservation was made for them.

The Objective Conditions

West Bengal prepared necessary objective condition for people's participation during the last two decades. Panchayats in West Bengal are ahead of other states in many respects. In the first place, panchayats are free from the clutches of the landed gentry and high caste people. Atul Kohli writes. "The new panchayats in West Bengal represent a break from the past political pattern in rural India. The panchayats in West Bengal or in most arts of India, have seldom been so free of domination by landlords or rich easants".[8] Second, successful implementation of land reform programmes has brought about a change in the top categories of the land-owning class. According to the data collected by the National Sample Survey Organization 70 percent of the agricultural lands is owned by the small and marginal farmers while the national average is 34.30 per cent. Again, 56 per cent of the assigness of the vested land belong to the Scheduled Tribes. Third, relatively successful working of the pro-poor panchayats together with land reform has led to 'the churning of the submerged humanity'. Fourth, the implementation of the programme for registration of the names of share-croppers through *Operation Barga* with the active help of the panchayats and informal support from the peasant organizations and the working of party-based panchayats have unleashed people's initiative. Fifth, literacy campaigns have increased literacy to nearly 70 per cent and conscientised the poor.[9]

Gram Sabha and Gram Sansad in West Bengal

The West Bengal Panchayat Act, 1973 as amended in 1994, provides for two participatory bodies-*Gram Sabha* and *Gram Sansad. Gram Sabha* literally means village meeting–a meeting of the villagers to discuss their common problems. In many ways, it is comparable to the citizens' forum of direct democracy which existed in Greek city states.

Gram Sabha is an institution in the hands of the people to air their grievances and to watch the functioning of the panchayats. It also offers the panchayats an opportunity to share their difficulties with the people who have elected them. This is more necessary in a situation of rising expectations and limitation of funds. It can go a long way in legitimizing the authority of the panchayats and ensuring transparency of their activities and inculcating in the people respect for political institutions.

The *Gram Sabha* has been incorporated by all the states in their amended laws on panchayats, although there are variations in respect of numbers of meeting to be held, the issues to be discussed in the meetings and the like, West Bengal has, however, taken a step forward by making provision for *Gram Sansad* apart from *Gram Sabha.* All the voters of each of the electoral constituencies of a *Gram Panchayat* constitute a *Gram Sansad* and all the voters of a *Gram Panchayat* constitute a *Gram Sabha.* A *Gram Sansad* is required to guide and advise the *Gram Panchayat* in regard to the schemes for economic development and social justice undertaken or proposed to be undertaken in its area and may :

(a) identify or down principles for identification of the schemes which are required to be taken up on priority basis for economic development of the village;

(b) identify or lay down principles for identification of the beneficiaries for various poverty alleviation programmes;

(c) mobilize mass participation for community welfare programmes and programmes for adult education, family welfare and child welfare;

(d) promote solidarity and harmony among all sections of the people irrespective of religion, faith, caste creed or race; and

(e) record its objection to any action of the *Pradhan* or any other member of the Gram Panchayat for failure to implement any other development scheme properly or without active participation of the people of the area.

Table–2

Year-wise data on Meetings of Gram Sansads as on 31.12.2001

Yr.	*Total no. of GP*	*Total no. of GS*		*Avg. no. of electors per GS*	*Total no. of meetings held In May*	*Avg. no. of attendance in each meeting With % In May*	*Total no. of GS which did not hold of meeting*	*Total no. of meetings held in Nov. with %*	*Avg. no. of attendance in ech meeting Nov. with %*	*Total no. of meetings adjourned in Nov.*	*Total no. of GS which did not hold meetings in Nov.*
		Before Elec. 98	*After elec. 98*								
1	2	3	4	5	6	7	8	9	10	11	12
1996	3313	36125	-	808			-	32101(89)	145(18)		4024
1997	3313	36179	-	804	28412	121(15)	-	30816(88)	142(18)		5363
1998	3329		44506	741	10435(29)			44104(99)	122(16)	1175	403(1)
1999	3330		44634	746	43346(97)	90(12)		43872(98)	94(13)	2496	762(15)
2000	3360		45167	748	42910(95)	88(12)	2257	43246(96)	96(13)	4929	1921(4)
2001	3360		45167	750	43770(97)	86(12)	1397	42829(95)	79(11)	11056	2338

Source: Panchayats and Rural Development Department, Government of West Bengal

Table–3

Year-wise data on Meetings of Gram Sabha in West Bengal as on 31.12.2001

Year	*No. of Gram Sabha*	*Avg. no. of electors per Gram Sabha*	*Total no. of meetings held with (%)*	*Avg. no. of attendance in each meeting with (%)*	*No. of Gram Sabha meeting adjourned*	*No. of Gram Sabha which have not held any meeting*
1	2	3	4	5	6	7
Dec. 1996	3329	9988	2094(63)	2986(30)		1054
Dec. 1997	3329	10013	689(21)	2987(30)		644
Dec. 1998	3329	9706	2761(83)	2952(29)	115	568
Dec. 1999	3330	9985	2952(89)	526(5.5)	133	378(11)
Dec. 2000	3360	10015	3102(92)	522(5)	584	258(8)
Dec. 2001	3360	10093	2513(75)	NA	962	847(25)

Source: ibid.

Table–4
Gram Sansad Meetings in West Bengal

District	*No. of gram pancha yats*	*No. of gram sansads*	*Avg. no. of voters in gram sansads*	*No. of meetings held with quorum*	*%*	*No. of postponed meetings*	*%*	*Total no. of meetings*	*dance*	*Average atten %*	*%*	*Average atten*	*%*
Cooch Behar	128	1710	743	1360	80	36	2	1396	82	124	17	25	3
Jalpaiguri	146	2095	744	1769	84	288	14	2057	98	134	18	15	2
Darjeeling Hill Council	112	1041	382	1017	98	24	2	1041	100	-	12	11	3
Siliguri Div. Council	22	349	764	349	100	0	0	349	100	-	11	-	3
Uttar Dinajpur	99	1470	740	1098	75	372	25	1470	100	70	9	10	1
Dakshin Dinajpur	65	925	744	485	52	440	48	925	100	52	7	10	1
Malda	147	2021	738	1289	64	454	22	1743	86	63	9	10	1
Murshidabad	255	3614	784	2806	78	687	19	3493	97	144	18	-	-
Nadia	187	2639	798	1975	75	591	22	256	97	83	10	15	2
North 24 Parganas	200	2923	761	2003	69	824	28	2827	97	78	10	14	2
Sourth 24 Parganas	312	4324	769	2493	58	1639	38	4132	96	62	8	12	2
Howrah	157	2218	803	917	41	1286	58	2203	99	52	6	10	1
Hooghly	210	3001	801	2037	68	954	32	2991	100	91	11	17	2
East Medinapur	224	2970	804	1778	60	1157	39	2935	99	95	12	25	3
West Medinapur	290	3449	787	3046	88	370	11	3416	99	89	11	18	2
Bakura	190	2844	750	1821	73	583	23	2404	97	65	9	9	1
Purulia	170	1925	711	1352	70	507	26	1859	97	79	11	7	1
Bardhaman	277	3833	817	31874	83	621	16	3805	99	97	12	27	3
Birbhum	167	2108	764	1452	69	521	25	1973	94	60	8	8	1
Total	3358	45459	746	32231	71	11354	25	43585	97	86	12	13	2

Source: ISS, Panchayatiraj update, December 2002

The Gram Sansad meets twice in a year. The half-yearly meeting to be held in November considers the budget for the coming year and the written opinion of the members on the budget and the last audit report. The annual meeting of the *Sansad* to be held ordinarily in May considers the revised budget of the previous year, the accounts of the last six months, the activities undertaken last year and proposed to be undertaken in the coming year. The resolutions adopted at the meeting have to be read out at the meeting itself. The meetings of the *Gram Sabha* and the *Gram Sansad* are to be convened by the pradhan and in his absence, by the upapradhan. The inability on their part to convene the meeting empowers the State Government to remove them. If the panchayat is held responsible, the State Government can dissolve the Gram Panchayat concerned.

The *Gram Sabha* meets ordinarily in December every year after the completion of the half yearly meeting of the *Sansads* in November. The agenda items of the *Sansad* are included in the *Gram Sabha* meetings. It is the duty of the *Gram Panchayat* to place before the meeting of the Sabha the budget of the *Gram Panchayat*, annual plan, the last audit report, the income and expenditure of the last year. The *Gram Panchayat* has also to place before the meeting of the *Sabha* the decisions of the *Gram Sansads* along with the observations of the *Gram Panchayat*. The opinions of the *Sabha* have to be recorded in the resolution book. The resolutions of the *Sansad* and the *Sabha* are considered by the *Gram Panchayat* concerned the failure of which is recorded in the audit report as a case of gross irregularity.

The tables 2, 3, 4 above provide a view about the working of the *Gram Sansads* and *Gram Sabha*. The tables tend to show that the meetings of the *Gram Sansads* are being held almost regularly, although the percentage of postponed meetings is quite remarkable in some districts like Dakshin Dinajpur and Howrah. The average attendance is below the expectation. Interestingly, average attendance is better in the backward districts with low literacy rate. What causes concern is the attendance of women. One wonders if there is need for mandatory presence of at least 10 per cent of the women members in all meetings. It will put pressure on the *Gram Panchayats*. There is more than 36 per cent women members in the *Gram Panchayats*. Evidently, they are failing in their duties to mobilise women in *Gram Sansad* meetings.

There are a few studies which have taken note of the working of the *Gram Sabhas* established in terms of the amendment of West Bengal Panchayat Act in 1992. Webster's research indicated that apart from *para* meeting of the Gram Sabha, the informal mighty discussions in some localities and regular public meetings were other forms of participation.[10] Lieten remarked that although the *boktrita* culture was not altogether absent in the Gram Sabha meetings, participation used to take place. About one fourth of the males he could speak to stated that they participated in the meeting.[11] Another study[12] has shown that the *Gram Sabha* meetings are being held regularly. The beneficiaries are consulted about the schemes to be taken up and sites to be selected for launching projects.

The working of *Gram Sansads* has also been studied by several scholars. A recent study on the functioning of *Gram Sansads* in a cross-section of 20 villages in May 1999 brings out certain important issues. The study shows, while analyzing the occupational category of the voters who attended the meetings, that the largest single category was agricultural labourers followed by farmers with less than two acres of lands. Those with more lands or had non-framing sources of income constituted about 16 per cent of those present. The analysis of the findings of the study tends to show that the meetings were centered around very practical and concrete problems within a village or cluster of villages: proposals for road repair, where should a tube-well be installed, who should receive loan as opposed to broader issues such as economic liberalization, privatization of public sector etc. In quite a few meetings, thought not in all, the accounts of the previous year and the budgets for the next year for the entire village council area were also placed. The study observes, to quote. "Also, while deliberations are often characterized by lively debates, winners and losers, participants find reasons that they can accept in collective actions, even though this does not coincide with their most preferred choice".[13] The researchers have noticed that the participants actively voice demands for new projects, suggest how allocated funds should be spent and debate how projects should be designed. The *Pradhans* and the local representatives are not spared. They have to answer a lot of questions and often face allegations about the misuse of funds and selection of beneficiaries. The responses of the panchayat leaders to the criticisms indicate that they could not take the voters present in the meetings for granted. There had been occasions when they had to make frank admission about their errors. A distinct feature of the *Gram Sansad* meetings is that those who participated were largely members or supporters of some political party or the other. These who do not belong to any political party stayed away from the meetings. Again, majority of the members present belonged to the party of the elected member. The average percentage of the participants without any political affiliation was approximately 20 per cent. The study notes that participatory governance essentially involves greater involvement of villagers deciding on how to spend money received from outside and ensuring that it is well spent. It has been observed that a village council raises on its own on an average 2-4 per cent of the money spent by it in a year.[14]

The study done by this author reveals that more than one third of the villagers is not aware of the *Gram Sansad.* The reactions of the respondents tend to show that there are three reasons for low attendance of the members in the meetings, namely, lack of time, the impression that the decisions are not taken in the meetings and the reluctance on the part of a section of the *Gram Panchayat* members to listen carefully and patiently to the proceedings of the meetings.[15]

Thorlind's study presents a different picture. *Gram Sabha* and *Gram Sansads* do not function effectively. *Gram Sansad* is still in a process of learning and adoption, but they may become important instruments for democratic accountability and participation in the future. It requires awareness among the disadvantaged classes, and practical learning of democratic procedures from their own work as panchayat members.[16]

Participatory Decentralised Planning

Participatory development has received a new momentum following the decision of the Government of West Bengal to implement decentralised grassroots planning through Community Convergent Action (CCA). In order to implement the programme the Government carried out pilot surveys in four blocks in four districts, namely, Jalpaiguri, Purulia, West Midnapore and Nadia Based on the Kerala model of peoples' campaign for decentralised planning and the experience learnt form the village based planning conducted in the district of Midnapore in 1980s the exercise has re-charged *Gram Sansad.* In this new mode of planning

Gram Sansad is the nodal organization. It is the forum where the sector-wise reports prepared on the basis of social development data collected from the villages are discussed. The six sectors identified included education, health, women's development, agriculture, irrigation, animal husbandry, fishery, cottage and small scale industry and trade and infrastructure. The special *Gram Sansad* meetings were held in many *Gram Panchayats* during the year 2001-2002 to see how the idea of village level planning is likely to work in the field.

It is learnt from the field studies and from the informal interactions with the field workers that initially the villagers had some misgivings. The collection of data and interaction with the villagers were wrongly understood as a calculated move by the Government to take away lands from the people who have lands. The field workers had taken long sessions with them to remove their misgivings and the result was positive.

It has also become evident that the *Gram Panchayats* were also confused. They took it as another government-sponsored programme for which they would get money from the government. The task of the *Gram Panchayats* would be to implement the programme.

There was some reluctance on the part of the bureaucracy to accept the idea of people as the participants in the planning process. It was argued by a section of the bureaucracy that the villagers do not have necessary competence and skill for this purpose. When the work started, the bureaucracy accepted the logic, although their participation was not full-throated.

The fact remains that the CCA exercise has generated tremendous enthusiasm in many of the *Gram Panchayats*. It has been helpful in reducing political differences among the villages and thus reducing political tensions in the countryside. The Jalpaiguri experience indicates that this kind of exercise can be effective in containing secessionist activities also.[17]

Concluding Observations

Participation to be meaningful and genuine calls for the creation of certain objective conditions in the society and motivation among the participants. The delicate democratic plant, as both the liberal and the

Marxist scholars agree, cannot grow in an atmosphere of inequality and poverty. This is not enough. Participation in a meeting calls for education and skill. It may be recalled that J.S. Mill, one of those who conceived the idea of local self-government in the 19th century, stressed the need for universalisation of education as a precondition for the successful growth of democracy. Education has, therefore, to be universalized. It is good that steps are being taken to universalize primary education through the *Sarba Shiksha Abhijan* throughout the country.

To make participation of the people more effective, the following specific measures, apart from the general measures suggested above, may yield desired results. In the first place, as the panchayats are party-based, the parties should come forward and play effective role. They should move from door-to-door before the meetings as they do before the elections. Second, in the meetings the panchayat leadership should demonstrate patience and tolerance. They should listen to the constructive criticism of the people. Chandrasekhar and Inabhanathan's study[18] has shown that the intolerance led to the cancellation of the *Gram Sabhas* in the past in Karnataka. Third, an atmosphere has to be created where the people would feel free to speak about their problems. Fourth, information about positive examples of the functioning of the *Gram Sabha* and *Gram Sansad* needs to be widely circulated and supported by the government at the state and national levels in order to create positive climate for promoting opportunities for self-government at the village level. The press should focus on such meetings. Fifth, the government official should be so oriented as to be responsive to the people. Sixth, the advice and decisions of the *Gram Sabha* should be made binding on the *Gram Panchayats*. In case that is not possible, it should be the statutory responsibility of the *Gram Panchayats* to explain to the member why they failed to implement the decisions taken at the Sansad meetings and this has to be recorded. Seventh, as the villagers are not used to participate in a situation like this and the village is not tuned to it, the synchronization of the meeting with the cultural programmes in tune with the rhythm of the rural life might be helpful. The last, though not the least, is the generation of motivation among the members. This can be attempted in two ways, first, by making them realize the usefulness of this meeting, and second, by ensuring that the decisions of the meeting are carried out.

References

1. 'Introduction', in Prabhat Datta (2003) *Towards Good Governance and Sustainable Development*, Das Gupta & Co. Kolkata.
2. Prabhat Datta and Panchali Sen (2003) in *ibid.*
3. Prabhat Datta (2001) *Panchayats, Rural Development and Local Antonomy: The West Bengal Experience*, Das Gupta & Co., Kolkata.
4. Prabhat Datta and Chandan Datta (2002) The Panchayat System in West Bengal in G. Palanithurai (ed) *Dynamics of New Panchayti Raj System in India*, Vol. 1, Concept New Delhi.
5. E.M.S. Namboodiripad (1962), 'Political Parties and Panchayati Raj', *Indian Journal of Public Administration* (Oct.-Dec.).
6. Surjya Kanta Mishra (1992) *An Approach to alternative Rural Development : Land Reforms and Panchayats*, Information and Cultural Affairs Department, Government of West Bengal, Kolkata.
7. Prabhat Datta (1993) *The Second Generation Panchayats in India*, Calcutta Book House, Kolkata.
8. Atul Kohli (1983) 'Parliamentary Committee and Agrarian Reform', The evidence from India 'West Bengal', *Asian Survey*, p. 394.
9. Prabhat Datta (2001) *New Horizons in Rural Development Planning in West Bengal*, Das Gupta & Co. Kolkata.
10. Neil Webster (1992) *Panchatati Raj, Decentralisation of Development Planning in West Bengal*, K.P. Bagchi, Calcutta.
11. G.K. Lieten (1996) *Development, Devolution and Democracy: the Village Discourse in West Bengal*, Sage (India), New Delhi.

12. Prabhat Datta (2001) *op. cit.*

13. Swapan Pramanik and Prabhat Datta (1994), *Panchayats and the People: The West Bengal Experience*, Sarat Book House, Kolkata.

14. Maitresh Ghatak and Maitraya Ghatak (2002) 'Recent Reforms in the Panchayat System in West Bengal: Toward Greater Participatory Governance? *Economic and Political Weekly*, January.

15. Prabhat Datta (2001), *Panchayats, Rural Development and Local Antonomy: The West Bengal Experience Kolkata*, Das Gupta and Co. Pvt. Ltd.

16. Robert Thorlind (2000) *Development, Decentralisation and Democracry*; NIAS, Copenhegen.

17. Prabhat Datta (2001) *op. cit.*

18. B.K. Chandrasekhar and A. Inabhanthan (1991), 'People's Participation is Rural Development', *Hindu*, October, 10.

6

Perspectives on Urban Governance in West Bengal

Since the adoption of the Habitat Agenda (1996), urban governance has become a major priority item in most of the developing countries for improving the functioning of the existing local self governments and promoting decentralisation and devolution of powers and functions to municipal and city governments. Good governance agenda in urban governance have laid stress on participatory and transparent governance besides decentralisation and devolution of powers. The United Nations Development Programme (1997) policy document argues that good governance and human development are indivisible. The former is a necessary ingredient to achieve equitable and sustainable development.

Decentralisation and participation are the twin principles of democracy and constitute the keystone in the arch of democratic governance and form the basis of the development discourse at least for the last two decades. The proponents of democracy in the early nineteenth century stood for local government as it embodied these twin principles. They spoke highly of the instrumental values of local government.

The Urban Policy of the Government of West Bengal

The governance programme including the design and plan of action of the Government of West Bengal in the urban sector was first mooted by the Urban Development Strategy Committee.

Its recommendations had far-reaching implications on urban decentralisation and set the tune of the new perspective on urban governance and development in the State. The important recommendations include the following:

(a) the difference in per capita investments between Kolkata Metropolitan Area (KMA) and non-KMA should be brought down by pumping the more funds to the non-KMA urban local bodies (ULBs) to restrict migration to the metropolis and to develop the non-KMA ULBs as growth centres;

(b) use of local resources and materials should as far as possible be maximized;

(c) special efforts should be made to upgrade the quality of life of the urban poor and the weaker sections;

(d) development activities should be decentralised, and

(e) preparation of developmental programmes and their implementation should be the responsibility of the ULBs.

After having carefully considered the recommendations of the Committee the Government of West Bengal developed its approach to urban governance. It is based, as the Minister-in-Charge observes, "on decentralised and balanced development people's participation in planning and execution of development works, transparency, responsibility and accountability in municipal administration and democratic decentralisation in decision-making authority".[1] Incidentally, it was possibly to implement the recommendations of the Committee that the State Government decided to have two independent departments, namely Municipal Affairs and Urban Development. Broadly speaking, the Government of West Bengal adopted five-pronged policy on the urban front as spelt out below:

(1) holding of elections at regular intervals to ensure unhindered democratization of urban governance;

(2) decentralisation of planning and development focusing on human development and sustainable development;

(3) ensuring people's participation in the planning, implementation and monitoring of urban development activities;

(4) giving special emphasis on the improvement of the quality of life of the down-and-out in the urban areas and

(5) making urban governance more efficient, modern and transparent.

Incidentally, West Bengal Government adopted quite a few measures in urban governance, which were subsequently included in the 74th amendment of the Constitution. West Bengal is one of the few States, which has implemented most of the provisions of the 74th amendment of the Constitution. The 74th amendment is definitely a watershed mark in the history of urban governance in India, as it constitutionalises urban local bodies as institutions of self-government and provides a few safeguards to strengthen the system.

Democratic decentralisation in urban West Bengal came to a creaking halt during the period between 1947 and 1977. Almost all the urban local bodies in the State stood suspended for long. The urban local bodies received a new lease of life following the holding of elections and devolution of powers and funds on them by the Left Front Government.

Decentralisation of Functions

The Twelfth Schedule of 74th Constitution Amendment Act empowers State legislatures to assign functions to the municipalities in the respective State. The Twelfth Schedule included 18 items and provides an illustrative list of functions. The State Governments were accordingly expected to review the functions entrusted to municipalities and formulate a new set of municipal functions while amending the respective legislations.

A study of conformity laws of the different states, however, reveal that only a few states, namely, Kerala, West Bengal and Tamil Nadu have made a comprehensive law devolving functions to municipalities. Kerala has devolved 11 additional functions with 98 sub-functions. West Bengal has an elaborate listing of 49 obligatory functions. Additionally, the Act also lists 40 functions, which have been devolved. The opportunity provided by the Constitution Amendment has indeed been utilized by these States and provides examples worth replicating in other States.

Decentralisation within Decentralisation

West Bengal is the first State in India to accept and operationalise the cabinet form of city governance through the Mayor/Chairman-Council model in all ULB. The Mayor/Chairman-Council model is rooted in the philosophy of democratic decentralisation and collective responsibility at the operational level.[2] It is an institutional contrivance, which is meant to promote more transparency and better accountability through decision-making mechanism.[3] K.C. Sivaramakrishnan wrote that only in Kerala and West Bengal there was a conscious attempt made to vest elected Mayor and municipal Chairpersons with executive powers so that authority and responsibility could go together.[4]

The Mayor/Chairman-Council system was introduced in three States–West Bengal in 1984, Maharashtra in 1998 and Madhya Pradesh in 1998. Maharashtra has gone back to the original scheme. The Mayor/ Chairman-Council models adopted in these States exhibit serious variation in matters like authority structure, relationship between different points of authority and power of the Mayor and Mayor-in-Council vis-à-vis the Commissioner. With the exception of West Bengal, the two other State Governments seem reluctant to share powers with the local governments.[5]

Citizen's Participation

West Bengal has a tradition of citizens' participation in urban governance, which received a jolt during the days of the Congress rule. Mention may be made of the existence of Citizens' Councils as a participative institution in some of the municipalities in the State. It has worked well in a few municipalities. There is a detailed discussion about the Ward Committees in West Bengal in a separate chapter of the book.

Implementing the Health Project Through People's Participation

Decentralisation and participation have been the guiding principles of implementation of the World Bank–sponsored Indian Population Project VIII currently in operation in a few ULBs in the State. Earlier, the World Bank supported another similar project known as the Calcutta Urban Development Project (CUDP) III in 1985-86, which benefited 16 lakh slum dwellers in 31 ULBs within the KMA. The IPP VIII, which targets the mothers and children in the slum areas, takes care of 38 lakh slum dwellers covering the areas beyond the purview of the CUDP III. This programme has been successfully implemented and yielded described results, as we notice form the data in the table.

Table 1 Health Development Index in the Slum Areas

Item	*1984-85 (in per cent)*	*2000-01*	*Percentage of Success*
Infant mortality rate	55	22	59 (Decline)
Child immunization	39	68	95 (Increase)
Crude birth rate	19	14	25 (Decline)
Crude death rate	06	04	32 (Decline)

Source: Municipal Affairs Department, Government of West Bengal

Engineering Participation and Development

Participation of women living below the poverty line is the basic principle of SJSRY. As per the guidelines of the programme there will be three community structures, namely, Community Development Society, Neighbourhood Committee and the Neighbourhood Group. West Bengal

Table 2 Urban Poverty in India

States	*1993-94*	*1999-2000*
All-India	30.37	28.76
Andhra Pradesh	35.44	32.28
Assam	10.13	12.45
Bihar	45.03	45.10
Gujarat	28.86	21.70
Haryana	13.40	13.79
Karnataka	32.41	24.55
Kerala	28.20	31.89
Madhya Pradesh	46.02	46.29
Maharashtra	33.52	32.16
Orissa	36.99	34.27
Punjab	6.79	6.74
Rajasthan	30.60	24.36
Tamil Nadu	37.83	29.83
Uttar Prdesh	34.23	36.39
West Bengal	20.97	16.74

Source: Economic and Political Weekly. August 2001.

had made significant progress in this regard. The SJSRY programme provides for the formation of the thrift and credit groups formed solely with the women members. In West Bengal this sub-programme has been successfully implemented as is evident from the Indian Institute of Public Administration's recent study. The study observes, "Inspite of various setbacks, the Government of West Bengal had done commendable job in setting up community organizations. The State has also shown some flexibility in order that maximum benefits are extended to the poor under the constraints imposed by the schematic budget and procedures." Urban poverty in West Bengal has substantially come down in the last few years, as the table clearly indicate.

Participatory Decentralised Planning

The Seventy Fourth amendment of the Constitution empowers the state legislatures to make such laws as would lead to devolution of power and responsibility to the municipalities in respect of preparation of plans for economic development and social justice. It is a clear constitutional recognition of the objectives of planning. The Constitution also lays down the institutional arrangement for planning thus:

"There shall be constituted in every State at the district level a District Planning Committees (DPC) in different States to consolidate the plans prepared by the Panchayats and Municipalities in the district and to prepare a development plan for the district."

Clearly, the constitutional amendment provides a new perspective on planning. The table below attempts to capture the nature of changes in terms of functions and tasks:

Table–3

Functions/Tasks	*Pre-Constitutional Amendment Scenario*	*Arrangements as could be Envisaged*
Basic 'needs identification Services Provision	Functional departments of state governments and/or special purpose Parastatal agencies	Local governments (i.e. Gram Sabha, Gram Panchayat. Ward Committee)
Project planning And implementation	-do-	Local government and departmental Agencies under the Administrative Control of local Governments.

(Contd.)

(Contd. Table)

Functions/Tasks	*Pre-Constitutional Amendment Scenario*	*Arrangements as could be Envisaged*
Delivery and maintenance	Same as above: Municipal bodies also Concurrently involved In urban areas	Community Groups, private entities on contract with local government.
Development Planning	Union/state	Local governments
Programmes	governments/NGOs	Local government, Citizen groups, CBOs.
Beneficiary Identification	functional departments, Parastatals, GP only For JRY.	Gram Panchayat/Gram Sabha
Implementation	Functional Departments, Parasatatals, NGOs, CBOs.	Functional departments under the supervision & Control of Local Govt. Community Groups.
Area perspective Development planning	Union & State govts. Urban Development Authorities, complete Neglect of rural areas.	District and Metropolitan Planning Committees (DPCs & MPCs)
Integrated spatial Planning	Functional departments. Municipal bodies.	Local government At their respective Levels. Plus DPC.
Resource planning	-do-	-do-

The constitutional amendment has authorized the state legialatures to make provisions with respect to the composition of the DPC and the functions to be assigned to them. Significantly, there are many major states where the DPCs hve not yet been constituted. The table below presents the status of DPCs as on October 1 2001.

Table–4

Sl. No.	*State/Uts.*	*Whether DPCs have been constituted*	*If yes, who is the chairperson of DPC*
1.	Andhra Pradesh	No constituted	
2.	Arunachal Pradesh	No constituted	
3.	Assam	No constituted	
4.	Bihar	No constituted	
5.	Chhattisgarh	No constituted	

(Contd.)

(Contd. Table)

Sl. No.	*State/Uts.*	*Whether DPCs have been constituted*	*If yes, who is the chairperson of DPC*
6.	Goa	No constituted	
7.	Gujart	No constituted	
8.	Haryana	Only in 3 district (No. of districts:19)	Deputy Commissioner
9.	Himachal Pradesh	No constituted	
10.	Jammu & Kashmir		
11.	Jharkhand	No constituted	
12.	Karnataka	Yes. Only in 10 districts (no. of districts:27)	Zilla Panchayat president
13.	Kerala	Yes	Zilla panchayat president
14.	Madhya Pradesh	Yes	Minister-in-charge of district
15.	Maharashtra	No	
16.	Manipur	Yes. Only in 2 district (no. of district: 9)	Zilla parishad president
17.	Meghalaya	Amendments not applicable	73rd and 74th
18.	Mizoram Amendment not applicable	73rd and 74th	
19.	Nagaland Amendment not	73rd and 74th applicable	
20.	Orissa	No	
21.	Punjab	No	
22.	Rajasthan	Yes	Zilla parishad president
23.	Sikkim	Yes	Zilla parishad president
24.	Tamil Nadu	Yes, Not operationalization	
25.	Tripura	Yes	Cabinet ministers
26.	Uttar Pradesh	Yes	Ministers
27.	Uttaranchal	No	
28.	West Bengal	Yes. In 16 district No. DPC in Darjeeling district, Metro Planning Commission in Calcutta District	Zilla parishad president
29.	A & N Islands	Yes	Zilla parishad president
30.	Chandigarh	Government has decided not to constitute DPCs as 90% of population is covered by municipalities	
31.	D & N Haveli	No	
32.	Daman & Diu	Yes	Zilla Parishad president
33.	NCT of Delhi		
34.	Lakshadweep	Yes	Development Commissioner
35.	Pondicherry	No	

Source: ISS Documentation and Information Centre.

West Bengal is one of the very few States in the country which started decentralised planning experiment after 1978. New planning structure at the block and district level came up in 1985-86. There were three structures, namely, District Planning and Co-ordination Committee, District Planning committee and Block Planning Committee. The planning bodies used to prepare overall development plans of the district and after threadbare discussion in the State Planning Board (SPB) the plans were finalized and schemes executed accordingly. We have discussed it in a previous chapter.

Consequent upon the 74th amendment of the constitution, the West Bengal District Planning Act was passed in 1994 and necessary rules were also framed. The Act lays down that the DPC will:

(a) consolidate plans prepared by the Panchayats and Municipalities in the Districts; and

(b) prepare a draft development plan for the District as a whole" Each urban local body is, therefore, required to prepare its development plan, which will be integrated at the district level. Imperatively, a municipal development plan will address macro-economic development agenda taking into account its distributive aspects. It will be followed by an infrastructure development plan for supporting and sustaining economic development including social sector development.

The Planning Processes

The decentralised planning processes for urban areas start from the state level to the district level and from the district level to the ward level. At the state level the SPB will interact with other department and the DPCs. At the district level the DPCs will interact with the District Planning and Co-ordination Sub-Committee. This body has to take into account social planning for SC, ST and women, mobilizing resources available in urban and rural areas, indication of priorities assigned to work in the DDP and the phasing out of the programme of development as such. This Sub-Committee is responsible for preparation of district plans co-ordinating and consolidating annual plans and programmes of the ULBs as recommended by the Urban Development Sub-Committee (UDSC).

The UDSC is an offspring of the District Planning Act and rules made thereunder:

The Sub-Committee is required to:

(a) examine, co-relate and integrate plans as drawn up by the different municipalities of the distrct;

(b) deliberate upon the issues relating to peripheral areas and resolution of conflicts;

(c) draw up guidelines for planning, building controls and aesthetics relating to municipalities;

(d) draw up plans for improvement of slums especially in the area of sanitation and environment;

(e) consider measures for environmental improvement with special emphasis on control of water and air pollution;

(f) consider issues relating to sources of water supply, disposal of sewage, solid waste and other disposable waste.

In West Bengal all the subjects under the 12th schedule have been transferred to the ULBs. The services of the district level officers of the line departments have been placed at the disposal of the Zilla Parishad/ ULBs. They are required to help them in the exercise of plan formulation.

In the processes of formulation of plan at each tier, the next tier hs no authority to reject any proposal/scheme of the own plan of the preceding tier if it conforms to the rules and regulations within the broad financial parameters. The higher tier may suggest alternative showing the justification of such revision. The DPC cannot reject any such proposal of the ZP/ULB outright. It may suggest modification. The DPC may suggest the executing agencies, through which the institutions of self-government may implement schemes. Field level functionaries of the different departments have been given suitable *ex-officio* status. They can execute schemes themselves through the line department field functionaries whose services have already been placed under their disposal.

A development plan to be effective and meaningful calls for mobilization of resources and participation of the people. Resource

Table-5 Financial Autonomy Ratio of Local Bodies, Village Panchayats and Urban Local Bodies

State(s)	*Financial Ratio of LBs (PRIs+ULBs)*	*Autonomy*	*Improve-ment Ratio*	*Financial Ratio of VPs*	*Autonomy*	*Improve-ment Ratio*	*Financial Autonomy Ratio of ULBs*	*Improve-ment Ratio*	
	1992-93	1997-98		1992-93	1997-98		1992-93	1997-98	
Andhra Pradesh	0.86	1.09	126.60	26.31	40.45	153.74	0.38	0.83	217.93
Bihar	—	—	—	—	—	—	—	—	—
Gujarat	46.46	46.46	95.68	46.66	51.91	111.25	46.39	41.13	88.65
Haryana	22.21	44.46	118.98	63.06	53.45	84.76	78.7	85.21	108.20
Karnataka	6.15	32.01	75.55	15.93	12.37	77.66	46.20	36.42	78.83
Kerala	43.83	4.65	48.46	28.51	22.49	78.89	62.05	41.80	67.37
Madhya Pradesh	21.89	21.24	34.22	4.71	3.84	81.50	40.03	23.85	59.58
Maharashtra	19.21	3.34	17.39	15.96	19.63	122.97	23.34	3.38	14.48
Orissa	19.73	11.85	63.03	6.81	4.80	70.44	57.09	61.76	108.18
Punjab	64.08	88.66	138.37	27.73	37.23	156.89	89.38	113.03	126.45
Rajasthan	19.46	20.28	104.21	4.35	1064	37.61	74.35	77.75	104.57
Tamil Nadu	31.27	39.76	127.14	10.02	10.84	108.20	41.91	52.62	125.56
Uttar Pradesh	15.98	14.47	90.55	0.90	0.51	57.35	27.59	28.44	103.11
West Bengal	9.76	68.50	701.75	3.19	4.11	128.90	17.96	163.08	907.94
Total (all States)	11.41	4.81	42.11	10.61	10.60	99.90	14.35	5.02	3501

Source: Mainstream, Oct 21, 2000.

mobilization has three distinct but complementary elements–resource as grants-in-aid n the form of entitlement, resource outlay for special projects, resources for execution of externally aided projects, on the one hand and institutional finance, on the other. Added to it is the mobilization of internal resources.

Metropolitan Planning

The Metropolitan Planning Committee (MPC) is a product of the Seventy Fourth Amendment of the Constitution. A metropolitan area has been defined as n area having population of ten lakh or more comprised in one or more districts and consisting of two or more municipalities.[6] The credit for reviving the concept and the provisions for the Metropolitan Planning Committee goes to the Joint Parliamentary Committee. We have discussed the subject in a separate chapter.

Financial Decentralisation

No talk of decentralisation is meaningful is the financial base of the ULBs is not improved and the dependence on the higher-level government is not reduced. In order to make theULBs not only instruments of planning but also instruments of development there has been substantial flow of funds from the State Government. West Bengal is one of the states where there were two Municipal Finance Commissions even before the amendment of the constitution, which provided for the constitution of the State Finance Commissions. West Bengal is one of the States where the Second SFC has submitted the report. M.A. Oommen has prepared an index of financial autonomy ratio of the ULBs. West Bengal's performance is remarkable as is evident from the table above.

Application of Geographical Information System (GIS)

Information technology has brought about a remarkable change in the collection, storing and dissemination of data and information. The Human Development Report, 2001 notes that people all over the world have high hopes that new technologies will lead to healthier lives, greater social freedom, increased knowledge and more productive livelihoods. The Sixth Left Front Government has laid special stress on application of IT to all spheres of administration. There is strong need for improving the quality of democratic governance in urban local bodies primarily by

Table–6

State/Union Territories	Birth rate			Death rate			Natural Growth rate		
	Total	*Rural*	*Urban*	*Total*	*Rural*	*Urban*	*Total*	*Rural*	*Urban*
India	26.1	27.6	20.8	8.7	9.4	6.3	17.13	18.2	14.5
Bigger States									
Andhra Pradesh	21.7	2.0	20.6	8.2	9.0	5.7	13.5	13.1	15.0
Assam	27.0	28.0	18.9	9.7	10.1	6.2	17.3	17.9	12.7
Bihar	30.4	31.3	22.6	9.1	9.3	6.6	21.4	22.0	16.0
Gujarat	25.4	27.0	22.0	7.9	8.8	5.9	17.6	18.2	16.1
Haryana	26.8	27.7	23.3	7.7	8.0	6.4	19.1	19.7	16.9
Karnataka	22.3	23.7	19.2	7.7	8.7	5.5	14.6	15.0	13.6
Kerala	18.0	18.1	17.7	6.4	6.5	6.3	11.5	11.6	11.4
Madhya Pradesh	30.7	32.1	23.4	10.6	11.2	7.4	20.1	20.9	15.9
Maharashtra	21.1	16.6	20.3	7.5	8.7	5.6	13.6	2.9	14.7
Orissa	24.1	24.6	20.3	10.6	11.1	7.1	13.4	13.5	13.3
Punjab	21.5	22.5	18.6	7.4	7.9	6.1	14.1	14.6	12.5
Rajasthan	31.1	32.5	24.9	8.4	8.9	6.4	22.7	23.6	18.5
Tamil Nadu	19.3	19.8	18.2	8.0	8.7	6.6	11.3	1.1	11.6
Uttar Pradesh	32.1	33.1	26.1	10.5	11.0	7.7	21.6	22.1	19.0
West Bengal	20.7	22.9	14.3	7.1	7.2	6.8	13.6	15.7	7.5
Smaller States									
Arunachal Pradesh	22.3	23.2	13.5	6.0	6.4	1.9	16.3	16.7	11.6
Goa	14.3	14.4	14.1	7.2	7.6	6.6	7.1	6.8	7.5
Himachal Pradesh	23.8	24.3	16.8	7.3	7.5	5.2	16.4	16.8	11.6
Jammu & Kashmir	NA	NA	NA	NA	NA	NA	NA	NA	NA
Manipur	18.6	19.4	16.4	5.4	5.0	6.6	13	14.3	9.8

Contd.

(Table 6 Contd.)

Meghalaya	28.7	31.1	15.7	9.1	10.2	3.3	19.5	20.9	12.4
Mizoram	17.0	18.7	14.8	5.5	6.9	3.7	11.5	11.8	11.1
Nagaland	11.8	-	11.8	2.3	-	2.3	9.5	-	9.5
Sikkim	21.6	21.9	14.7	5.8	5.9	3.4	15.8	16.0	11.3
Tripura	17.0	17.5	14.4	5.7	5.7	5.7	11.3	11.8	8.7
Union Territories									
Andaman & Nicobar Island	18.1	17.8	19.2	5.5	6.2	3.5	12.6	11.5	15.7
Chandigarh	17.9	24.5	17.1	3.9	2.6	4.1	14.0	21.9	13.0
Dadra & Nagar Haveli	32.4	35.2	23.5	5.9	7.0	2.3	26.5	28.1	21.2
Daman & Diu	26.9	24.9	28.8	7.1	8.9	5.4	19.9	16.1	23.3
Delhi	19.4	20.7	19.3	4.8	4.5	4.9	14.6	16.2	14.4
Lakshadweep	25.1	25.1	25.0	4.7	4.3	5.0	20.4	20.8	20.0
Pondicherry	17.7	18.0	17.5	6.9	7.9	6.1	10.8	10.1	11.4

-Not presented due to part-receipt of returns.
-NA–Not available due to non-receipt returns.
Source: Sample Registration System, Government of India, 1999.

ensuring people's participation in planning and development and by making the local government to respond to the needs of the target groups. The State Government has decided to take necessary steps for the implementation of GIS in 51 urban local bodies at the first instance. It will be useful for successful implementation of participatory decentralised programme in the urban areas. The data collected, stored and updated would help planning process in an effective way.

The Constitution of the Reforms Committee

The Government of West Bengal constituted the Administrative Reforms Committee, the first of its kind in the country, to suggest measures, *inter alia*, for extending and consolidating the democratic and participating base of the urban local government. Some of the major recommendations have been implemented while others are under active consideration of the Government.

Human Development in Urban West Bengal

West Bengal's performance in relation to human development dimension of urban governance is commendable. The important indices of human development such as infant mortality rate, couple protection rate, literacy rate, birth rte, death rate have recorded achievement as shown in the table and data below:

Data on Urban West Bengal

Monthly Per Capita consumption expenditure (1999-2000)

National average	Rs. 854.96
West Bengal	Rs. 866.60

Monthly Per Capita Expenditure pattern: Food–1999-2000

National average	Rs. 48.06%
West Bengal	52.28%

Persons in Labour Force (Male)–1999-2000

National average	78.6%
West Bengal	80.5%

Percentage of People below the Poverty Line (1999-2000)

National average	23.62
West Bengal	14.86

Households with Semi-pucca house

National average	19.50%
West Bengal	50.19%

House with safe drinking water

National average	81.38%
West Bengal	86.23%

Household with safe drinking water (SC/ST) (1991)

National average	81.99%
West Bengal	87.27%

Household with access to electricity, safe drinking water & toilet (1991)

National average	50.5%
West Bengal	57.2%

Urban Literacy (2001)

National average	80.06%
West Bengal	81.63%

Adult Urban Literacy rate (1991)

National average	70.68%
West Bengal	74.14%

Expectation of Life at Birth (1992-96)

National average	66.3
West Bengal	67.9

Estimated Sex ratio at birth (1991) Females per thousand males)

National average	926
West Bengal	962

Birth Attended by Health Professions (1998-99)

National average	33.6%
West Bengal	40.4%

Couple Protection Rate

National average	48.2%
West Bengal	66.6%

Source: National Human Development Report–2001 Planning Commission, Govt. of India, March, 2002.

Summing Up

The Government of West Bengal has introduced decentralisation from within and from without as is evident from the introduction of the Mayor/Chairman-in-Council form of urban governance and Ward Committees. Going beyond the mandate of the Constitutional Amendment the Government has made it mandatory to constitute Ward Committees in all municipalities irrespective of the size of the population. The municipal legislations empower the Ward Committees to constitute beneficiary committees to ensure people's supervision over the process of implementation of the urban development.

West Bengal is one of the few big states to constitute District Planning Committees and is the first State in the country to constitute Metropolitan Planning Committee (MPC). The MPC has started working and a number of sectoral committees has already been formed.

To achieve the objective of decentralised and participatory governance and development, the ULBs need to take more meaningful initiative in resource mobilization. The most important source of taxes of the ULBs is property tax. The Municipal Reforms Committee collected data about the property tax performance of the ULBs. It is found that out of 113 ULBs the performance of 76 is less than 40 per cent of the total demand. The dependence of the ULBs on the State Government is very high as is evident from a comparative study of the revenue receipts of different municipal bodies from own source and Government grants (non-plan) during 1997-98 to 1999-2000. Government to the extent of more than 51 percent, in 1998-99 out of 98 ULBs 80 were similarly dependent. In 1999-2000 the number of the such ULBs rose to 90 out of 100. Many ULBs are yet to properly utilize statutory powers relating to imposition of tax on advertisement and toll tax on ferries and bridges. While own sources of revenue constitute about 89 per cent of the total revenue for ULBs in Gujarat, their share is as low 28 per cent for ULBs in West Bengal. In West Bengal per capita municipal revenue collection is Rs. 36 compared to Rs. 441 in Gujarat and Rs. 252 in Punjab. It needs to be kept in mind that the ULBs are now institutions of self-government performance of which will now be judged from different angles. Initiative in all respects is the life-blood of the elected local government. Increasing dependence of the ULBs on the higher-level government will weaken the basis of local government as conceived in the amendment of the Constitution.

West Bengal's achievement in the spheres of decentralised and participatory governance at the local level may be attributed to two things: the character of the regime rooted in the ideological commitment of the Left Front partners and the strong political will to strengthen the elected local government. Incidentally, some scholars think that there is inherent contradiction between democratic decentralisation and democratic centralism. Democratic centralism, as Isaac rightly says, is the organizational principle of the Communist Party. It is voluntarily accepted by the party because of their conviction that only a party organized on this principle can successfully negotiate the twists and turns of politics and provide resolute leadership for revolution. In contrast, democratic decentralisation is a principle of governance, a commitment exemplified by the radical decentralisation programme of the Government of West Bengal.[7]

The participatory governance and decentralisation is facing a serious challenge from the liberalization policy of the Indian State and the current fiscal crisis of the State Government. There had been a substantial decline in the social sector expenditure of the country.[8] Take for example, the case of education. The share of expenditure from all the Central Government departments devoted to education was 4.1 per cent in 1990-91. It came down to 3.8 per cent in 1998-99. India taken together the expenditures of the central and state governments, spent 6 to 8 per cent of its Gross Domestic Product on the social sector in 1990s–lower than that in 1980s. It was low compared to other developing countries and certainly compared to East Asian countries. It was low compared to the ratios recommended by the United Nations Development Programme.

References

1. Asok Bhattacharya, 'Urban Development Strategy in West Bengal' *Urban Management*, January, 2000.
2. For details see, Prabhat Datta, *Urbanisation and Urban Government in West Bengal*, Institute of Local Government and Urban Studies: Kolkata, 2000.
3. Marina Pinto, *Metropolitan Governance in India*, Sage : New Delhi, 2000.
4. K.C. Sivaramakrishnan Power to the People: *The Politics and Progress of Decentralisation*, Konark Publishers, New Delhi, 2000.
5. Archana Ghosh 'Towards Municipal Autonomy,' *Panchayat Update*, November, 1999.
6. Prabhat Datta 'Metropolitan Planning Committee: West Bengal Shows the Way', *Mainstream*, July 13, 2002.
7. T.M. Thomas Isaac with Richard W. Frankel, *Local Democracy and Development*, Left Word, New Delhi, 2000.
8. Abusaleh Shariff et.al. 'State–Adjusted Public Expenditure on Social Sector and Poverty Alleviation Programmes' *Economic and Political Weekly*, December-22, 2002.

7

Institutionalising Citizens' Participation in Urban West Bengal

For the last 20 years the concept of participation has been widely used in the development discourse and for much of the period the concept has referred to participation in the social arena, in the community or in the development projects. Increasingly, the idea of participation is related to the rights of citizenship and to democratic governance.

It needs to be emphasised that participation of the people in governance and development has become more relevant in recent years in the context of the paradigmatic shift in the role of the state in the developing countries following the World Bank and the International Monetary Fund-sponsored Structural Adjustment Programme. Earlier, particularly since the second half of the 19th century the state was conceived as a welfare state, a social service state. Currently, following the adoption of the structural adjustment programme in the developing countries, the state in these countries is looked at in the role of a facilitator, which suggests the need for enhanced participation of the stakeholders in the development process both rural and urban. The state's role as a facilitator in the context of the urban areas suggests the need for enhanced participation by the different stakeholders in the urban developmental process.

With respect the citizens' participation in urban governance three areas are particularly relevant. The first two areas relate to development projects and local services. Participation in this regard is looked at as a means of strengthening their relevance, quality and sustainability. The World Bank Learning Group on Participation defines participation, "as a process through which the stakeholders influence and share control over development initiatives and the decisions and resources which affect them". In the case of the development projects the objectives of participation include effectiveness, efficiency, cost sharing, capacity building and empowerment. In the case of the local services the emphasis is on coverage, effectiveness, efficiency, community awareness, capacity building and empowerment. The third area relates to public policy and planning. Here the stress is on effectiveness, equality, capacity building and empowerment.

There are, as Meera Mehta suggests, three strands of ideas, which have emphasised the need for participation'. They are not exclusive and overlap in actual practice.[1]

Alternative Development

The concept of alternative development grew in sixties when the world was stirred by movement politics. The wide variety of movements essentially represented "the rise of the civil society as a collective actor working for political agenda outside the established framework of party politics". There came alongside an intellectual movement which worked on developing alternative development approach for the developing countries. In this approach the emphasis is on people-centered development, which focuses only on the community or the people, completely negating or avoiding the role of the state. This is a very narrow view. There is need for re-inventing the government in the changed context. The role of the state has to be viewed in the context of the need for evolving mechanisms for moving from exclusion of a large majority to their empowerment.

Reassertion of the Civil Society

Of late, there has been a special interest in the civil society particularly in the urban areas. This may be attributed to the failure of the urban government to cater to the needs of the citizens. The concept of partnership has gained considerable ground in public administration. The role of the third sector in development, that is, the non-government organisations, is being increasingly acknowledged. It is widely believed that this sector has good potential for reaching low-income group population and those in the informal sector. The NGOs may play important role in improving the participatory character of urban governance.

Facilitating and Enabling Government

Earlier, particularly since the second half of the 19th century the state came to be viewed as the provider. This role of the state has undergone a change. The state is now looked at from the perspective of facilitator which suggests the enhanced participation by the different stakeholders in the urban development process.

The concerns of development have also broadened to include wider definitions of environmental quality and a new focus on the poor and the down-and-out. There is now greater concern for equity in distribution and resource mobilisation.

Case for Participation

Participation is not an end in itself. It is a means for the achievement of a certain objectives. Participation as an instrument of goal-achievement serves a number of purposes as stated below:

- Increases efficiency in public service
- Ensures democratic accountability
- Promotes democratic values
- Enhances transparency in governance
- Acts as an instrument of social audit
- Makes administration more responsive to the people
- Develops respect for political institutions
- Ensures better implementation of the poverty alleviation programmes

Incidentally, participatory municipal budgeting in Brazil has led to an increase in the share of the households with access to water services from 80 per cent to 98 per cent. The percentage of population with access to sanitation got almost doubled from 46 per cent to 85 per cent during the first seven years. 70 cities have established participatory budgeting which allows citizens to participate in the process of resource allocation. Participatory structures have been created. There is a body called Municipal Council of Government Plan and Budget. It is constituted by the elected citizens from the different regions of the city.

But participation to be effective and meaningful calls for at least some degree of socio-economic equality in the society. In an unequal society there may be participation of the people which really means participation of a segment of the people, participation of the few, participation of a class.

Sen and Dreze write that participation is intimately connected with demands of equality. They argue that political participation can be more effective and more equally enjoyed if there is some equity in the sharing of economic resources as well.[2]

There is a view that participation may also act as a co-optational device. The ruling class or classes may seek to legitimize their authority to rule (or exploit) on the plea that the decision has been taken either in consultation with the people or people themselves have taken the decision.

Citizens' Participation

One of the most popular state reforms that has opened spaces for a wider and deeper participation of citizens at the local level has been the decentralisation process. Decentralisation has a number of merits having political and administrative implications. In the first place, it decongests government at the center making the national leaders free from the onerous details and unnecessary involvement in local issues. In this way co-ordination is facilitated and action at the local level is expedited.

Second, it helps increase people's understanding and support of social and economic development activities and in this way, people can contribute to their own activities.

Third, social and economic development programmes at the local level becomes more realistic and target group oriented.

Fourth, decentralisation plays a meaningful role in training the people in the art of self-government, and thus acts as an instrument of political education of the citizens.

Fifth, it not only increases popular capacity to ensure responsibility and accountability but also improves delivery of services by allowing careful consideration of local needs and creating conditions for innovations.

Sixth, it makes local development plan more responsive to local conditions and helps implementation by facilitating local resource mobilization.

Seventh, it helps achieve flexible implementation through quicker decision-making.

All but 12 of 75 developing countries with more than five million inhabitants have implemented some form of decentralisation, with varying degrees of financial and political power. Parallel to these developments, enabling legal frameworks and institutional channels for citizenship at the local level have been developed in many of these countries as shown below:

Legal Enabling Environment for Citizens' Participation

Philippines	Local Government Code (199 1)
India	73 & 74th Constitutional Amendments (1993)
Honduras	Municipal Law (1990)
Bolivia	Popular Participation Law (1992)
Namibia	Local Authority Act (1992)
Uganda	Local Government Act (1997)
Tanzania	Local Authorities Act (1992)

Institutional Channels for Participation in Some Countries

Tanzania	Ward Development Committee
Zimbabwe	Village Development Committee
Uganda	Resistance Councils and Committee
India	Grain Sabha and Ward Committee
Nepal	Village Development Council
Columbia	Over-Seeing Committee
Bilivia	Vigilance Committee
China	Villagers Committee and Residents Committee

The Seventy Fourth Amendment of the Constitution

The Seventy Fourth Amendment of the Constitution marks a distinct watershed in the concept and practice of citizens' participation in urban governance. It seeks to institutionalise citizens' participation through the formation of Ward Wards Committees in all urban local bodies. The amendment breaks a new ground by providing for an institutional framework for citizens to actively participate in their own administration and development through a two-tier system of local governance-the municipality and the Ward Committee. The former is an elective body at the level of the municipality consisting of the elected representatives of the people (councilors) and the latter is a nominated body at the level of the Ward.

The Seventy Fourth Amendment authorizes the State Governments to decide on the composition, territorial area and manner in which the seats of the Ward Committees will be filled. The State Governments have also been given the power to decide how the members of the Ward Committees would be nominated. The argument that has been given in favour of the provision of nomination is that it will encourage the experts who do not like to join partisan politics, to join the Ward Committees giving them necessary vigor, vitality and relevance. One may question the logic on the ground that there is a lack of democratic element. While accepting the argument it needs to emphasised that two sets of democratic bodies at the local level may cause conflict and confrontation leading to unhealthy situation. It would ultimately impede development.

Another provision of the 74th amendment of the Constitution is that the municipalities with three lakh or more population are required to constitute such committees. And again, there is no bar on clubbing wards to constitute Ward Committees. These two provisions tend to show that this arrangement is for big municipalities only and in this way there comes into being big wards where this clubbing of wards takes place. This being the case, one has reasons to believe that the amendment of the Constitution seeks to promote administrative decentralisation rather than democratic decentralisation.

Ward Committees in State Legislations

The Constitutional Amendment empowers the State legislatures to decide on the constitution and composition of the Ward Committees (WCs). While the elected councilors are automatically members of these committees, the State Governments have made different arrangements for the members of the public to be included in the Ward Committees. The table below provides a view of the status of Ward Committees in some major city corporations as on 31.07.2001.

It is found from the table that Ward Committees are yet to be constituted in Bangalore, Ludhiana, Lucknow and Kolkata. Rules have not been framed with regard to the formation of the Ward Committees in

Table-1 : Status of Wards Committees in Some Major Corporations as on 31.7.2001

Municipal **Corporation**	*No. of* **Wards**	*Last Election* **held**	*Constitution* **of WC**	*Number of nominated members* **of WC**
Hyderabad	100	Election due sine 1991	*	Not less than 10 Wards per WC • No other persons excepting the elected Councillors
Ahmadabad	43	June, 2000	*	• Rules not yet framed
Faridabad	25	July, 2000	*	• Rules not yet framed
Bangalore	100	April, 2001	Not constituted	28 Wards Committee • Not more than 5 nominated by the State Government • 2 from NGOs.
Thiruvananthapuram	81	October, 2000	Constituted	81 Wards Committees • Not more than 50 nominated by the Chairperson in consultation with the Councillor • 3 nominated by the Chairperson.
Bhopal	66	1999	Constituted	11 Ward Committees • 2 nominated by the Councillor
Chandigarh	20	1996	*	• Rules not yet framed
Greater Mumbai	221	1996	Constituted	16 Wards COmmittees • 3 nominated by the Mayor

(Contd.)

(Table Contd.)

Ludhiana	70	1997	Not Constituted	Not less than 5 Wards per WC • Municipal Commissioner (ex-officio) and other officers nominated by the Commissioner
Jaipur	70	1999	*	• Rules not yet framed
Chennai	155	1996	Constituted	10 Zonal Committees • No other persons excepting the elected Councillors
Lucknow	110	October, 2000	Not Constituted	11 Wards Committees • No other persons excepting the elected Councillors
Kolkata	141	November, 2002	Not Constituted	141 Wards Committees • 4 to 14 nominted by the Mayor and the Councillor

Table-2
Composition of Ward Committee

Members nominated by

State	*Councillor*	*Local body*	*State Government*
Kerala		Not more than 50 persons (in consultation with the councilor) Not more than 3 prominent citizens	
West Bengal	3 to 11 (depends on the size of the ward)	1 to 3 (depends on the size of the ward)	
Karnataka			Not more than 5 persons
Rajasthan		Not exceeding 5	
Tamil Nadu	Not more than 2 members (Non voting) in Municipalities Not more than 10 members (Non voting) in Municipal Corporation		
Uttar Pradesh			Not exceeding 5
Maharashtra	Not more than 3 members		

Source : B.N. Singh & Shipra Moitra 'Formation of Wards Committee'.

some urban local bodies, namely Ahmedabad, Faridabad, Chandigarh and Jaipur. In Chennai and Delhi, WCs are actually zonal committees. Large size cannot ensure people's participation. In Maharashtra, there is distinction between municipal wards and administrative wards. Administrative ward is the geographical unit of the Ward Committees and 3-4 municipal wards constitute an administrative unit. Elections are due in many corporations. It is a violation of the mandatory provision of the constitution. There seems to be lack of political will to institutionalize citizens' participation through Ward Committees.

On the provision of nomination as shown in the table 2 below there are peculiar arrangements. In States like Rajasthan and Uttar Pradesh, the State Governments have been given power to nominate. Such a situation cannot ensure democratic decentralisation.

The table below shows the size of Ward Committees and their population in some major municipal corporations :

Table 3. Ward Committees in some Major Municipal Corporations

Municipal Corporation	*Municipal Wards (No.)*	*Ward(s) Committees (No.)*	*Population 2001*	*Population per WC*
Brihan Mumbai	221	16	1,63,68,084	10,23,005
Calcutta	141	141	1,32,16,546	93,734
Delhi	134	12	1,27,91,458	95,458
Chennai	155	10	64,24,624	6,42,462
Pune	111	13	37,55,525	2,88,886
Kanpur	110	11	26,90,486	2,44,589
Lucknow	110	11	22,66,933	2,06,084
Varanasi	80	08	12,11,749	1,51,468
Ludhiana	70	14	13,95,053	99,646

Source : Shiptra Moitra 'Participatory Governance at the Local Level : Gateway to Sustainable Development', Urban Management, December, 2002.

It is impossible to ensure citizens' participation in a committee with a population size of 6,42,462 as in Chennai. There are more than two lakh populations in a few Corporations. Kolkata has the smallest number and that too, 93,734 which cannot facilitate citizens' participation. Kolkata Corporation has not yet constituted WCs.

One wonders if the architects of the 74th amendment of the Constitution really wanted citizens to participate in urban governance.

Presumably, they wanted administrative decentralisation in order to create conditions for effective management of the ULBs rather than democratic decentralisation of powers and citizens' participation at the level of urban local bodies and down below.

The Parallel Bodies : Advance Locality Management in Maharashtra

In Maharashtra, Mumbai Corporation has adopted an innovative approach called Advance Locality Management (ALM) involving clean environment. Incidentally, it is interesting to recall the background of ALM. A few residents of Joshi Lane at Ghakkopar, Mumbai were worried about the filthy surroundings in their lane. In October, 1996 they decided to form a Select Committee (SC) to solve the problem. The SC found that the problems in their lane were generated due to the abusive tendencies of the residents themselves. The SC decided to address the issue through intervention and contribution. The SC approached the municipal corporation which decided to work jointly. It was later extended to five nearby lanes voluntarily. In July, 1997 the Municipal Corporation accepted the scheme for the implementation in the entire city. It is an initiative of improving the quality of life in city where the Corporation collaborates and co-operates with the citizens. The scheme lays downs the conditions which a locality or area is required to fulfill for being recognized as ALM[3]. Thus it is a parallel structure existing along with the Ward Committees.

Mohalla Samitis in Madhya Pradesh

Madhya Pradesh provides for constitution of a Mohalla Samiti in every municipal area. The State Government decides on the number of these samitis, the number of members as well as the territorial areas. The State Government has been authorized to determine the powers and functions of these bodies. All the members are elected. At present such committees are formed in slums only. The elected municipal councilor is a member of the Mohalla Samiti within his ward. In modification of the 74th amendment of the Constitution, the State Government has left the decision of formation of the Ward Committee to the local bodies concerned. There is also no time limit. But in the case of Mohalla Committees there is a clear stipulation that such Samitis must be constituted within three months from the date of notification of a municipal area. The Samitis will prepare the proposals for development of the Mohalla and submit the same to the concerned Ward Committees. They can raise resources for local developmental works with the consent of the local body.

Area Development Society in Kerala

In Kerala there are Area Development Societies (ADS) at the Ward Level for every 200 risk families. Each of the Committees has a governing body with five members. They are elected from the elected members of Neighbourhood Group (NHG). The ADS is an advisory committee with the Ward Councillor as the Chairman. It provides guidance, coordinates and integrates of all poverty alleviation programmes. There is a Community Development Society at the municipal level consisting of Chairpersons of all ADSs. Thus the ADS is a parallel body with a difference. There is a provision for organic linkage between the ADSs and the constitutionally mandated WCs.[4]

Ward Committee in West Bengal

West Bengal has taken a step further by, making the constitution of Ward Committee mandatory for all municipalities irrespective of size of the population. The Ward Committee is a municipality in miniature, "guide, friend and philosopher of the municipality" concerned. The local councillor chairs it. It consists of elected councillors and such other members as may be nominated by the elected councillors of the ward and the municipality/Notified Area Authority (NAA) from amongst the residents of the ward. The nomination of the members will be made in the following manner:

Total number of other members of the Ward	*To be nominated by the Councillor elected Committee*	*To be nominated by the Municipality from the ward*
7	5	2
8	5	3
9	6	3
10	7	3
11	8	3
12	9	3
13	10	3
14	11	3
15	11	4
16	12	4
17	13	4

While making nomination care has to be taken to ensure proper representation of engineers, physicians, educationists, social workers, sportspersons, women, persons from economically backward sections of the society or any other persons from among the residents of the ward.

It has to be constituted within one month from the date of the first meeting of the Board of Councillors after a general election. After the formation of the committee, the councillor of the municipality/Notified Area Authority concerned is required to place the names of the members of the committee in the next general meeting of the residents of the ward. The proposals, if any, from any resident of the ward regarding change of any name or any other matter relating to constitution of the committee will be considered by the councillors or the municipality/ N.A.A, as the case may be. The councillors or the municipality/N.A.A., as the case may be, may replace any of the members of the committee.

The Tenure of the Committee

Tenure of the Committee is the same as that of the Board of Councillors of the municipality/N.A.A. In the case of any casual vacancy caused by the factors mentioned in the West Bengal Municipal (Ward Committee) Rules 2001, it would be filled up by the councillors of the Municipality/N.A.A. as the case may be, either in the annual general meeting or in an ordinary meeting of the ward convened for that purpose.

Among the total numbers of the members of the committee, the councillors has to nominate, at least 2 representatives of the Community Development Societies (CDS), in case the total number of members is 7-9, 3 representatives of the CDS in case in case of the number of members being 10-17, who are the residents of the concerned ward. It is further laid down that no member of the CDS can, however, be nominated in more than one committee. In this connection, it is also necessary to mention that where the members of the CDS are not available, the members would be nominated from amongst the women members belonging to the below-poverty-line families from the ward concerned.

Rules of the Business

The first meeting of the committee will be convened by the Chairman of the committee within the 15 days from the date of the constitution of the committee. Apart from normal business, the committee is required, at its first meeting, to select a member-secretary for the committee from among the members. The member-secretary is authorised to convene the subsequent meetings of the committee in consultation with the Chairman and will perform the secretarial functions of the committee. The committee must meet at least once in every month, the date, place and time of which is fixed by the Chairman. It is clearly laid down that no meeting shall be held unless at least seven clear days', before the day of the meeting, notice specifying the date, place and time of such meeting and the business to be transacted there, has been given to the members. One of the important tasks of the committee is to convene one half-yearly and one annual general meeting of the residents of the ward by intimating every resident of the ward and also by public proclamation specifying the time and venue of the meeting. The half-yearly meeting will by held in the month of October-November each year to apprise the residents of the activities of the Municipality/N.A.A. in general and the ward in particular. This meeting will discuss the proposals for preparation of the development plan for the next year. The annual general meeting will be held within June 30 every year to apprise them the activities of the Municipality/N.A.A. in general, and the ward in particular, during the preceding year and to assess the popular needs of the ward for the current year. In order to make the meetings meaningful and effective, it is clearly mentioned in the rule that it is a duty of the Municipality/N.A.A. to furnish the following documents to the committee for public information and deliberation thereon :

(a) a detailed report about the activities of the Municipality/ N.A.A. in the ward area during the preceding year;

(b) a copy of the annual administration report along with the annual financial statement of the Municipality/N.A.A. for the preceding year.

The committee has to maintain a minute book to record the proceedings of the meetings. The minute book will contain the names of the members who attended the meetings, the business transacted, the decision of the committee on each item of business, the date of meeting and the time of commencement and closing of the meeting.

Functions

The committee has been given a wide range of supervisory and monitoring powers within the ward, subject to the general supervision of the Borough Committee of the municipality. Such powers include, *inter alia*, detection of violation of the various provisions of the Act such as unlawful construction, public nuisance, tax evasion, arresting wasteful use of various municipal services such as tap water, street hydrant, street lights, parks, playgrounds etc., collection and removal of garbage, removal of the accumulated water in streets, health immunisation services, improvement of slums including its clearance wherever necessary etc. The committee is also required, as per direction of the Borough Committee or the municipality/N.A.A., as the case may be, to monitor and supervise within the ward the following activities:

(a) work of assessment, collection of property tax, other taxes, fees and other sums due to the municipality/N.A.A.

(b) maintenance and repair of roads and drains;

(c) execution of public works;

(d) maintenance of sanitation and public health;

(e) the prevention and control of dangerous diseases;

(f) issue of birth and death certificates;

(g) all urban poverty alleviation programmes of the State and the Central Government

(h) tree planting in the municipal properties;

(i) maintenance of parks, tanks, and other municipal properties; and

(j) generation of internal resources.

Planning

The Ward Committee has also been given specific role with regard to participatory planning. Within three months from the date of the constitution, the committee is required to prepare a list of schemes for development of the ward during the next five years and also annual priority of the schemes in the ward area.

Execution of Development Schemes

The Ward Committee has to execute development schemes in the ward area. In order to ensure client participation there is a provision for the constitution of beneficiary committee consisting of the citizens of the ward. The committee is constituted by the Ward Committee, which under the supervision of the former, looks after the work and may offer any suggestion relating to the concerned work. It is also the duty of the committee to make the work schedule of any development scheme, available to the beneficiary committee.

Powers of the Ward Committee

The Chairman of the Ward Committee has been authorised to:

(a) call for any information insofar as it relates to any matter within the ward;

(b) call for and consider all periodical statements relating to the receipts and disbursement;

Any member of the committee is entitled to draw the attention of the Chairman to any requirement of any locality or to any lapse in execution of the work or to any waste of municipal fund or municipal property and may suggest any improvement, which he considers desirable. It is laid down in the West Bengal Municipal (Ward Committee) Rules 2001 that the Committee may require, with the permission of the Municipality, any officer of the Municipality, to attend a meeting at which any matter dealt with by such officer in course of his duties, is being discussed. When any officer is thus required to attend any such meeting he may be called upon to make a statement of facts or furnish such information in his possession relating to any matter dealt with by him or produce or report as the Committee may require.

The Municipality has some duty towards the Ward Committee. The Rule lays down that the Municipality has to make available the following information:

(a) decisions of the Standing Committees;

(b) decisions or resolution of the Municipality;

(c) ward-wise budgetary allocation made by the Municipality;

(d) copy of the ward map;

(e) details of municipal properties ward-wise;

(f) Annual Financial Statement and Annual Administration Report

(g) demand and collection figures of tax and non-tax revenue of the ward; and

(h) such other information as required by the Committee.

The Ward Committee has also been involved in the disaster management programmes. The Municipality, on a written requisition from the Chairman of the Committee, is required to make available an advance amount to meet the emergent needs of natural calamity, accident and the like.

The Committee has been given a major role in respect of resource mobilisation. It is required to consider the opportunities for creation of new sources to augment municipal income by way of :

(i) using lands vested in the Government or Municipality/N.A.A. and any land belonging to any Government department subject to permission of such department for;

  (a) tree plantation on long term and short term basis; or

  (b) constructing market complexes, shops and buildings for commercial use; or

  (c) integrating scattered small scale industries in industrial complexes; or

  (d) constructing parking spaces for buses, trucks, cars etc; or

  (e) construction of housing complexes; or

  (f) any other measure the Committee considers feasible;

(ii) using private, public water bodies for promotion of pisciculture or entertainment purposes;

(iii) installing unconventional energy sources like solar electricity or bio-gas or any other alternative for commercial distribution;

(iv) using private lands for commercial purpose on joint venture of Municipality/N.A.A. and the concerned owner;

(v) running municipal transport system on roadways and waterways for carrying goods and passengers in such routes which are not covered by adequate public transport system and are financially viable; and

(vi) such other measures which the Committee considers feasible and viable.

The Committee has to submit a detailed proposal for creation of internal resources to the Municipality/N.A.A. It is authorised to interact with the members of the other Ward Committee for this purpose, if necessary. It is obligatory on the part of the Municipality/N.A.A. to spend 60 per cent of the income from the newly created internal resources, as per proposal of the Committee, in the ward/wards, where such new internal resources have been created, after deducting the cost for implementation of such project, if any.

The author has studied the working of Ward Committees in two urban local bodies, namely Rajpur-Sonarpur and Berhampore. The findings are presented below :

Rajpur-Sonarpur Municipality

Rajpur-Sonarpur is located close to Kolkata Municipal Corporation and forms part of the Kolkata Metropolitan Area. Rajpur was a part of the south suburban municipality till 1876. A Municipality of more than 100 years old, it has a long tradition. Sonarpur spreading over 10 Gram Panchayat areas became part of the present Rajpur Sonarpur Municipality on December 16, 1993. It covers an area of 55.30 square kms. Thus the Municipality has both the characteristics of rural and urban areas. There was a lot of doubt about how things would shape in the municipality which has to cater to needs of two different types. It was felt by many that it was an incongruous mixture of rural and urban areas which might generate frustration and discontentment.

As per 2001 census report the total population in the municipality is 3,36,390. The density of population is 6,083 per square km. The literacy rate is 85.68 per cent. The sex ratio is 938 per 1000 males.

It is now one of the best performing ULBs in the state. According to the figures collected from the office of the Municipality per capita development expenditure has gone up to Rs. 250.

Having been located close to Kolkata it is one of the fast-expanding ULBs in the State. With a geographical area of 45 square kms., population in the ULB has been on the rise ever since its inception. The present population is little over 3 lakh with holdings being I lakh. All these have resulted in the construction of multi-storied buildings. Drainage is one of the major problems of the ULB.

The ULB is divided into 5 boroughs each one of which has independent offices. There are 33 wards.

Supply of drinking water has received top most priority in the municipality as is evident from a close look at the annual development plan. The citizens are engaged in various kinds of activities. Apart from service holders, there are artisans, daily wage labourers, small traders and self-employed professionals. Agriculture continues to be the mainstay of people living in one or two wards. In the poverty pockets education is still to make a dent.

It has had the benefit of Calcutta Urban Development Project III and Indian Population Project VIII. These two projects have benefited many people below-the poverty-line. Health services reach out to a large section of them, although it is inadequate compared to the needs of the people.

Roads are good. We have been told that the Ward Committees supervise road construction and repair work. It has improved the quality of construction and repair.

The ULB has made it mandatory to involve the beneficiary committee in all development work. The Ward Committees keep watch on the working of the beneficiary committees.

We interacted with 43 members belonging to WCs in Rajpur-Sonarpur municipality. It is found from the table no. 3 that middle-aged members predominate the Committees. They constitute more than 70 per cent of the members.

The members belong to diverse occupational groups as the data in table no. 1 tend to show. It seems that the different segments of the society get represented in the body. The caste background of members as shown in table-2 also bears it out.

There are not many women members. Only 13.95 per cent of members were women (table 4). This is not desirable after the reservation of seats for women in all ULBs in terms of the 74th amendment of the Constitution. The Board does not seem to have taken the gender component into account while making nomination. At least one third of the members in the WCs should have been women. Is it due to lack of political will to empower women through the WCs or there is reluctance on the part of women to take up this kind of work? While taking to the political functionaries we have not received any satisfactory definitive answer. Our impression is that the patriarchal values are still very strong among political leaders and this is not absolutely unexpected in a country like ours. Significantly, even the socialist revolution has also failed to bring about necessary change in this direction. It is evident from the speech of Albania's Prime Minister. In a party meeting he confessed that even the party members are not free from the patriarchal values.

The formation of the WC started in 1997. Most of them were formed in 2000: Almost all of the members (93.4 per cent) are first timers. As a result they are yet to perceive their roles properly. It is evident from the analysis of data about their reactions to the objectives of the Ward Committee. Although many of them are aware of the legal status of the WC as a constitutional body, a good number of them do not know the role of the ULBs in terms of the Constitution of India. This merits serious consideration because they will not be able to play their role properly if they cannot perceive it. The traditional role of the ULBs as providers of municipal services continues to remain ingrained in the minds of the WC members. It underscores the need for imparting suitable training to them at the ULB level. The concerned ULB can take up the job in consultation with Institute of Local Government and Urban Studies (ILGUS). The ILGUS may, however, organise training for the secretaries of the WC.

The data in table 6 show that 86.05 per cent of the WC members have reported that they are aware about the rules of the WC. This awareness has to be understood in the sense that they have only heard about them. While interacting with them intensively it was noticed that most of them have not read the rules. It will adversely affect the working of ULBs. The State Government has laid down detailed rules in clear terms and it is the declared policy of the Government to involve the WCs in the working of the ULBs as much as possible. Participatory development and governance have been highlighted as the effective arrangement for properly addressing the urban problems which are causing concern of the policy makers. There has been a revolution of rising expectation among the urban dwellers as a result of the amendment of the Constitution and the policy of liberalisation adopted by the Indian State has reduced the role of the State in the sector. It is creating a peculiar contradictory situation which has to be tackled. The vibrant WCs with the clear perception of the role of the members can be effective in a situation like this because they are in regular touch with the people.

It is good that almost all the members seem to be aware of the major problems in their areas. They have knowledge about the categories of the residents and their occupations in their respective wards.

We have tried to tap their perception about the issues calling for attention and we wanted them to prioritise. Interestingly, drainage problem has been identified as a problem to be attended to with top most priority, as the data in table 7 tend to indicate.

It is true that this is a very acute problem in this ULB. Most of the streets get flooded during rainy season. What strikes us is the lack of adequate concern for education and health, which form part of the priority agenda of the Government of West Bengal. There is a consensus in the State that the earlier Left Front Government (LFG) could not properly address the issue effectively. The sixth LFG is committed, and seem to be determined to improve the situation through the modality of decentralised development. This calls for an effective role of the WCs.

It is found from the data collected that only 23.26 per cent members of the Ward Committees have their independent offices. This is deplorable because without a permanent office, the WCs cannot be expected to function effectively. WCs are required to interact with the people. It is possible only when there is an office where the citizens would be coming to discuss their problems. It has to be kept open during specified hours. The recent revision of the Ward Committee rules lay down that the ULB concerned has to make provision for it. WCs cannot be citizens' committees in the true sense of the term if the citizens are denied a place where they will interact. Again, WCs have to meet at regular intervals. It is gathered that meetings are held in the house of the Chairman or Secretary or member. Significantly, meetings in the ULB under study are held at regular intervals. There are WCs, which meet more than once in a month.

There is no budgetary allocation of the WC as a result of which small expenses incurred in holding meetings are borne by the Chairman/ Secretary or member. This practice cannot be encouraged. Some funds need to be given to them, otherwise the concept of participatory governance and development will turn into a mere formality, if not mockery.

We tried to ascertain from the respondents if there has ever been, any issue of serious debate in the meeting leading to sharp differences of opinion. The answer has largely been in the negative indicating that there is consensus among the members on matters pertaining to development. It is definitely a good indication and helps achieve the goals of development quickly and easily.

The proceedings of all the meetings are carefully recorded and read out in the next meeting. We have seen the proceedings of the meetings and found them in order.

It is also known that annual general meetings are regularly held in all the wards. The date and venue of the meetings are communicated to the citizens through notices. We have found that in some wards the Councillors concerned as the Chairpersons of the Ward Committee take personal interest. The Ward Committee members are asked to make door-to-door campaign for the meetings. As expected, meetings in such wards are well attended. In most of the meetings, as reported, the attendance has not been beyond 25 per cent of the total citizens. Women attendance has not gone up beyond 10 per cent. In the meetings two reports, one on annual administration report and the other on the present budget are generally placed.

The meetings are conducted by the Chairman who requests the members to participate. Participation has not generally been encouraging. Only a few people participate and almost all the participants refer to the problems like drainage, sewerage and sweeping and the like. Major human development issues hardly figure in the discussion.

In Rajpur-Sonarpur there is a unique feature of the Ward Committee. Apart from the annual general meeting the municipality organizes Ward Conventions where all the members of the Ward Committee assemble and interact on the issues concerning their Wards. Such Conventions are held once in a year. It is chaired by the chairman himself. In the annual Ward Conventions they identify the schemes and prioritise them and examine how to fund the programmes. They discuss the question of mobilization of resources and promise help to the municipalities in resource mobilization. The Conventions try to locate areas where more resources can be mobilized. This is an important event and will be very useful for the purpose of participatory decentralised planning.

The proceedings of the Ward Committee and those of the Ward conventions are transmitted to the Municipality for the perusal of the latter. The reactions of the municipality are not, however, made known to the Ward Committee. We have been told that the proceedings of the conventions are carefully considered by the Municipality

It is interesting to note that about 79.07 per cent of the Ward Committee members visit municipality offices regularly (table 9). They discuss the problems of their Ward with the authorities and try to collect information about the schemes, which can be implemented in their wards. This indicates that the members take active interest in their work

In order to examine the extent and level of interaction between the Municipality and the Ward Committee we asked a few other questions. For example, we wanted to know if the Municipality representative other than the local councillor, visits their wards. 74.42 per cent of the respondents have replied in the affirmative. We also wanted to find out from the respondents if the municipality seeks their help 86.05 of the respondents have told us that Municipality seeks their help (table 10).

One of the problems of municipality being located close to Kolkata is the tendency to use lands and buildings illegally because land prices are very high. There is a widespread tendency to encroach upon public space, if available. It is difficult to prevent this kind of illegal construction without involving the Ward Committee. In Rajpur Sonarpur Municipality the WCs appear to be active in dealing with the situation. 81 per cent of the members, as the data in table II show, draw the attention of the Municipality and discuss it in the meeting of the WCs.

As in other states slums form part of the urban areas. And there has been a sustained effort in our plan document to reduce poverty in rural and urban areas. Thus came a number of schemes during the different plan periods. Now there is a comprehensive centrally sponsored slum development plan called Swarna Jayanti Sahari Rozgar Yojana. This programme is implemented by the Community Development Societies (CDS) created for that purpose. And formally speaking, there was earlier no specific role of the Councillor not to speak of the WC, other than the general role of the ULB. The recent revision of the WC rules as noted above) has sought to develop a linkage between the WCs and the CDSs. In West Bengal there is UPE cell in each ULB, which is supposed to supervise the implementation of all anti-poverty programmes. Insofar as the implementation of the SJSRY programme is concerned the Councillor has nothing much to do because he is not a member of the community structures in terms of the guidelines for the programme. In West Bengal an attempt has been made to involve the Councillor. This arrangement seems to be working well here. The WC discusses the poverty issue and 93.02 per cent of them participate in the implementation of the SJSRY programme (table 14).

In order to encourage savings among the poor people in the slum areas there is a provision of self-help programme called Thrift and Credit Group. We wanted to know from the members if they are aware of the scheme. 83.72 per cent of them reported awareness. To go deep into matter we asked them to let us know about the problems of implementation of the programme, if any. A little more than 60 per cent of the respondents have told us that the major handicap is the attitude of the banks, which are supposed to provide loan to the BPL families. 23.26 of them have, however, pleaded ignorance (table 15). This is not certainly desirable.

In Rajpur-Sonarpur Municipality Beneficiary Committees are functioning in each Ward. It is gathered from the discussion with the members that the young citizens have been inducted into the committee. They keep watch on the activities being undertaken by the Municipality and keep the Ward Committee posted about how the schemes are implemented.

The members have told us that they discuss about the developmental works being undertaken by the Municipality in their wards. They do not, however, seem to be aware of all the programmes.

Berhampore Municipality

Berhampore Municipality was established on July 1, 1876 following the merger of the cantonment area with other areas like Saidabad, Kashimbazar, Kalikapur, Khagra, Gar Berhampore, Gorabazar and the like. In July 1876 there were 14 non-official members and the Government nominated 5 members on the body, thus the total number of members being 19. In those days there were 6 wards.

In 1932 came the Bengal Municipal Act. At that time Berhampore was divided into 30 zones covering an area of 15.65 square kms. In 1993 came the West Bengal Municipal Act as result of which the numbers of zones were reduced to 23 wards out of which 7 are reserved for women, 1 for SC woman and 1 for SC. According to the population criterion in terms of the West Bengal Municipal Act, 1993 Berhampore municipality is categorised as the Grade C municipality with 30,872 holdings. The sex ratio is 958 per 1000 males. The distance from Kolkata is 186 kms.

There are 5 municipal primary schools in addition to 12 other primary schools. There are 16 secondary schools and 2 colleges. A town with a fairly long tradition, Berhampore has 2 public libraries. Literacy rate is 86.05 per cent. There are some slum pockets in the municipal areas. There are 11,308 families in the slum areas, the total slum population being 55,942.

Being a very old town the municipality has many problems the most important of which is congestion and narrow roads. Other infrastructures like drainage and sewerage are very old. 75 per cent of the households have been provided with tap water connection. Some of the roads have recently been widened. The traffic problem has to some extent been eased after the construction of a bye-pass road by the side of the river Bhagirgithi.

As per the latest census data the total population in the municipality is 1,60,168 with a population density of 9,893 per square kilometers. The census data of 1991 showed that they were engaged in different kinds of occupations as follows:

Service holders	28.01 per cent
Agriculturists	0.22 per cent
Agricultural labourers	0.38 per cent
Cottage industry	0.47 per cent
Urban-based occupations	26.97 per cent
Marginal employees	0.27 per cent

The data in table-I indicate that more than one third of the Ward Committee members have been drawn from sectors other than teaching and service. While talking to them we have gathered that some of them are small traders, retired persons and the like. Unlike Rajpur-Sonarpur Municipality the professionals like doctors are absent. It is not that they are not available. Either they have not agreed or the ruling party does not want them. The number of service holders is insignificant unlike the situation in Rajpur-Sonarpur. It may be attributed to the location of the Municipality. Rajpur-Sonarpur having been located close to the capital of the state, many people are service holders.

However, the general caste members as the table-2 shows, far outweigh the members belonging to SC/ST. In fact, the general caste members have overwhelming domination in the ULB area.

The younger members dominate the WCs. The data in table 3 show that 34.15 per cent of the members belong to the age group 31-40, almost double the percentage of the members in Rajpur-Sonarpur Municipality. Nearly 30 per cent of the members belong to the age-group 18-30, thus a little more than 63 per cent of the members are below 40 years. While talking to the Chairperson and the elected members we have gathered that they have given special consideration to this factor while nominating members in the WCs. Most of them are, however, unemployed and insisted that some payment should be made to them for doing the work of the Ward Committee. It is good that the municipality has been able to motivate them. There is a general feeling in Kolkata Metropolitan Area that the young members do not take much interest in this kind of local governmental activity. This seems to be reflected in the age-group distribution of the members of the WCs in Rajpur-Sonarpur Municipality.

The gender-wise distribution of members as made in table-4 reveals that there is lesser representation of women in Berhampore WCs. In Rajpur-Sonarpur their members in the WCs are double the numbers in Berhampore. There is nearly absolute predominance of the male members. Even in respect of reserved constituencies the female members are numerically insignificant.

It does not speak well. It reinforces the assumption that there should be reservation of seats for women even in the WCs. The informal discussions brought out that there is lack of interest on the part of women to join WCs. Women do not consider themselves properly suited for this kind of job due to their heavy domestic commitment. The women representatives should take special care in this regard. Women need to be motivated and roped in. The WCs can be turned into a training ground of the future women councillors.

The data in table 5 clearly bring out that nearly 20 per cent of the WC members in Berhampore do not know the exact legal status of the body. In course of informal interaction with many of them it has become clear that they do not have any knowledge about the distinction between a constitutional body and a non-constitutional body. They cannot be held responsible for the lack of awareness. The ULB has not tried to make them realise the legal significance of the body. In fact, some of the councillors we could interact with, are ignorant about it. When the State Government has been emphasising on strengthening this body and developing them as nurseries of genuine democracy it is high time to generate awareness among the WC members about the legal status of this body. It is one of the ways of creating respect for the grassroots participative body.

What causes greater concern is the lack of awareness among 41.46 per cent of the members about the rules of the WC. None of them has seen the copy of the rules. Only a few of them have come to know about them from the councillors. We wanted to find out if they did not have time to read the rules. The answer was that they did not know about it. They evinced interest but they did not have any information. It is, again, a failure on the part of the ULB.

We tried to tap their perception about the priority of issues in their agenda. Nearly 40 per cent of the members could not respond, as they do not have any idea about it. Amongst those who responded, nearly one third laid stress on drinking water and road. Education is not a priority agenda item. They seem to be aware of the problem of massive unemployment in their wards but do not know what to do. All of them are sure that employment has to be generated; otherwise there would be youth unrest. But that is the end of it. They seem to believe that it is the task of the government, not that of the ULB.

All the members do not visit the municipal office for the work of the WC. About one fourth of them has reported that they do not go to the municipal office. They have told us that they interact with the councillors, attend meetings and take part in the discussions. They have never felt it necessary to visit the municipal office. On further investigation it became evident that two of such wards belong to the councillors who are members of the Chairman-in-Council. Presumably, the WC members do not experience any difficulty in getting their work done.

The situation is not really substantively different from that obtaining in Rajpur Sonarpur Municipality. Clearly, the linkage between the WC and the municipality is yet to be firmly established. It may be suggested that the municipality should take initiative in this regard for establishing an organic linkage between the WC and the municipality.

According to the revised rules the WCs are authorised to look into the matters pertaining to illegal construction in their wards in terms of drawing attention of the municipality to the matter. We tried to elicit reactions of the WC members on this issue. The data in table II tend to demonstrate that 63.41 per cent of the members have reported that they do not do anything in this regard. It shows that the WC members are failing in their duty. It is definitely not an encouraging phenomenon. The WC members of Rajpur Sonarpur are more alert in this regard and a large number of them play their role. It may be due to the fact that there has, of late, been construction boom around Kolkata. The promoters, who are the real actors in the real estate business, connive with the 'influentials' to carry on illegal construction. Although this activity is not widespread in Berhampore, real estate business has started picking up in Berhampore. If it is left unnoticed, it may play havoc in near future causing immense harm to the town.

One of the basic problems that the urban local bodies have been facing in India since the days of the British rule, is the lack of necessary financial resources. It was one of the basic reasons why the institutions failed to work effectively during the days of the colonial rule. The same problem recurs in post-colonial India. The 74th amendment of the Constitution has sought to solve the issue by appointing the State Finance Commission. The local bodies also get a share from the Central Finance Commission. Still the local bodies starve off of funds. In West Bengal the performance of the local body in this regard is dismal. The data collected by the Department of International Development, Government of United Kingdom show that West Bengal lags significantly behind the other major states. While the 'own sources of revenue' constitute about 89 per cent of the total revenue for ULBs in Gujarat, 88 per cent for ULBs in Punjab, 77 per cent for ULBs in Kerala, 71 per cent for ULBs in Assam, the share is as low as 28 per cent for ULBs in West Bengal. Similarly, in West Bengal the per capita revenue collection is a mere Rs. 36 as compared to Rs. 441 in Gujarat and 252 in Punjab, Rs. 132 in Kerala.[5]

As a result the municipalities have become largely dependent on the State Government. A comprehensive study of the receipts of different municipal bodies from own source and Government Grants (non-plan) during 1997-98 to 1999-2000) tends to show that during 1997-98, out of 96 municipalities 81 were dependent on the State Government to the extent of more than 51 per cent, in 1998-99 out of 98 municipalities, 80 were similarly dependent. In 1999-2000 the number of dependent municipalities rose to 90 out of 100.[6]

All the data make a strong case for more resource mobilisation by the municipalities. It should also be stressed here that the constitutional concept of municipalities as the institutions of self-government loses its significance in a situation of increasing dependence of the municipalities on the State Government. The State Government has revised the WC rules empowering the WCs to play an important role in this regard. In response to the question of whether the WC members are aware about their role in this regard it has been found that one third of them is not aware. It is a matter of concern and the municipality should sit with the members of the WC to discuss their roles and responsibilities in this matter.

In West Bengal there are good numbers of tax defaulters as a result of which arrears keep on accumulating. The WCs are supposed to help the municipality in this regard. In Berhampore, the WCs extend help in this regard as the reactions of the members in table 12 tend to show. It may be mentioned that Berhampore's performance in respect of resource mobilisation is commendable. There is, however, no study to measure the performance of the WCs in this regard. We have gathered this information in course of discussion with the members of the WCs.

The performance of the WCs of Berhampore municipality appears to be better than that of Rajpur-Sonarpur municipality in some respects. One wonders it is due to the inclusion of large number of younger members in the WCs or greater political attention to the problem.

As in Rajpur-Sonarpur municipality we wanted to know from the respondents about their role in the SJSRY programme, although formally speaking, it is a matter under the charge of the three-tiered slum committees set up for that purpose. Roughly, one third of them takes interest in the programme. On the question of awareness about the Thrift and Credit Society in the slum areas, more than 50 per cent of them have responded in the negative. It is difficult to explain this variation. The second programme, however, involves greater involvement.

Concluding Observations

Participation is about power and its exercise by the different social sectors in the space created for the interaction between the citizens and the local government. There are structures for participation. Ward Committee is one of such myriad of structures. To make it effective we need to take two kinds of steps, namely, creation of necessary objective and subjective conditions and identification of barriers to participation. In Tanzania Mukandela has found that decisions over who should participate in the Ward Development Committee hinders effectiveness in achieving high level of participation. In our country Manor and Crook have shown that participatory procedures affect the opportunity of citizens to participate.

To ensure genuine participation of the citizens what appears to be very important is political will and motivation of those who are the wielders of powers at the local institutional level. They have to create both objective and subjective conditions for participation. It may so happen that there is adequate political will and motivation at the top but at the local level where participation takes place, the leaders may be, reluctant to take the people into confidence and to share power with them. There should be penal provision in the legislation in line with the West Bengal Panchayat Act, 1973 to compel the recalcitrant local leaders, if any. If an ULB does not constitute Ward Committee for which the concerned municipal body is responsible, the Government should have power to dissolve the ULB after giving necessary hearing. If the Councillor concerned is found responsible, the Government should be authorised to dismiss him after giving necessary hearing.

There is need for developing accountability mechanisms. In Bolivia there is provision for Vigilance Committees in the legislation. In Kerala also, there are local vigilance Committees which sign off local projects before making payments to the contractors. It enables the citizens to realise that their opinion has value. It will encourage them to participate.

The media, both print and electronic, have to be utilised for generating awareness of the citizens. Material have to be developed for popular education. The citizens have the right to information. Incidentally, the right to information campaign organised by the non-government organisations in Rajasthan has been helpful in raising awareness of the rural people although there is reluctance on the part of the political leaders to transmit information to the people despite clear legal provision. Legal guarantee of the right to information does not always mean much unless there is a demand from the people backed by the organised strength. The non-government organisations can play effective role in this regard.

The findings of the study clearly indicate that although the WCs have started working, the members are still to perceive their roles properly. The lack of infrastructures and funds often creates problems. It is good that the recently revised rules of the WC have taken note of the problem and have made it a duty of the ULBs to provide for office space of the WCs. In fact, institutionalisation of citizens' participation will not make much sense if office is not provided for the institution.

There seems to be lack of awareness on the part of the ordinary citizens about the WC. The concept of WC as a constitutional body for grassroots participation is yet to be popular among the citizens. It is, therefore, necessary to make awareness campaign for this purpose. The annual general meetings, wherever held, have become a ritual. Rule has been amended to provide for two meetings in a year. The government appears to be keen to ensure that citizens will decide on the priorities for development planning in their wards. The holding of annual general meetings should be preceded by widespread publicity campaigns through house-to-house contact, posters, leaflets etc. The meeting notice may be given individually to generate interest of the members.

The way the general meetings are held, does not create necessary conditions for participation. It has been noticed that this kind of meetings takes the shape of election meetings. A podium is built. The WC members and the Councillors sit in the dais and the ordinary citizens sit on the floor and thus a distance is created between the members of the WC and the citizens of the Ward. The way the meeting is arranged and conducted often discourages the members to participate.

To ensure better participation the following steps may be suggested.

(a) Attempt should be made to bridge the distance between the ULB and the citizens as far as possible. It would be good if podium is not erected and all of them take their seats on the even space

(b) As there is lack of awareness among the citizens the meeting should start with a briefing of what needs to be done in the meeting in terms of the legal provisions to enable the members to play their roles effectively. It would be better if the relevant sections of the Act and rules are photocopied and distributed among the members along with the meeting notices.

(c) The elected councillors and the nominated WC members have to be made to realise that in a democratic system of governance power ultimately belongs to the people. Our constitution starts with the words "we, the people of India". They need to legitimise the authority to rule. The WCs are institutional arrangements for this purpose.

References

1. Meera Mehta (1999) 'Participation and Urban Governance' is O.P. Mathur (ed.) *India : the Challenge of Urban Governance*, National Institute of Urban Affairs, New Delhi.

2. Jean Dreze and Amartya Sen (2001) *India : Participation and Development* OUP, New Delhi.

3. Sneha Palniker (2000) 'Promoting People's Participation for Local Governance in Urban Area'. *Habitat*, April.

4. Shipra Maitra (2002) 'Participatory Governance at the Local Level Gateway to Sustainable Development', *Urban Management*, December.

5. *KUSP Inception Report*, Municipal Affairs Department, Government of West Bengal, 2002.

6. Source : Institute of Local Government and Urban Studies, Government of West Bengal.

7. R.C. Crook and James Manor (1998) *Democracy and Decentralisation in South Asia and West Africa : Participation, Accountability and Performance*, Cambridge University Press, Cambridge.

Table-1 Occupational Background of the W.C. Members
(Rajpur-Sonarpur Municipality)

Sl. No.	*Nature of Occupation*	*Numbers*	*Percentage*
1.	Business	1	2.33
2.	Doctors	4	9.30
3.	Service Holders	9	20.93
4.	Teachers	4	9.30
5.	Social Workers	8	18.60
6.	Others	17	39.53
	Total	**43**	**100.00**

Table-2 Caste Background of the W.C. Members
(Rajpur-Sonarpur Municipality)

Sl. No.	*Nature of Caste*	*Numbers*	*Percentage*
1.	General Caste	33	76.74
2.	Scheduled Caste	3	6.98
3.	Other Backward Caste	7	16.28
	Total	**43**	**100.00**

Table-3 Age Groups Distribution of the W.C. Members
(Rajpur-Sonarpur Municipality)

Sl. No.	*Age-Group*	*Numbers*	*Percentage*
1.	18-30	3	6.98
2.	31-50	8	18.60
3.	41-50	18	41.86
4.	Above 50	14	32.56
	Total	**43**	**100.00**

Table-4 Gender Distribution of the W.C. Members
(Rajpur-Sonarpur Municipality)

Sl. No.	*Gender*	*Numbers*	*Percentage*
1.	Males	37	86.05
2.	Females	6	13.95
	Total	**43**	**100.00**

Table-5 Perception about the Status of Ward Committee
(Rajpur-Sonarpur Municipality)

Sl. No.	*Perception*	*Numbers*	*Percentage*
1.	Constitutional Body	42	97.67
2.	Not a Constitutional Body	1	2.33
	Total	**43**	**100.00**

Table-6 Awareness about the Rules of the Ward Committee
(Rajpur-Sonarpur Municipality)

Sl. No.	*Response*	*Numbers*	*Percentage*
1.	YES	37	86.05
2.	NO	6	13.95
	Total	**43**	**100.00**

Table-7 Perception of Priority about the Issues to be Addressed
(Rajpur-Sonarpur Municipality)

Sl. No.	*Issues*	*Numbers*	*Percentage*
1.	Drainage	27	62.79
2.	Drinking Water	5	11.63
3.	Education	2	4.66
4.	Health	5	11.63
5.	Road	4	9.30
	Total	**43**	**100.00**

Table-8 Reactions about the Utilisation of Services of Ward Committee by the Municipality
(Rajpur-Sonarpur Municipality)

Sl. No.	*Reactions*	*Numbers*	*Percentage*
1.	YES	37	86.05
2.	NO	6	13.95
	Total	**43**	**100.00**

Table-9 Whether the Ward Committee Members Visit Municipality
(Rajpur-Sonarpur Municipality)

Sl. No.	*Reactions*	*Numbers*	*Percentage*
1.	YES	34	79.07
2.	NO	9	20.93
	Total	**43**	**100.00**

Table-10 Visit of the Municipality Representative to the Ward
(Rajpur-Sonarpur Municipality)

Sl. No.	*Responses*	*Numbers*	*Percentage*
1.	YES	32	74.42
2.	NO	11	25.58
	Total	**43**	**100.00**

Table-11 Action taken by the Ward Committee against Illegal Construction
(Rajpur-Sonarpur Municipality)

Sl. No.	*Actions*	*Numbers*	*Percentage*
1.	No Action	7	16.28
2.	Inform the Ward Committee	1	2.33
2.	Inform the Municipality	35	81.40
	Total	**43**	**100.00**

Table-12 Help of the Ward Committee in Dealing with Tax Defaulters
(Rajpur-Sonarpur Municipality)

Sl. No.	*Responses*	*Numbers*	*Percentage*
1.	YES	32	74.42
2.	No	11	25.58
	Total	**43**	**100.00**

Table-13 Awareness about the Role in Resource Mobilisation
(Rajpur-Sonarpur Municipality)

Sl. No.	*Responses*	*Numbers*	*Percentage*
1.	YES	36	8372
2.	No	7	16.28
	Total	**43**	**100.00**

Table-14 Role of the Ward Committee Members in SJSRY Programme
(Rajpur-Sonarpur Municipality)

Sl. No.	*Responses*	*Numbers*	*Percentage*
1.	YES	40	93.02
2.	No	3	6.98
	Total	**43**	**100.00**

Table-15 Awareness about the Thrift & Credit Society
(Rajpur-Sonarpur Municipality)

Sl. No.	*Responses*	*Numbers*	*Percentage*
1.	YES	36	87.72
2.	No	7	16.28
	Total	**43**	**100.00**

Table-1 Occupational Background of the W.C. Members
(Behrampore Municipality)

Sl. No.	*Nature of Occupation*	*Numbers*	*Percentage*
1.	Teachers	4	9.75
2.	Social Workers	5	12.20
3.	Others	32	78.05
	Total	**41**	**100.00**

Table-2 Caste Background of the W.C. Members
(Behrampore Municipality)

Sl. No.	*Nature of Caste*	*Numbers*	*Percentage*
1.	General Caste	36	87.80
2.	Scheduled Caste	2	4.88
3.	Other Backward Caste	3	7.32
	Total	**41**	**100.00**

Table-3 Age Groups of the W.C. Members
(Behrampore Municipality)

Sl. No.	*Age-Group*	*Numbers*	*Percentage*
1.	18-30	12	29.27
2.	31-50	14	34.15
3.	41-50	6	14.63
4.	Above 50	9	21.95
	Total	**41**	**100.00**

Table-4 Gender Distribution of the W.C. Members
(Behrampore Municipality)

Sl. No.	*Gender*	*Numbers*	*Percentage*
1.	Males	38	92.68
2.	Females	3	7.32
	Total	**41**	**100.00**

Table-5 Perception about the Status of Ward Committee
(Behrampore Municipality)

Sl. No.	*Perception*	*Numbers*	*Percentage*
1.	Constitutional Body	33	8049
2.	Not a Constitutional Body	8	19.51
	Total	**41**	**100.00**

Table-6 Awareness about the Rules of the Ward Committee
(Behrampore Municipality)

Sl. No.	*Response*	*Numbers*	*Percentage*
1.	YES	24	58.54
2.	NO	17	41.46
	Total	**41**	**100.00**

Table-7 Perception of Priority about the Issues to be Addressed
(Behrampore Municipality)

Sl. No.	*Issues*	*Numbers*	*Percentage*
1.	Bustee	3	7.32
2.	Drinking Water	7	17.07
3.	Education	3	7.32
4.	Employment	2	4.88
5.	Health	4	9.75
6.	Road	6	14.63
7.	No Response	16	39.03
	Total	**41**	**100.00**

Table-8 Reactions about the Utilisation of Services of Ward Committee by the Municipality
(Behrampore Municipality)

Sl. No.	*Reactions*	*Numbers*	*Percentage*
1.	YES	37	86.05
2.	NO	4	13.95
	Total	**41**	**100.00**

Table-9 Whether the Ward Committee Members Visit Municipality
(Behrampore Municipality)

Sl. No.	*Reactions*	*Numbers*	*Percentage*
1.	YES	31	75.61
2.	NO	10	24.39
	Total	**41**	**100.00**

Table-10 Visit of the Municipality Representative to the Ward
(Behrampore Municipality)

Sl. No.	*Responses*	*Numbers*	*Percentage*
1.	YES	37	90.24
2.	NO	4	9.76
	Total	**41**	**100.00**

Table-11 Action taken by the Ward Committee against Illegal Construction
(Behrampore Municipality)

Sl. No.	*Actions*	*Numbers*	*Percentage*
1.	No Action	26	63.41
2.	Inform the Ward Committee	1	2.44
2.	Inform the Municipality	14	34.15
	Total	**41**	**100.00**

Table-12 Help of the Ward Committee in Dealing with Tax Defaulters
(Behrampore Municipality)

Sl. No.	Responses	Numbers	Percentage
1.	YES	37	90.24
2.	No	4	9.76
	Total	**41**	**100.00**

Table-13 Awareness about the Role in Resource Mobilisation
(Behrampore Municipality)

Sl. No.	Responses	Numbers	Percentage
1.	YES	31	75.61
2.	No	10	24.39
	Total	**41**	**100.00**

Table-14 Role of the Ward Committee Members in SJSRY Programme
(Behrampore Municipality)

Sl. No.	Responses	Numbers	Percentage
1.	YES	28	68.29
2.	No	13	31.71
	Total	**41**	**100.00**

Table-15 Awareness about the Thrift & Credit Society
(Rajpur-Sonarpur Municipality)

Sl. No.	Responses	Numbers	Percentage
1.	YES	20	51.22
2.	No	21	48.78
	Total	**41**	**100.00**

8

Institutional Reforms in Metropolitan Governance in Kolkata

Institutional designs of urban local government have been an issue of debate for ages. There was a concern in the Aristotelian thought for the most appropriate constitution for the Greek City State. Institutional structures are very important because they are the vehicles through which objectives are implemented. The urban local government can be of two types–bureaucratic and democratic. In the case of the former, the power is concentrated in the hands of the bureaucratic head, in the case of the latter, in the hands of the elected leadership. To Aristotle, the structure of politics is the structure of institutions contributing its appropriate part of the final end embodied in the state. Thus, a democratic state would ideally call for a democratic local government, just as an oligarchical state would go for oligarchical local government.

Urban centres in the West sprang up from the industrial revolution. In our country they emerged from colonial commerce with emphasis on presidency towns. In small towns it took the form of municipalities. It adhered to the English pattern with the chairman as the chief executive. He is also the head of the deliberative body. In England, the members of the Council of a local body are, as a whole, involved in the process of decision making. It is the committees of the Council, which exercise important powers within their areas. The executive powers of the municipal bodies are, in practice, exercised by the functional committees, which have emerged as specialized agencies for detailed deliberations on different sets of problems and have come to occupy an important position in due course. They have, in reality, supplemented the working of the Council. The Mayor, who also presides over the meetings of the

Council is little more than the city's ceremonial head. It is known as the "Weak Mayor" system. The Mayor is weak in the sense that whatever powers he possesses, are mostly of a residual character and in administrative affairs his role is that of an advisor. Incidentally, the Weak Mayor system was in vogue in the municipal administration of USA. But since the close of the nineteenth centuries most of the medium-sized cities of the USA adopted the City Manager Plan in which the Council formulated the policy framework and the professionally qualified city administrator was responsible for the implementation of the policies. Later on, the larger cities like New York, Boston, Philadelphia opted for what is popularly known as the Strong Mayor system. It is an arrangement in which the Mayor elected by the people is invested with wide administrative powers and responsibilities.[1]

Commissioner Form of City Governance

In big cities the colonial rulers in India introduced Municipal Corporation. It was structured on the principle of separation of policy-making and policy implementation functions, which can be entrusted to two authorities. The Corporation, as the deliberative body, lays down broad policies, frames byelaws, sanctions the budget and oversees administration. The executive authority is vested in the hands of the commissioner who is appointed by the State Government. He occupies the status of a co-ordinate municipal authority and derives power directly from law. The structure of Corporation seems to be based on the assumption that policy and administrative functions are distinct and divisible and can be entrusted to two different authorities. In practice, these two functions are intertwined. However, it is known as the commissioner form of city governance. In this scheme the commissioner enjoys enormous powers as the administrative head and by virtue of the statutory position in the municipal authority.

It was a model different from the widely accepted British model where the council was supreme in both legislative and executive spheres. It was devised to meet the peculiar needs of the colonial government who had high stakes in towns and cities.

This kind of arrangement originated long ago in the presidency towns in India when the then ruling class had a stake in administration and could not afford to transfer executive authority to a partially elected council. Executive dominating in the big city government was in tune with the politics of imperialism. In this kind of city governance the conflict of authority is inbuilt. 'With the inauguration of constitutional democracy after independence the retention of the government appointed commissioner as a co-ordinate and independent municipal authority had hardly any justification. When a civil servant is placed as co-ordinate statutory municipal authority, it is an unwarranted trespass into the domain of the representative local council. If he is defended as a check on the popular element, the argument reveals a distrust of representative government itself. As the history of Corporation government in India shows, the statutory division between deliberative and executive powers has been a constant source of friction between the Commissioner and the Corporation".[2]

Demerits of the Commissioner form of city Governance

This form of governance is not only against the spirit of democratic ethos but also unfit for ensuring high level of efficiency. The other difficulties of this model are as follows:

- The Commissioner is unable to provide administrative leadership because he is not a permanent and professional official.
- He cannot be expected to provide political leadership because he is not elected.
- There is also no absolute separation of powers. Given the large council and many committees with heterogeneous character that operate as unco-ordinated centres of decision making, the Commissioner cannot function like the American City Manager.
- The authority structure is anomalous and archaic. The Mayor is weak. It generates conflicts and tensions between the elected Councilor and the appointed officials.

Search for an Alternative form of Government

The difficulties led to a search for an alternative institutional arrangement. The Rural-Urban Relationship Committee examined the matter and the Committee reported that the cabinet system of government at the municipal level has been favoured by the Mayors and the Corporations of the important Corporations such as Mumbai, Kolkata, Delhi, Poona, Nagpur and a few others. The Sixth Conference of the

Municipal Corporations held in 1967 adopted a resolution urging upon the Government of India to draw up a model bill for the Mayor-in-Council form of governance. The Metropolitan Council in Delhi passed a bill, which provided for executive powers to be vested in the Mayor-in-Council. The Commissioner is principal officer of the Corporation.[3]

Merit of the Mayor-in-Council

The Mayor-in-Council form is similar to the cabinet form of government. The cabinet system of government in municipal administration seeks to establish a plural executive as distinguished from a singular executive :

- It resolves the debate on the so-called dichotomy between administrative efficiency and popular responsibility. In this case, the elected political executive takes the decision.
- Decision making is more open, people-oriented and quicker. The Mayor has the freedom to lead, act and push through his agenda in the corporation.
- It ensures accountability. The Mayor-in-Council is accountable to the corporation, which provides responsible local governance.
- The system is believed to get better results than those achieved through standing committees.
- The plural executive scores over the single executive. It makes room for political accommodation.
- The system can succeed if the ruling party has a comfortable majority so that there is political stability.
- It is not easy to keep out politics form city governance. City governance is political because it is involved in resource mobilization, resource accumulation and allocation. It could be that the Mayor-in-Council can induct right type of persons and trigger off a process of healthy and dynamic restoration of nexus between development and politics.
- It is said to unify four kinds of roles–political, executive, decision making and participatory in a single municipal organization.

The Mayor-in-Council model, as it appears from the foregoing discussion, is strictly different from the concept of Mayor-in-Council in the American context. In the USA, it is deliberative and policy-making body called the council in the municipal organization. It is generally small in size and the Mayor is the sole executive bearing the trait of the presidential form of government. The Mayor-in-Council form of city governance as conceived in India is a small collective body chosen out of the bigger council called the corporation.

The issue was discussed in a seminar on the cabinet system in municipal government organized under the auspices of Indian Institute of Public Administration, New Delhi in 1969. Although there was lack of unanimity, the general consensus was that the deliberative wing of the municipal corporation should be separated from the executive wing, the executive powers should be vested in a determinate authority of the cabinet type and that the Mayor should be so positioned as to enable him to provide leadership with a reasonable tenure.

It may be recalled that the urban government system in India, which owes its origin to the colonial rule, has developed the model of the commissioner system (popularly known as the Bombay model) in municipal corporations. The state appointed commissioner enjoy enormous powers as the administrative head and by holding statutory position in the municipal authority structures. On the contrary, the Mayor who holds a democratic office, does not have real powers and authority to decide on the municipal agenda. The 74th amendment of the Constitutions conceptualizes urban local bodies as the institutions of self-government. But the studies conducted show that the ULBs have been so designed as to enable the officials to play important role. The Mayor-in-Council, on the contrary, empowers the elected representatives of the people.

Mayor-in-Council System in West Bengal

West Bengal was the first state in India to introduce the Mayor-in-Council system in Kolkata and Howrah Municipal Corporations in 1994. It was later extended to the other municipal bodies in the state in 1995. In 1998 Maharashtra adopted the model and introduced the system in Mumbai and Nagpur on a trial basis. The next state to follow suit was Madhya Pradesh which introduced the system in all ULBs in August 1998. Maharashtra has gone back to the original arrangement. A close look at the legislations of the three states indicates that there are differences in terms of authority, power structure, hierarchical relationship between different points of authority of the Mayor and the Mayor-in-Council vis-à-vis the commissioner with the state government, financial authority of the Mayor and MIC members etc.

In Kolkata, the Mayor-in-Council system was introduced through the Calcutta Municipal Corporation Act, 1980. This Act seeks to resume the old thread of supremacy of the political wing in Corporation Government. It resembles the concept of Swaraj as popularized by Surendranath Banerjea in 1923. This Act, as Mohit Bhattacharya says, "reflects a political mood to keep step with the forces of change."[4]

The declared objective was to remove a basic ailment, namely, lack of responsive and responsible government for the citizens of Kolkata. It was felt that unless the city government could be made accountable to the local people, it would be impossible to fight against the existing undesirable outcomes of the municipal administration.

Historically, Calcutta's city government has been conceived in terms of a strong executive since the British days. But the concept of the executive has somehow remained elusive. As Calcutta suffered badly form the ravages of a famine, the city was given a strong government with a powerful chief executive, a general committee and the council as its component parts. The design was embodied in the 'Mackenzie' Act of 1989. Surendranath Banerjea took over as the minister-in-charge of the Local Self Government under the Dyarchy. He wanted to bring 'swaraj' to the city government of Calcutta. The Calcutta Corporation Act, 1923 was an attempt to liberalize the city government in tune with the spirit of the Montague–Chelmsford Reforms. Following the model of the British local government the Act made the Corporation all powerful and the Chief Executive Officer was accountable to it for his actions.

After India become independent Calcutta was the first to be shorn of its reformed mantle and driven back to the Bombay Model. The Calcutta Corporation was superseded in 1948 and a Commission of Inquire was set up to investigate the affairs. It recommended a structure similar to Bombay. The Calcutta Corporation Act was based on the Banerjea model and in this way, the supremacy of the political will was reaffirmed.

Legal Basis of the System

In terms of the Kolkata Municipal Corporation Act the municipal authorities include the Corporation, the Mayor-in-Council and the Mayor.

The standing committees have been abolished. There is a provision for Municipal Consultative Committee to advise the Mayor-in-Council, if necessary. The Commissioner is no longer the statutory municipal authority. He exercises powers and functions under the supervision and control of the Mayor. At the first meeting of the Corporation the elected members elect form among themselves one member to be Mayor and one member to be the Chairman. The position of the Chairman is similar to that of the Speaker in the legislative assembly and the position of the Mayor may be said to correspond to that of the Chief Minister of the State. The Mayor presides over the meetings of the Mayor-in-Council. The members of the Mayor-in-Council have hardly any existence without the Mayor. If the Mayor ceases to hold office, the entire Mayor-in-Council goes away. The Mayor is the key figure in the MIC. The present Act based on the philosophy of the strong Mayor endows the Mayor with immense powers and a reasonable tenure. He is the controlling authority and source of executive powers of the Corporation. There are, however, certain quasi-judicial authorities like the Municipal Assessment Tribunal, Municipal Building Tribunal etc. which lie outside the jurisdiction of the Mayor.

The Mayor can be removed from office under the special circumstances by a resolution carried by a majority of the total number of elected members of the Corporation at a special meeting called for the purpose upon a requisition made in writing by not less than one-third of the elected members of the Corporation. But no such resolution can be moved before the expiry of six months from the date of assumption of his office by Mayor. Again, if such a resolution is not carried out by a majority of the total number of elected members, no further resolution for the removal of the Mayor can be moved before the expiry of the period of six months form the date of the initiation of the former resolution.

In terms of the Calcutta Municipal Corporation Act, 1951 the standing committees and the commissioner were responsible to the Corporation and were overshadowed by the dominant nature of the commissioner. It needs also to be noted that in terms of the said Act the statutory powers enjoyed by the Mayor were confined to the presiding over the meetings, accessing all records, obtaining all reports form the commissioner on municipal administration and hearing of appeals on disciplinary matters. "The dual government of Calcutta based on separation of powers between the Councilors and the Commissioner is indefensible on many grounds. It is especially in appropriate as a tool for civic planning and development... The provision of an independent Commissioner has repeatedly been demonstrated to provide at best only a negative check on the parochialism and bias of the Councilors with the result of either a cold war between the Councilors and the Commissioner or the subservience of the latter to the former... Under the present systems, there is no institutional device or agency to absorb and reconcile the differences between the Councilor and the Commissioner to their mutual disadvantage, and for the benefit of the city."[5]

The Mayor-in-Council system in Kolkata consists of the Mayor, Deputy Mayor and not more than 10 elected members. The members of the Mayor-in-Council who are formally appointed by the Mayor are political heads in charge of functional departments. The Councilors find it easier to attend to grievances of their constituencies by interacting directly with them.

The MIC streamlines decision making because the focus and locus of authority are clearly defined. There is better interaction between the members of the MIC and the bureaucracy. The technocrats and administration have easy access to the political executive.

The executive power vests in the Mayor-in-Council. It is collectively responsible to the Mayor. The Mayor picks up the members of the Council and allocates portfolios. Sometimes the Mayor can exercise his powers without prior approval of the Mayor-in-Council but he has to inform it of the action taken. The MIC can constitute any number of consultative committees. These committees help the Mayor in the discharge of his functions.

The Act provides for only a single statutory committee, the Municipal Accounts Committee. It consists of five to seven persons who are elected by members of the Corporation form amongst themselves in accordance with the system of proportional representation by means of a single transferable vote. Members of the Mayor-in-Council are not eligible for being elected. It seems that the architects of this body wanted it to supervise the functions of the Mayor-in-Council from the point of view of audit and accounts.

The Mayor-in-Council meets once in a week to discuss major policy issues referred to it by the members and the Commissioner. The Commissioner is the Secretary of the MIC. He attends meetings and maintains minutes.

The Commissioner is the chief administrative officer of the Corporation and he is subordinate to the Mayor. He is appointed by the State Government in consultation with the Mayor-in-Council from amongst the persons who are or have been in the service of the government or (b) if so directed by the State Government by the Mayor-in-Council in consultation with the Public Service Commission or (c) by the Mayor-in-Council with the prior approval of the State Government from amongst officers who are or have been in the service of the Corporation. The Commissioner, if appointed by the state government, may be dismissed by the Mayor-in-Council in which case the State Government has to terminate the appointment.

The Mayor-in-Council is collectively responsible to the Corporation. The accepted methods of enforcing the responsibility are question, calling attention notice, resolution, adjournment, no-confidence motion etc. A Councilor has right to ask any question on any matter relating to the administration of the Corporation or the municipal government in Kolkata.

The Borough Committee

The Kolkata Municipal Corporation Act, 1980 provides for a second tier of governance–the Borough Committee. Each Borough committee consists of the Councilor of the wards in that Borough other than the Chairman of the Corporation and the members nominated from amongst the elected member of the Kolkata Municipal Corporation to form a panel of presiding officers to preside over the meetings of the Corporation in the absence of the Chairman. The Borough Committee functions under the guidance and supervision of the Mayor-in-Council. The MIC has built-in checks and balances seen in the form of the Mayor and his council vis-a-vis the Borough Councils or the Commissioner vis-à-vis the Municipal Secretary. The members of the Borough Committee have to do house-keeping job and therefore interact more intimately with the rate payers. They function as pressure groups and act as a check on the functioning of the MIC. The Borough Committees are required to discharge their functions under the overall supervision of the Mayor-in-Council. The present system, in fact, combines the deliberative role of a councilor or a member of the Corporation with limited executive responsibility as a member of the Borough Committee. There are 15 Borough Committees charged with the responsibility of performing statutory functions. The Borough Committees do not have any power to plan for the development but they can always discuss their developmental needs and forward the suggestions to the Mayor and the members of the Mayor-in-Council (MIC).

The Ward Committee

There are Ward Committees which function under the general supervision and control of the Borough Committees. Each of the committees is chaired by the councilor concerned. There are two sets of nominated members, one set nominated by the councilor concerned and the other set by the Corporation. The Ward Committees are required to identify the problems of the ward, fix priority of the development project, prepare annual and five year development plans, motive people to pay municipal taxes, advise the Corporation in mobilization of resources and listen to people's grievances.

Financial Devolution

Another important characteristic feature of MIC system in Kolkata is financial devolution. Expenditure proposals have to get routed through the department. This gives the political and administrative heads of the departments an opportunity of being familiar with the financial position. Each department has its own internal financial unit headed by a municipal accountant. This unit exercises powers of financial control delegated to it. In addition there is detailed scheme of vetting and sanctioning powers. The councilor who is elected by the citizens of a ward has been given powers of fixing priority and sanctioning development expenditure to the tune of Rs. 1,20,000 per year, which will be executed by the Borough Committee.

Apex Body for Utility Services

There is another institutional arrangement under the MIC system for consultation and co-ordination at the Corporation level, namely, Apex Body for Utility Services established by a MIC resolution in 1985. It consists of representatives of the various statutory public authorities providing utility services to the citizens of Kolkata, namely, Kolkata Metropolitan Development Authority, Kolkata Metropolitan Water and Sanitation Authority, Irrigation and Waterways and Public Works Department of the Government of West Bengal, Calcutta Electric Supply Corporation, Calcutta Port Trust and Kolkata Telephones. It is chaired by a member of the MIC. It recognizes the role of the political authority and responsibility for the management of the civic services.

The Mayor-in-Council form of city governance in Kolkata Municipal Corporation grew out of idealism because it was envisaged as a form of good local government, which would create efficiency and democracy at the grassroots. It was dictated by the expediency of governance at the higher level and trigged off by the need to have more transparency and better accountability through a streamlined decision making mechanism. The point was made clear by the Minister-in-charge while piloting Calcutta Corporation Bill, 1979. It was stated in the aims and objects of the Act that the chief functionaries of the Corporation of Calcutta or members of the standing committees, elected for a year at a time, could hardly ensure a continuity of administration and left matters mostly to the bureaucratic machinery. This needs to be tuned to the trend of democratization of self-government institutions.

It brought back the old thread of supremacy of political wing in the corporation government which was what Surendranath Banerjea attempted to do through his concept of Swaraj in 1923. The Calcutta Municipal Act, 1923 based on this philosophy, made provision for a politically responsible executive. It was hoped that it would throw up desired leadership that would make the system work. But the system failed due to a number of factors.

Challenges to the MIC System

The Mayor-in-Council system ran into rough weather a number of times after the change of political power from the hands of the Left Front to those of the Trinamool Congress-BJP combine, the most recent being in June 2003 as result of factional feuds in the All India Trinamool Congress. Earlier, one members of the Mayor-in-Council charged the Mayor that he had indulged in nepotism and malpractices while accepting tender for generation of electricity. This led to bad blood between them. The issue did not take bad turn as the party leadership intervened and handled the matter deftly and quickly. However, this time matter assumed a very dangerous turn. The Mayor had to sack his entire 10-member MIC after the municipal Commissioner was assaulted and threatened by seven members of the MIC. It was reported in the newspapers that the seven members stormed the chamber of the Commissioner, heckled him and dragged him out by his sleeves. He was taken to the conference room and asked to explain an order which undermined the powers and authority of the MIC. The Commissioner refused to discuss the issue which caused anger of the members who prevented him form leaving the room. The matter came to such a pass that the Commissioner had to file an FIR. The members were arrested. The controlling officials of the various departments decided to boycott the members of the MIC.[7]

The immediate provocation was the Commissioner's move to disregard an official note issued by the member of the MIC (Health). This note resulted from the order of the Commissioner to entrust all responsibility relating to health in borough 15 to the deputy health officer. In this note the MIC (Health) asked the Commissioner to remove the deputy health officer of borough 15 on the basis a decision of the Borough Committee. The Commissioner refused to act. The Commissioner ignored the note saying that he had no authority in terms of the Kolkata Municipal Corporation Act to instruct him. He argued that as per the legal provisions of the Act he works under the superintendence and control of the Mayor only. He told the press persons that he discussed the matter with the Mayor who approved his action. The Commissioner distributed the note among the member of the Mayor-in-Council.

Some of the members of the Mayor-in-Council demanded the withdrawal of the Commissioner by the State Government. The State Government cited the legal provisions to argue that it was the Mayor-in-Council which is required to adopt resolution for this purpose. The Mayor stood by his side and refused to yield to the pressure of the Mayor-in-Council.

The party formed an enquiry committee which was asked to submit report next day. The dismissed members sat in demonstration before the official chamber of the Mayor. The Mayor had to relent and bring back all the members. The portfolios were re-organized.

On another occasion the relationship between the Kolkata Municipal Corporation and the State Government assumed an undesirable turn. It was in April, 2003 that the State Government amended the legislation providing for payment of water tax by the citizens. The Kolkata Municipal Corporation initially accepted the proposal to introduce water surcharge on the basis of a proposal from the State Government. It was mentioned by the Mayor in his budget speech. But the TMC refused to accept it and directed the Mayor not to proceed further in this regard. This caused tension between the State Government and the Kolkata Municipal Corporation.

Another bone of contention resulted from the decision of the State Government not to pay electricity bill of the Kolkata Municipal

Corporation from the month of April, 2003. Earlier the State Government used to pay this bill and it was later on adjusted against the grant from the State Government. However, the Calcutta Electric Supply Corporation (CESC) acted promptly saying that it would disconnect electric connection from the offices and establishments of the Mayor, Kolkata Municipal Corporation. The KMC retorted back saying that in the event of the power supply being disconnected water supply in the metropolitan area would be disrupted. It was told that they would take up the matter with the citizens of the affected wards. The Kolkata Municipal Corporation threatened the State Government saying that it would also not be able to provide basic municipal services to the State Government offices if the latter did not pay property and other taxes and surcharge. Presumably having realized the political implications of the move the State Government softened its attitude. The matter was resolved when the State Government requested the CESC not to take such drastic step. The State Government seemed to have soft pedaled because in the case of Howrah and Bally ULBs the power supply was discontinued.

The success of the MIC system depends lot more on the Mayor, on the kind of leadership he provides and the team spirit he evolves. He is not just first among equals. He is more than a leader of the team as he is the head of the political executive. He has to carry his council and the Commissioners with him.

No less important is the party system which is the basic to the MIC pattern. The MIC system has started working from 1985 after the first elections under the Kolkata Municipal Corporation Act, 1980 were held. It was a Left Front dominated council in which the majority of the members belonged to the CPI(M). The working indicated that this arrangement is far better than the previous one. The priority of the development schemes is decided politically after careful consideration of the proposals of the different departments. Secondly, the time taken for consideration and approval of schemes has been considerably reduced. Thirdly, as the members are fully responsible for mobilizing political support the officers are free from avoidable worries and blames. Fourthly, it is easier to achieve policy and plan coordination and execution. This is done through a body called Apex Body for Utility Services having representatives of various statutory public authorities like Calcutta Metropolitan Development Authority and Calcutta Metropolitan Water and Sanitation Authority. The change of political party at the helm of affairs of the KMC has brought into light some of the weaknesses of the

MIC from of city governance. But the fact remains that it is more useful and effective form of city governance.

References

1. Marina R. Pinto, (2000). *Metropolitan City Government in India*. New Delhi: Sage Publications India Pvt. Ltd.
2. Mohit Bhattacharya, (1973). *Cabinet System in Municipal Government*, Kolkata: The World Press.
3. Sibranjan Chartterjee, (1988). "The Mayor-in-Council Form of City Government in Calcutta: Its Nature and Working", *Nagarlok*, July-September.
4. Mohit Bhattacharya, (1990). "The Mayor-in-Council System: Calcutta's New Government Outfit". In *Development and Administration* edited by Marina R. Pinto and R. Srinivasan. Bombay: Himalaya.
5. Ali, Ashraf, (1966). *The City Government of Calcutta: A Study of Inertia Bombay*: Asia Publishing House.
6. D.N. Banerjea, and S. Sen Gupta. (1986). *A Treatise on the Calcutta Municipal Corporation Act*, 1980.
7. *The Statesman*. (2003). 10 June.

9

The Kolkata Metropolitan Planning Committee

The Metropolitan Planning Committee (MPC) is a product of the Seventy Fourth Amendment of the Constitution. A metropolitan area has been defined as an area having population of ten lakh or more comprised in one or more districts and consisting of two or more municipalities. Interestingly, while 65th Constitution Amendment Bill contained the provision on metropolitan planning, the 73rd Constitution Amendment Bill initiated at the instance of the then Prime Minister, Mr. Narasimha Rao, was silent about it. The credit for reviving the concept and the provisions for the Metropolitan Planning Committee goes to the Joint Parliamentary Committee.

The Rationate for MPC

The Committee argued that there has been significant increase in the number of metropolitan cities in the country over the last few years and metropolitan areas encompass not only the main city corporations but also a number of other local bodies, both urban and rural, surrounding the main city corporation. To ensure that there is an orderly development of the vast area, proper plans need to be drawn up in association with the plan of the city. The Central and the State Governments make a lot of investment in these areas. These investment plans need to be co-ordinated with the development plans and requirements of the city.

All these underscore the need for a suitable planning machinery at the metropolitan area (MA). It will take care of the interaction between the various local bodies both local and urban, in the respective metropolitan areas. The existing arrangement in the form of development authority cannot respond to the problem because these bodies do not have a uniform functional pattern In some states they are planning bodies, while in others, they exercise executive function. Secondly, they do not have democratic character. The Committee, therefore, recommended the insertion of Article 243ZE for establishing an MPC and a new clause 243P to define metropolitan area.

Constitutional Provision

Article 243ZE says that there shall be constituted in each metropolitan area a Metropolitan Planning Committee to prepare a draft development plan for the metropolitan area as a whole. The State Legislature has been authorized to make provision with respect to the composition of the MPC, representation of the Central Government, State Government or of other organizations and institutions in the Committee and the functions relating to planning and co-ordination to be assigned to the Committees and the manner in which the chairpersons will be chosen. While the State Legislature has been empowered to decide on the manner in which the seats are to be filled, the Constitution stipulates that not less than two-thirds of the members of such committees shall be elected by and from amongst the elected members of the municipalities and chairpersons of the panchayats in the metropolitan area to the ratio between the population of the municipalities and of the panchayats in that area.

Surprisingly, despite clear constitutional provision MPCs are yet to be set up in the States except West Bengal. Some States have enacted necessary legislations. Maharashtra Government passed a similar enabling law as a sequel to the Public Interest Litigation challenging the failure of the Government to set up the MPC. Earlier, the Maharashtra Government promulgated an ordinance in June, 1999 to enable the creation of a 45-member MPC in Mumbai, Pune and Nagpur. But the MPC has not yet been set up.

State-Level Variations

The chart below shows state level variations in the composition of MPCs :

MPC: State Level Variations

Name of the State Act	*No. of Members*		*Chairperson*	*Secretary*	*Composition: Nominated Members and Special Invitees*
	Elected	*Nominated*			
Karnataka Municipal Corporation Act. 1976 (Act. 14 of 1996)	20	10	Not yet priscribed	Commissioner Bangalore Development Authority	1) Nominated Members: Representative from Govt. of India, State Gov. and organisations & institutions nominated by the State Government. 2) Special invitiees (permanent): All MPs, MLAs, MLCs from concerned Metropolitan Area
Kerala Municipalities Act, 1994 (Act 8 of 1995)	10	5	Elected from among the elected members	Officer nominated by the State Govt.	Nominated Members: secretary to the State Govt. or an eminent person experienced in local administration, one officer each from Town

(Contd.)

(Table Contd.)

					Planning Dept. and PWD, one of the collectors of Districts comprising the metropolitan area, other members as desired by the State Govt. to carry out the limited functions assigned to them.
Maharashtra Metropoli-Tan Planning Committees (Constitution and Functions) Act. 1999	30	15	Nominated by the State Govt.	Nominated by the State Govt.	1) Ex-Officio Members: Secretary, UD Department and Divisional Commissioner of the concerned Revenue Department 2) Nominated Member: 6 from the Municipal Commissioners, etc. and CEOs of Planning & Development Authorities, 2 from

(Contd.)

(Table Contd.)

MLAs and MLCs from
The concerned
Metropolitan area and 4
Experts from urban
Administration, industry,
Trade and urban
Community
Development
3) Special Invitees
(Permanent): 5 from
MPs, MLAs and
Ordinary residents of the
Concerned metro area,
CEOs of MIDC, Mhada,
MPCB, MSEB, MSRTC.
Director or Deputy
Director of Dept. of
Town Planning,
Representatives of
Central Govt.
Organizations like
Railways, Telephone,
Port Trust.

(Contd.)

(Table Contd.)

UP Munici-Pal Corpo-Ration Act. 1959 (Act 12 of 1994)	14 to 20	7 to 10	To be chosen through rules Prescribed by the State Govt.	Not specified	Nominated Members :1 officer from the Central Ministry of UD recommended by the Secretary, other state officers from UD Dept., Forest Dept., PWD & State Electricity Board, State Chief Town and Country Planner, Director–State Environment Depts., Managing Director UP Jal Nigam, General Manager -Jal Sansthan, Vice Chairman of Metropolitan Development Authority.
West Bengal Metropoli-Tan Planning Committee Act. 1994	40	20	Chief Minister; Vice Chairperson Minister-in-charge MA & UD	KMDA is the Secretariat	Nominated Members: Chief Minister, Minister-in-Charge, Municipal affairs & Urban Development, Mayor-KMC, Presidents from 2 District Panchayats, 2 MPs, 2 MLAs, 8 Central & State Govt. officials, 3 experts.

Source: Network–Update, November-December 2001

Reasons for the Unhappy Situation

The general reasons for this unhappy situation seem to be bureaucratic confusion about the purpose and role of the MPC, lack of political interest and the lurking fear of the parastatal bodies in almost all the metropolitan areas that their authority will be undermined. All these reasons appear to be based on misconception and misreading of the constitutional provisions. There should not be any confusion about the role and responsibility of the MPC as the Constitution is very specific on the point. The MPC cannot acquire political identity of its own because it is a body where the Central Government and the State Government are represented. It has also accepted the role of the civil society. The parastatal bodies have to accept that in a democratic system they cannot play policy-making role.[1] If the MPCs are constituted, they can execute the plans formulated by the MPC. They can act as the technical secretariat of the MPC, as has been done in West Bengal.

West Bengal Shows the Way

West Bengal is the first State in the country to set up MPC by holding elections on October 7, 2001. The enabling legislation was enacted in 1994. It provides for Kolkata Metropolitan Planning Committee which will prepare draft development plan having regard to (a) the plans prepared by the municipalities and panchayats in the metropolitan area (b) matters of common interest between the municipalities and panchayats including co-ordinated spatial planning of the area, sharing of water and other physical resources, the integrated development of infrastructure and environmental conservation (c) over-all subjects and priorities by the Government of India and the State Government (d) extent and nature of investments likely to be made in the metropolitan area by the agencies of the Government of India and of the State Government and other available resources, whether financial or otherwise.[2]

Kolkata Metropolitan Area comprises the whole of Kolkata Municipal Corporation (KMC) and certain areas within the districts of the North 24 Parganas, South 24 Parganas, Howrah, Hooghly and Nadia. It is inhabited by 1, 25, 17, 253 people of whom 1, 07, 00, 552 reside in urban areas and 18, 16, 701 in rural areas.

Results of the Election

The election was held on the basis of proportional representation and on a single transferable ballot paper. The electorate consisted of the elected representatives of the KMC, Howrah and Chandannagar Municipal Corporation, all the 38 constituent municipalities of the KMA, Pradhans of 133 Gram Panchayats, Sabhapatis and Sabhadhipatis of the respective Panchayat Samitis and Zilla Parishads, a part of which falls under KMA. There was no party symbol but the political parties took active interest n the elections. The results of the elections are shown below:

Results of Election to KMPC

District	*Total Seats*	*Left Front*	*Trinomul + B.J.P.*	*Congress*
Kolkata	14	6	8	0
Nadia	2	2	0	0
Hooghly	4	3	1	0
Howrah	6	6	0	0
South 24 Parganas	3	3	0	0
North 24 Parganas	11	8	2	1
Total	40	28	11	1

Composition of the KMPC

The KMPC consists of 60 members. To ensure representation of the organizations and authorities who are in one way or the other related to the development planning of the KMA provisions have been made for the inclusion of the railways, port authorities and the overlapping district planning committees apart from the Central and State Government functionaries. The Chief Minister is the Chairperson of this body. The Minister-in-charge of Municipal Affairs and Urban Development is the Vice Chairperson. The KDMA is the Secretariat of the KMPC and the Secretary, KDMA has been appointed as its Secretary.

The KMPC in its first meeting held on December 4, 2001 under the chairmanship of the Chief Minister constituted the executive committee and five other sectoral committees. The executive committee

(EC) is headed by the Minister-in-charge of Municipal Affairs and Urban Development Departments, Government of West Bengal. The EC is required to co-ordinate on behalf of the KMPC the development activities within KMPA, review and monitor the work of all five sectoral committees, consider and finalize the sectoral plans and submit the same to KMPC for approval and to convene the meetings of the KMPC and provide necessary support to it.

There are five sectoral committees (SCs):

a) Drainage, Sewage and Sanitation Committee

b) Traffic, Transportation, Railways and Waterways Committee

c) Water Supply Committee

d) Education, Health, Employment and Bustee Committee and

e) Environment, Wetlands, Urban Amenities and Heritage Committee

Each of the Committee consists of experts, political leaders and government officials.

The EC and SCs may formulate procedures and methodology for the discharge of their functions. The SCs are authorized to invite experts in respective fields for the purpose of preparing sectoral plans. They are also required to ensure that plans are prepared within the scheduled time frame. They will report the progress of their work to the EC from time to time. It is laid down in the notification that in order to promote sectoral interdependence the sectoral committees will interact with each other and also take into consideration plans, programmes and likely investments/agencies in both public and private sectors in their respective subjects.

References

1. *Decentralisation and Municipalities*, (2001) National Commission to Review the Working of the Constitution, New Delhi.

2. R. Bandyopadhya (2001), 'Kolkata Metropolitan Planning Committee', *Urban Management*, Institute of Local Government & Urban Studies, Kolkata.

10

People's Participation in Forest Management in West Bengal

Till about the end of the 18th century the Indian State treated forests as an open access resource. A complex range of rules and regulations managed it. The State which began to expand its control over forests since 1800, continued to consolidate its position through enactments, the first of which was the Forest Act, 1865. It facilitated the acquisition of forests by the State. The 1878 Act sought to curtail the customary rights of the rural communities to manage forests. The forest policy statement of 1894 further strengthened the hands of the State by giving it the right to forcibly take over all forests including private and community forests. The Forest Act of 1927 denied people any rights over the forest produce simply because they were domiciled there. The colonial forest policy was based on the belief that the people were not only incompetent to manage forests but also a threat to forests. Unfortunately, this attitude continued unabated even after independence. The Forest Policy of 1852 retained the concept of reserved forests now justified in the name of national needs and placed them under the control of the State. Interestingly, although the idea of 'village forests' was accepted to serve the needs of the people in and around the villages, the villagers were denied the right to manage such forests.

Such a forest policy of the State had hit the general people. They were prohibited from using forest resources even to meet their needs. The fuel wood and fodder crisis complicated the situation. The people who were traditionally involved in protecting the forests, became alienated. The forest dwellers had to bear the biggest brunt of it. This led to social conflicts on the use of forest resources in 70s and increased pressure on the State to re-orient forest policies.

It was a time when the international community had started realising the need for protecting environment including forests for human survival. Along with it came international resource commitments to the protection of the forests in the developing world. The financial support came in the form of massive social forestry programme. By 1988 over 60 million rupees had already been spent on it, but the programme could not produce satisfactory results particularly with regard to fuel wood and fodder crisis.

The New Forest Policy

The National Forest Policy of 1988 reversed the State's earlier forest management priorities of meeting industrial and commercial requirements for forest produce and maximising revenue ignoring local needs. The new forest policy emphasised on the environmental protection and conservation and meeting the requirements of fuel wood, fodder, minor forest produce and small timber of the rural and tribal population and creating a massive movement, with the involvement of women, for achieving these objectives.

The National Forest Policy of 1988 was the first to realise that the people who were living in and around forests, must have a stake on the forests. In the new policy it was stated that the people dependent on forests, were to be consulted and their views were to be taken into account in the management and development of forests. The execution of the forest management plan will be done through the village committee to which the funds would be provided by the Forest Department. The people were to be given the right to take the usufruct free of cost and to have a share in the timber and other major forest produce when harvested as per the Joint Forest Management (JFM) plan. Andhra Pradesh was the first state to allow 100 per cent of non-timber forest produce and 50 per cent of the timber from the reserved forests to the people who would help in the protection and development of forests. Such a policy was influenced by a number of local, national and international factors as noted below :

(a) The agitations organised by the local people, the Chipko movement in Uttar Pradesh hills and Appikko movement in Andhra Pradesh asserted people's rights to manage forests. The local people had challenged the rights of the State Government officials to interfere with their forests ;

(b) The powerful Non-Government Organisations extended their support to local people's movements. The State was left with no alternative but to pay attention to the problems of the increasingly marginalised forest dwellers.

(c) There was, again, the increasing international acceptance of people's participation as an effective method for forest protection and conservation. The foreign assistance programme in the field, particularly the World Bank's social forestry project, insisted on ensuring people's participation in forest management.

The Joint Forest Management Programme (JFM) envisages active association of rural communities in planning, management and rejuvenation of degraded forests. The JFM resolutions assure the participating villagers free access to most non-timber forest produce and 25-50% share of net income from the sales of poles/timber on final harvesting. In return, the villagers are expected to protect the forests after forming an organisation conforming to the membership and structure set up by the Forest Department[1].

Experiments in participatory management of forests began in West Bengal at Arabari in Midnapore and Purulia in the early 1970s. The Arabari experiment culminating in 1987 aimed at rejuvenation of degraded sal forests through active participation of forest fringe committees. A total of 11 villages with 618 families were involved in the experiment. The Government supported the experiment by launching a special socio-economic project and issued order for the sharing of 25 per cent of the usufructs with the people. The experiment improved the strained relationship between the Forest Department and fringe committees, resuscitated 1186 ha degraded sal forests and enhanced the income of the local people through a set of activities of employment generation and sharing of non-timber forest produce (NTFP). K.C. Malhotra's study on the contribution of NTFP to the village economy of Midnapore in West Bengal had shown that 16.44 per cent of the annual income of the households under survey came from NTFP[2].

The question of protecting forests is connected with the question of managing the forests, which came to the forefront after the Earth Summit in Rio in 1992. The Summit emphasised the need for involving the communities in the management of forests.

The introduction of the West Bengal Social Forestry project in 1980s gave peoples' participation in forests management a big push. The objective of the forestry project was to promote peoples' participation in the management and development of forests. The objectives of the social forestry under the JFM can be summed up thus:

(a) to reduce pressure on natural forests;

(b) to involve indigenous people depending on forests for their subsistence needs in planning, development, exploitation and protection of forests; and thereby

(c) to preserve/conserve bio-diversity by means of people's participation

It brought about a change in the mindset of the forest officials by making room for interaction with the fringe committees. The Forest Department organised the fringe committees into forest protection committees (FPCs). To allow the forests to regenerate, people have to forego a lot of immediate benefits. The Government had to provide them with some employment support through resource building activities to help them sustain their efforts. The Government had also to share with them a part of the revenue generated from the forests through their efforts.

The State Government passed a resolution in 1989 specifying the composition, rights and responsibilities of the (FPCs.) This resolution applied to South Bengal districts. Owing to regional, climatic and socio-economic differences, region–specific JFM resolutions were framed. Thus came separate resolutions for the Darjeeling hills, North Bengal plains, sunderbans and wild life protected areas. In 1996 separate resolutions were framed for setting up eco-development committees with a view to protecting and developing wildlife protected areas through the participation and involvement of the fringe people.

The FPC : Composition and Functions

The Divisional Forest Officer (DFO) in consultation with the Forests and Land Reforms Standing Committee (Bon-O-Bhumi Sanskar Sthayee Samiti), selects beneficiaries for the constitution of FPCs. The beneficiaries are to be drawn from the economically backward people living in the vicinity of the forests concerned. The concerned Gram Panchayat is required to extend necessary support and help.

The Executive Committee (EC) of the FPC consists of the following:

1.(a) Chairpersom (Sabhapati) or any member of the Bon-O-Bhumi Sanskar Sthayee Samiti of the local Police Station to be nominated by the Sabhapati

(b) Head of the GP (Pradhan) or any member of the local GP to be nominated by the Pradhan

(c) Elected representatives of the beneficiaries (not exceeding 6)

(d) Concerned Beat Officer who acts as the Member-Secretary

The FPC has to be approved by the DFO on the recommendation of the Forest and Land Reforms Standing Committee (Bon-O-Bhumi Sanskar Sthayee Samiti). The latter is responsible for monitoring and supervising the FPC.

Duties

2. (i) The Forest Protection Committee shall maintain a register showing necessary particulars of beneficiaries as well as Members of the Committee, e.g. name, father's name, address, age, number of family members, name of nominee, etc. The nomination forms duly filled in and approved by the Executive Committee should be pasted in the register. Such registers are also to be maintained in the concerned Range Offices of the Forest Department for permanent record;

(ii) The Forest Protection Committee shall maintain a minutes book wherein proceedings of the meetings of the Executive Committee held from time to time as well as the proceedings of the Annual General Meeting of the Forest Protection Committee will be recorded under the signature of the President of the Committee and such minutes duly attested by the Member-Secretary shall be sent to the concerned Range Officer for record;

(iii) The Forest Protection Committee shall hold an Annual General Meeting once every year where activities of the Committee as well as details of distribution of usufructuary benefits are to be discussed, besides electing representatives of the beneficiaries to the Executive Committee.

Functions (a)

(i) To ensure protection of forest(s)/plantation(s)/wildlife through members of the Committee;

(ii) To protect the said forest(s)/plantation(s) with the members of the Committee ;

(iii) To inform forest personnel of any person or persons attempting trespass and willfully or maliciously damaging the said forest (s)/plantation(s)/wildlife or commit theft thereon;

(iv) To prevent such trespass, encroachment, grazing, fire, theft or damage ;

(v) To apprehend or assist the forest personnel in apprehension of such person or persons committing any of the offences mentioned above

Functions (b)

(i) To ensure smooth and timely execution of all forestry works taken up in the area under protection by the Committee;

(ii) To involve every member of the Committee in the matter of protection of forest(s)/plantation(s)/wildlife as well as other duties assigned to the Committee;

(iii) To assist the concerned forest official in the matter of selecting/ engaging of labourers required for forestry works;

Functions (c)

(i) To ensure smooth harvesting of the forest produce by the Forest Department;

(ii) To assist the concerned forest official in proper distribution of the earmarked portion, i.e., 25 per cent of the net proceeds among the members of the Committee as per list maintained by the concerned Standing Committee;

(iii) To ensure that usufruct rights allowed by the Government is not in any way misused by any of the members and forest/ plantation sites are kept free from any encroachment whatsoever

Functions (d)

(i) To prevent any activities in contravention of the Indian Forest Act of 1927 and any Acts and rules made thereunder and the Wild Life Protection Act, 1972;

(ii) To report about the activities of a particular member which are found prejudicial and detrimental to the interest of particular plantation and/or forest to the concerned Beat Officer/Range Officer, which may result in cancellation of membership of the erring member ;

(iii) To assist the forest officials to take action or proceed under the Indian Forest Act of 1927 and the Wild Life (Protection) Act, 1972 and any Acts and rules made thereunder, against the offender, including any erring member of the Committee found to be violating the Act or damaging the forest/plantation

Usufructuary Benefits

(i) The member will have to protect the forest/plantation/wildlife for at least 5 years to be eligible for sharing of usufructs under this programme

(ii) The members shall be entitled to collect following items free of royalty without causing damage to forests/plantations:

(a) Fallen twigs, grass, fruits, flowers, mushroom, seeds, leaves and intercrops raised by FPCs, subject to any restrictions imposed from time to time, provided however such collection will not be allowed in National Park, core area to Tiger Reserve and sanctum sanctorum of sanctuary.

(b) Medicinal plants in North Bengal will be permitted to be collected by the FPC members free strictly on the basis of approved micro-plans, except in National Park, core area of Tiger Reserve and sanctum sanctorum of sanctuary;

(c) Members of FPC will receive 25 per cent net of sale proceeds of firewood and poles, which are harvested during thinning and cultural operations. The poles for the purpose of this order will be upto 90 cm bhg for all species except teak. For teak the upper limit of bhg is 60 cm.

(d) Timber would not be subject to revenue sharing. However, lops and tops derived out of clear felling as per approved Working Plan which comes under a category of firewood would be shared on 25 per cent net sale proceeds basis.

(iii) Entire sal seeds so collected shall have to be deposited with the West Bengal Tribal Development Co-operative Corporation Limited through the local LAMPS (where LAMPS are functioning) and LAMPS will pay the members, in approved tariff against their individual collection.

(iv) The concerned forest official will distribute to the eligible members their proportionate share of the usufructs from the harvesting after satisfactory performance of functions detailed hereinbefore.

The usufruct sharing will be subject to restrictions imposed from time to time on account of silvicultural and management requirement and from preservation of wildlife point of view.

In order to sustain community initiative, a series of measures have been taken by the Government. Mention may be made of micro-planning, shifting of management emphasis on non-timber forest products, preservation of bio-diversity. The degradation of forests has a more profound effect on the life style of women than men. Women in the forest communities have to perform double duty—cooking and nursing as well as collecting fuel wood and non-timber forest products. In the joint forest management there is a deliberate effort to ensure that women are not deprived of their constitutional rights to benefits accruing from the public lands. And for that it is provided :

1. gathering of NTFP has to be in proportion of three females for every male.
2. processing of NTFP exclusively by females.
3. in marketing of NTFP for every two females one male is involved.

More than four lakhs FPC members protect 5,299.45 square km. of forest area. The Eco-Development Committees (EDCs), comprising

18,072 members around Protected Areas, take care of 774.62 square km. of the area. In terms of percentage of recorded forest area FPCs and EDCs together cover 51.13 per cent of the total forest area of the state. In all FPCs wives are joint members with their husbands, and in some cases, they are primary members too. There are 17 all women FPCs in the South West Bengal, the region accounting for 80 per cent of the FPCs.

The factors contributing to the success of the programme :

- Realisation on the part of the officials that the custodial system of management of natural resources has failed and needs to be replaced by a system of stakeholders' participation.
- Change in the management objectives giving higher priority to the needs of the local people.
- Empowerment of people at the grassroots through the effective working of three-tiered panchayati raj system and thus effective political support.
- Motivation of the communities through intensive extension work.
- Adoption of micro-planning through PRA as a tool for involvement of committees in developmental activities and management of forests.
- Community/eco-development activities by way of infrastructural development, vocational training and input support for increased productivity of land-based systems, creation of assets for supplementary income and generation of employment in forestry and allied activities and management. Moreover, FPCs have become effective platforms for resolving intra-village and inter-village disputes and conflicts.
- Sharing of usufructs with the participating communities.
- Persistent efforts by the forest department, NGOs and natural leaders of FPCs to motivate and build awareness through face-to-face communication, group meetings, workshops.
- Regular monitoring by the Department.
- Formation of Self Help Groups (SHGs) among members of the FPCs in some areas.

- Increased availability of the NTFP from the forests protected by the communities.

Impact of JFM

- Rejuvenation of the degraded forestlands–the forest cover has increased from 12, 674 sq. km. in 1988 to 13,581 sq. km. in 2000.
- The tree crop in JFM forests is regularly harvested and the income shared with the people. The fringe communities have benefited from non-timber forest produce (NTFPs). There are 189 different types of NTFPs, which contribute to generating between 10-25 per cent of the total income of the poorest sections of the community. A study of WWF(2000) noted that the Trishula FPC in Bankura South Division earned Rs. 30,500 from selling lac host trees in 1996-97.
- JFM has strengthened grassroots democratic bodies of natural resource management and brought them to the forefront in rural Bengal. The formation of FPCs has produced a new element of community leadership for resource protection.
- Women play a significant role in the JFM programme. They have started strong self-help micro-credit movement. In some FPCs they have developed a common fund out of the sale proceeds of NTFP.
- The relationship between the forest department and the people has improved as a result of frequent interaction. FD works more as a facilitation than as an implementing agency.

A Case Study of the FPCs in the Hills District of Darjeeling

The author and an officer of the Forest Department, Government of West Bengal had done a study of 3 Forest Protection Committees in the hill districts of Darjeeling. The FPCs were selected on the basis of their performance. About one hundred members were interviewed. The FPCs are named after the areas of location, namely, Deorali, Chhatakpur and Phuguri. In terms of performance as assessed by the Forest Department Deorali comes first followed by Chhatakpur and Phuguri. It is found from the data collected that while health centres and primary schools have been set up in all FPC areas, other facilities such as drinking water, high schools and electricity have not reached all the people in the FPC areas. All the FPC areas have, however, roads leading to the market. These roads enable the poor people of the localities including the FPC members to sell their goods in markets where they get higher prices, if not, fair prices.

All the FPC members have been motivated to form FPCs for the purpose of building environment. When people in our society get together on non-economic considerations and for a general social cause, it speaks of high social consciousness of the people. It implies that democratic values have struck firm roots. It is the basic subjective pre-condition for the successful growth of the grassroots democratic institutions like FPCs.

It is found that the field officers did not properly draw the attention of all the FPC members to the Government resolution regarding the FPC in hills. The fulfillment of targets given to them by the higher officials might have been of greater concern for them. The members of the Deorali FPC who were introduced to FPC by the forest officers, denied having knowledge about the concerned Government order. Interestingly, in Chhatakpur where the neighbours and family members had motivated 90% of the members to form FPCs, the persons interviewed have reported to have very little familiarity with the Government order.

Strangely enough, the large numbers of members ignorant of Government order, know about the benefits which flow from the formation of FPC. A deeper probe is necessary to find out how they have come to know about it. More than 70% of the members of Phuguri (poor-performing) are unaware of the benefits. This may be one of the reasons for bad performance of the Phuguri. In Chhatakpur where some Non-Government Development Organisations (NGDOs) are reported to be active, the situation is not encouraging. One of the objectives of the NGOs or NGDOs is to empower the people. The FPC is a forum for empowerment of the people. The role of the NGDOs is not, therefore, understandable.

The data demonstrate that the performance of the FPCs has been good in those areas where the officers have taken initiative in making the people familiar about the FPCs. Presumably, when the FPCs are organised at the initiative of the people and officers do not interact with the members, the members get less motivated because assurance from officers and their observations carry greater value to them.

The Deorali FPC has been able to perform well because of effective and meaningful interaction with the Forest Department's officials. The latter have frequently visited the former and listened to the members patiently. It was reported that neither the senior officers nor the Beat Officers had ever visited the Chhatakpur and Phuguri FPCs.

The Beat Officers have, however, given patient hearing to those who come to see them in their offices. But the problem remained because while only a few members of the Chhatakpur and Phuguri had visited the Beat Officers, 63% of the FPC members of Deorali had done this. Higher motivation, primary education and more official attention might have contributed to good performance of the Deorali FPC. The findings indicate that the motivation by the officers is like a high powered engine of the FPCs.

Forest Protection

The data collected tend to show that patrolling with the Forest Department staff has been widely accepted as an important method of forest protection by the members of the Deorali FPC. The performance of the Phuguri and Chhatakpur in this regard is not encouraging. Their low level of motivation and infrequent interaction with the forest officials may be the reasons.

Interestingly, the average-performing FPC has the best of record in terms of catching forest offenders. Can it be presumed that extensive patrolling has brought down the offence in Deorali and Phuguri areas to almost nil?

Impact of Forest Protection

Forest protection seems to have paid good dividends. All the FPC members interviewed for the study, have reported improvement in the forest condition following the formation FPCs, although they differ among themselves on the extent of improvement. All the members of the Deorali FPC have reported full improvement while full improvement in respect of Phuguri has been reported by 68% of the members. The Chhatakpur FPC members have, broadly speaking, held the same view as that of Deorali FPC members, 92% members reporting full improvement.

As the data indicate, the condition of plantations has been remarkably uneven in different FPC areas even after the formation of the FPC. The situation has been perceived as bad by more than 58% members of Chhatakpur FPC. While the situation in Deorali is good, more than 50% of the members of Phuguri report medium and bad plantation condition. The glaring unevenness in the plantation condition may be attributed to the different level of motivation of the FPC members in the respective areas. It is also difficult to rule out differential attention of the forest officials as a contributing factor.

Labour Deployment

The FPCs are authorised to take decision about the deployment of labour. But it is found from the data that while in Deorali the FPC takes this decision, in Chhatakpur those who take the decision, are not members of the FPC. Are they village influentials or contractors? The situation is different in the case of Phuguri FPC where the Beat Officer takes such decision in most cases relegating the FPC to the background. This is an undesirable situation and calls for immediate correction because it might have led to discrimination in labour engagement as reported by the members. There has been no discrimination in the deployment of labour in the Deorali FPC which take decisions in matters pertaining to deployment of labour. Such discrimination has also been reported in Phuguri and Chhatakpur where such decisions are not taken by the FPCs.

Usufructs Sharing

Although, usufructs sharing forms part of the JFM programme it is not taking place in all FPCs. Surprisingly, 96% of the members of the Phuguri FPC report that they do not share usufructs. While this may be due to the ignorance of the members about the benefits they are entitled to, it may be creating a negative interest in them about the FPC.

It is, however, significant to note that while all the members of the Deorali FPC share usufructs, only 13% of them report knowledge about the disputes in usufructs-sharing. This speaks of the remarkable role played by the forest officials and indicates that there is harmonious relationship between the Forest Department and FPCs.

Women's Participation

Although there is no stipulation about women's participation in FPCs in the concerned government order, women have an important role to play in this regard because womenfolk in all poverty group population participate in the bread-earning and bread-making processes. They have a stake in forests because forests help them in many ways.

Women's participation in the FPCs under survey is neither even nor encouraging in all FPCs. Interestingly, while many women had attended Annual General Meetings of the Deorali FPC, hardly any one of them had opened their lips. Their presence in the meeting was not therefore felt. Surprisingly, only in the poor-performing Phuguri FPC meetings a few women had raised their voices. It has to be examined if it is due to their lack of education or lack of interest in FPCs or due to the resistance of the male members present in the meeting.

In an age of women empowerment throughout the globe and when India has taken special initiative in this regard by making constitutional provision for reservation of seats for women in grassroots democratic bodies, this situation calls for immediate attention. The Government may think in terms of amending the order providing for reservation of seats for women in FPCs.

It is not clearly understood why the political leaders who have to look for women for contesting reserved seats for them at the time of election to local bodies like panchayats and municipalities, do not care to develop FPCs as nurseries for recruitment and training of women keeping in view the elections in higher democratic bodies.

Political Interest

Politicians in the hills do not appear to have taken due cognizance of FPCs. It is difficult to explain the situation because in a democratic political system where votes matter, the politicians are expected to have some stake in FPCs. Presumably, the FPCs do not have adequate political clout in the villages. Can it be assumed that there is no challenge to establishment politics in hills?

The political affiliation of the FPC members has been insignificant. The Deorali FPC does not have any member having political affiliation. A little more than one third of the Phuguri members is reported to have links with political parties. Party politics does not, therefore, play any role in the functioning of the FPCs.

Benefits of the FPC Members

According to the Government resolution relating to the FPCs there is a *quid pro quo.* The members are entitled to some benefits such as right to raise intercrops, free collection of things like fodder, firewood, broomsticks grass, employment in forestry works, vocational training.

This is necessary to unleash initiative and ensure effective participation of all the members.

While the Deorali and Phuguri FPCs raise intercrops, no such activity is reported to have been undertaken by the Chhatakpur FPC which is an average performing one. Is raising intercrops difficult or impossible in the FPC areas? Are the members not aware of their entitlement to do so? It may be recalled that 75% of the members of this FPC have reported to have no knowledge about the Government order. No forest officer has, however, explained to them the need for forming FPCs.

As the data indicate, free collection of forest produce varies from FPC to FPC. The data show that Phuguri's share in this regard has been less than that of the other two FPCs. This may have been a factor contributing to the poor performance of this FPC. While all the FPCs have been evenly benefited from the support activities, in respect of other benefits such as vocational training, employment in forestry works, the situation in the average and poor-performing FPCs has some similarities. While not a single member of the Chhatakpur FPC has reported to have received vocational training, only 25% of the members of the Phuguri FPC have reported to have been trained under the vocational training programmes. In respect of forestry employment, while nobody from Chhatakpur got employed only 39% of Phuguri got some employment.

Development Interventions

While FPCs have come into being primarily at the initiative of the Forest Department for the purpose of protecting forests through the participation of the beneficiaries and by giving the protectors some benefits in lieu of their service, the protectors being the poverty group, the other Government development departments and self-government bodies have some programmes and activities targeted to them. It is an open secret that no amount of goodwill and motivation alone will improve the functioning of the FPCs unless and until the FPC members are assured of at least two square meals a day or if they are made to realise that their participation will help them maintaining their subsistence. In other words, they have to be helped to come out of the poverty situation.

It is true that the Forest Department's activities alone cannot raise them beyond the level of poverty. It is, therefore, necessary to examine the contribution of the other Government development departments and local self-governing institutions to the FPC members.

The Darjeeling Gorkha Hill Council (DGHC) and Panchayat institutions are two important local-self government institutions operating there and administering many development programmes for the poor. While all the FPC members of Deorali and 83.8% of the Chhatakpur FPC have reported that they get the benefit of the DGHC programmes, more than 70% of the Phuguri FPC have refused to answer the question. Though it is not clearly understood why they have taken this position one may try to find a feeble answer to this question in the political affiliation of the members of the Phuguri FPC.

Insofar as the activities of the Panchayats are concernecd the situation in the Chhatakpur FPC is the worst. Panchayats appear to be non-existent in this FPC area. Some of the benefits of two important panchayat programmes namely, JRY and IRDP have been reaped by a good number of members of the Deorali FPC. In Phuguri 82.8 % of the members are aware of panchayat programmes but only 14.8 % of them have enjoyed the benefits of the programmes.

Panchayat activities might have helped the Deorali FPC members to increase their incomes and thus to enable them devote more time to forest protection. They did not have to move out of their localities in search of employment.

Interestingly, the members of the Phuguri FPC had alone enjoyed the fruits of MP Fund Scheme. It may be due to the fact that a large number of the FPC members have secondary education, which raises consciousness, and/or because of interest of the Phuguri members in political activities. Therefore, secondary education and political interest may have been useful to them.

The data indicate that poverty-stricken FPC members cannot always be motivated to protect forests. It seems that they can be motivated to protect forests if they can be convinced that through the participation in the programme they will able to improve their living conditions.

The presence of the NGDOs has not been reported in all FPC areas. Only in Chhatakpur there are some NGDOs which have been able to provide some employment to a few people. But they have not been able to empower the people and to generate their interest in taking part in grassroots democratic bodies like FPCs as forums for their empowerment. All development agencies, be it government and non-government, should teach the people the art of sustainable development. In the context of the present global discourse on the 'third world' development it has assumed great significance. Sustainable development calls for empowerment of the people. Successful implementation of the JFM programme requires empowerment of the people. Though it is essentially a political work, the government servants cannot be onlookers when politicians do not play their role properly and NGDOs for reasons best known to them, do not take up the work.

The findings reveal while the distance between the forest officials and the people has been bridged and both have started interacting, this is not enough for the effective working of the FPCs. Horizontal interaction certainly goes a long way in paving the road for the healthy growth of FPCs, vertical interaction is the life blood of all grassroots democratic bodies. Democratic breeze should blow through the windows of FPC. The FPC members should meet more frequently, preferably twice in a month. One can think of identifying the agenda items for such meetings Successful working of the FPCs calls for taking two steps-sharing of power among the FPC members and regular conscientisation of the members.

References

1. For a detailed discussion see. Dolly Arora, "From State Regulation to People's Participation : Case of Forest Management in India" *Economic and Political Weekly*, March 19, 1994.

2. K.C. Malhotra *et al* (1991) Role of NTFP in Village Economy: A Household Survey in Jamboni Range, Midnapore, Indian Institute of Bio-Social Research and Development, Kolkata.

Note : The field study was funded by the Forest Department, Government of West Bengal and conducted jointly by the author and Shri S.S. Bist, Conservator of Forest, Hill Circle, Forest Department, Government of West Bengal in 1992.

Appendix-1

Extracts from *The Task Force on Panchayati Raj*, Planning Commission, New Delhi, 2001

Status of Panchayati Raj Institutions in the Country

The passage of the 73rd Constitution Amendment Act, 1992 marks a new era in the federal democratic set up of the country and provides Constitutional status to the PRIs. The main features of the Act are: (i) constitution of panchayats at village, intermediate (block) and district level; however, panchayats at the intermediate level may not be constituted in a State having a population not exceeding twenty lakh; (ii) regular elections to Panchayats; (iii) reservation of seats for Scheduled Castes/ Scheduled Tribes and Women (33%); (iv) setting up of an independent State Finance Commission for strengthening finances of local bodies at all levels; (v) constitution of an independent State Election Commission to hold PRIs elections on a regular basis; (vi) legal status to Gram Sabhas; and (vii) addition of Eleventh Schedule to the Constitution listing 29 Subjects within the jurisdiction of PRIs. Further, the 73rd Constitutional Amendment Act contains provisions for devolution of powers and responsibilities upon panchayats at the appropriate level with reference to (a) the preparation of plans for economic development and social justice; and (b) the implementation of such schemes for economic development and social justice, as may be entrusted to them. The Provision of the Panchayat (Extension to Scheduled Areas) Act 1996, (PESA) extends panchayats to tribal areas in nine States. It enables the tribal society to shape their own development and preserve and conserve their traditional rights over natural resources.

The status of PRIs in a State can be reviewed in terms of following parameters: (i) Conduct of Panchayat Elections; (ii) Devolution of Financial Powers; (iii) Devolution of Functions and Functionaries; (iv) Constitution of District Planning Committees (DPCs); (v) Act 40 of 1996 Provision of the Panchayat (Extension to Scheduled Areas) Act, 1996 (PESA); and (vi) Status and Empowerment of Gram Sabha.

Conduct of Panchayat Elections

Consequent to the enactment of the 73rd Constitutional Amendment Act, almost all the States/UTs except Arunachal Pradesh enacted appropriate legislations for setting up of strong, viable and-responsible Panchayats at different levels in their respective States. However, some States as well as Schedule VI areas in States are exempted from the purview of this enactment. Part IX of the Constitution pertaining to formation of panchayats is not applicable to the States of Jammu & Kashmir, Hill areas of Manipur, Meghalaya, Mizoram, and Nagaland. The State of Jammu & Kashmir is accorded a special status under Article 370 of the Constitution, while the States of Meghalaya, Mizoram and Nagaland are covered by the Scheduled VI of the Constitution and the traditional system of local self-government exists in these states. In the NCT of Delhi, the panchayati raj was suspended by the State Government and no effective steps have been taken to revive the PRIs till date. Each of the States/UTs has constituted the State Election Commission (SEC) to ensure elections to the PRIs once in five years.

In all the States, panchayats have been constituted according to the provisions except in the States of Arunachal Pradesh, Assam and UT of Pondicherry.

In the State of Arunachal Pradesh, the election for PRIs have not been held so far because the Panchayati Raj Bill of Arunachal Pradesh does not provide for reservation for Scheduled Castes (SCs) as this State has no indigenous SC population. The Central Government decided to exempt Arunachal Pradesh from making provisions for SCs in their Panchayati Raj Act. On 8.9.2000, the President accorded his assent on the Bill passed by the Parliament in this regard. The Government of Arunachal Pradesh has been requested to initiate appropriate steps in this regard at the earliest. The Ministry of Home Affairs has sought opinion of the Ministry of Law for according the Presidential Assent to the Arunachal Pradesh Panchayati Raj Bill, 1997. The Ministry of Law has advised to seek opinion of the Ministry of Social Justice and Empowerment. The matter is still pending.

The Assam Government enacted the Assam Panchayat Raj Act, 1994 incorporating almost all the features of the 73rd Constitutional Amendment Act, 1992. The term of Panchayats in the State expired in October 1997. However, State Government have put off the Panchayat elections several times citing different reasons such as the then ongoing Budget session 1998, subsequent monsoon rains and then law and order situation and subsequently Census operations. The State Government decided to hold election in November 2000. However passing an order on a petition filed in High Court at Guwahati, the Hon'ble High Court directed the State Government that before the notifications for elections were issued, the State Government should dispose of the Petition containing a plea for not holding Panchayat elections in Mising Autonomous Council Areas. The State Government constituted a Committee of five State Ministers to submit a report in this regard. The Union Minister for Rural Development has written to the Chief Minister of Assam to hold Panchayat elections in the State.

In Bihar, elections for Panchayats have not been held on time. On August 23, 1993, the Bihar Panchayat Raj Act, 1993, conforming to the Constitution (73rd Amendment) Act 1992 was enacted and brought into force. The Patna High Court vide their orders dated 19.3.1996, stuck down certain provision of the State Panchayati Raj Act. The State of Bihar filed Special Leave Petitions (SLPs) No. 9724-28 & 9819-25 of 1996 in the Hon'ble Supreme Court against the judgment dated 19.3.1996 of the Patna High Court. In the meantime, a PIL Writ Petition (Civil) No. 719 of 1995 filed by Rural Litigation and Entitlement Kendra against the Government of Uttar Pradesh and others come up for hearing and the above SLPs were also taken up with this Writ Petition. Thereafter, on 22.7.1997, Hon'ble Supreme Court directed that the matter should be decided by the Constitution Bench as the validity of the 73rd and 74th Amendment of the Constitution of India, vis-a-vis Bihar Panchayati Raj Act, 1993 is required to be considered for the purpose of disposing of the present SLPs. In the said Order, the Hon'ble Supreme Court observed that the matters may be placed before the Hon'ble Chief Justice of India for constitution of an Appropriate Bench for the disposal of these matters at an early date in view of the fact that Panchayat elections in Bihar can not be held until these matters are disposed of. On a petition filed by the Union of India, the Supreme Court clarified that there is no bar in holding Panchayat elections in Bihar in accordance with the prevailing law subject to the final disposal of pending SLPs. In pursuance of these Orders, the panchayat elections in State were held in April 2001.

Panchayat elections have not been held in Pondicherry, as the validity of provisions relating to reservation for backward classes in the Pondicherry Panchayati Raj Act were sub-judice. Judgement of the Chennai High Court has become available and the UT Administration has filed a clarificatory application in the Chennai High Court. On a similar issue pertaining to Tamil Nadu, the Hon'ble High Court at Chennai had passed orders making it possible for Tamil Nadu Government to hold elections. The MORD have advised the LIT Administration to take appropriate action to hold Panchayat elections at the earliest on the same lines. The UT Administration has not yet intimated the steps taken in this regard.

In the three new States, it is reported that elections to panchayats will be held by November 2001 in Jharkhand, and by December 2001 in Uttranchal. In Chhattisgarh, the panchayat elections were held in January 2000 and next round of elections will be due in 2005.

So far, about 2,32,278 panchayats at the village level, 5905 panchayats at the intermediate level and 499 panchayats at the district level have been constituted in the country. These Panchayats are being manned by 2.92 million elected representatives at all levels, of which one-third are women. This is the broadest representative base that exists in any country in the world.

Elections to PRIs on expiry of their first term have been held in the States of Haryana, Himachal Pradesh, Karnataka, Kerala, Madhya Pradesh, Rajasthan and Uttar Pradesh.

Devolution of Financial Powers to PRIs

Article 243 I of the Constitution provides for the constitution of a State Finance Commission (SFC) to review the financial position of Panchayats and to make recommendations regarding principles governing (a) distribution between the State and the Panchayats of the net proceeds of taxes, duties, tolls and fees leviable by the State; (b) determination of the taxes, duties, tolls and fees which may be assigned to, or appropriated by the Panchayats; (c) the grants-in-aid to the Panchayats from the

Consolidated fund of the State; (d) the measures needed to improve the financial position of the Panchayats; and (e) any other matter referred to the Finance Commission in the interests of sound finance of the Panchayats. The present status of the State Finance Commission is given in the Table-1.

Table-1 Status of First State Finance Commission

Status of SFC	*Name of States*
Constitution of SFC	All States except Arunachal Pradesh &NCT of Delhi
Submission of SFC Report	All States except Bihar
Report accepted in full	Himachal Pradesh, Kerala, Madhya Pradesh, Manipur, Punjab, Rajasthan, Tamil Nadu, Tripura, Uttar Pradesh and West Bengal
Report accepted in parts	Andhra Pradesh, Assam, Haryana, Karnataka, Maharashtra
Accepted with modifications	Orissa
Report under consideration	Goa, A&N Islands, Daman & Diu, Lakshdweep, Pondicherry
Report yet to be placed before Legislature	Gujarat

Source: Ministry of Rural Development, Government of India

The recommendations of the State Finance Commissions can be divided into three categories: (i) assignment of taxes, duties, levies and tolls to local bodies; (ii) sharing of revenue proceeds; and (iii) transfers on account of grants-in-aid and other financial assistance. The major recommendations of first SFCs with respect to devolution of taxes, grants and PRI's own taxes-Statewise, are given at Annexure-III.

Devolution of Functions and Functionaries

According to Article 243 (G) of the 73rd Constitutional Amendment Act, the States are required to devolve adequate powers and responsibilities on the PRIs in order to make them effective institutions of local self-government. The responsibility for preparation of Plans for economic development and social justice and its implementation in relation to 29 Subjects listed in the Eleventh Schedule have also been assigned to Panchayats. The List of 29 Subjects is given at Annexure-III. The State Governments are expected to place the functions of Departments dealing with these 29 Subjects including the officials, under the control of the Panchayats.

In view of this, the functional autonomy of PRIs along with their financial autonomy must be clearly delineated. Even in respect of the 29 Subjects identified in the Eleventh Schedule it is necessary for the State Governments to clearly identify what would be done by the different tiers of panchayats at each level. This should be based on the rule that what can be done at the lower level should be done at that level only and not at a higher level. Detailed instructions and guidelines would have to be issued by the concerned departments to their field officers in this regard. Furthermore, departmental functionaries required to implement the programmes at the panchayat level must be placed under their overall supervision and control. In States like Karnataka, Kerala, Maharashtra, Madhya Pradesh, Orissa, Rajasthan, Sikkim, Tamil Nadu, Tripura, Uttar Pradesh and West Bengal detailed instructions in this regard have already been issued and in several cases departmental functionaries have been placed with the panchayats. The Statewise position of devolution of funds, functions and functionaries to the PRIs is given at Annexure IV.

The State Governments of Madhya Pradesh, Uttar Pradesh, and Rajasthan have made considerable progress regarding devolution of three Fs i.e. function, functionaries and funds. Some of the recent initiatives taken by them are highlighted in Boxes 1 to 3.

Box-1: Panchayati Raj in Madhya Pradesh

- Activities of governance and development have been clearly demarcated between Panchayat Sector and the State Sector.
- 18 Subjects/Departments have been transferred to the Panchayati Raj Institutions (PRIs).
- All district and sub-district level officers and employees in respect of programmes transferred to PRIs are placed under control of PRIs at the appropriate level.
- Greater coordination among the three tiers through representation of 1/5 sarpanchs to Janpad Panchayat, Janpad Panchayat Adhyakshas to Zilla Parishad.
- Gram Panchayats are empowered to sanction development works upto Rs. Three lakhs, Janpad Panchayats upto Rs. Seven lakhs, while Zilla Panchayat upto Rs. Ten lakhs.
- Merger of District Rural Development Agencies (DRDAs) with Zilla Panchayats.

- Gram Panchayats recruit the Panchayat karmi designated as Secretaries. Shiksha Karmis are appointed by Janpad Panchayats and Zilla Parishad. No recruitment by State Government to 'dying cadres'.
- Budgetary allocations for transferred programmes/subjects are made available to PRIs. From 2000-01, tier-wise and district wise provision would be made in the Budget to ensure efficient flow of resources to PRIs.
- Greater transparency in selection of beneficiaries and implementation of programme through social audit by strengthening the Gram Sabha/Panchayat in the State. For instance, no technical evaluation required for Jawahar Gram Samaridhi Yojana (JGSY) (old JRY) works. Quality and utility of works subjected to social audit through Gram Sabhas.
- First and only State to introduce the concept of "Right to Recall" of elected representatives at Gram Panchayats once in their tenure for greater accountability to the Gram Sabha.

The Madhya Pradesh Government has also recently amended its Panchayati Raj Act. The amended Act provides for setting up of Standing functions. Duties and responsibilities of the gram panchayat in the area assigned to them are clearly defined and continue to devolve on them. The gram sabhas in the exercise of duties and responsibilities would have the benefit of Standing Committees which would be set up by the gram sabha itself by a process laid down by law, fully taking into account reservation for SC, ST and women and would supplement and strengthen the institutional framework available in the system.

Box-2: Recent Initiatives Taken by Government of Uttar Pradesh for Empowerment of PRIs

With a view to bring about a sustained process of decentralisation and people's participation, the State Government has devolved a large number of functions and powers to Panchayats.

New Responsibilities Assigned to Gram Panchayats:

- Functions and functionaries of eleven departments i.e. Education-primary, upper primary and non-formal education centres, State Tubewells, Handpumps, Youth Welfare, Medical and Health, Women and Child Development, Animal Husbandry, Fair Price Shops, Agriculture, Rural Development and Panchayats transferred to them.

- Identification of beneficiaries and disbursement of pensions and scholarships. Funds for works, maintenance of assets, and for payment of salaries and honorarium to teachers and Gram Panchayat Vikas Adhikaris.
- Transfer four percent of the State's total tax revenue directly to the Gram Panchayats which resulted in an unprecedented increase in the funds from Rs. 20 crore in 1996-97 to Rs. 328 crore in 1999-2000. Apart from this, funds out of the rural development schemes and Tenth Finance Commission Award have also been transferred directly to Gram Panchayats.
- Empowered Gram Panchayats to collect irrigation tax from State Tubewells and to impose surcharge on land revenue.
- For transparency in functioning, the villagers are entitled to obtain a copy of any document of Gram Panchayat at the nominal fee.
- Mandatory for Gram Panchayats to hold minimum one meeting every month.
- In case of Women Pradhans, husbands/male relatives were not allowed to attend the meeting by proxy.
- The works entrusted to gram panchayats will be done through six committees namely Planning and Development Committee, Education Committee, Construction Work Committee, Health and Welfare Committee, Administrative Committee and Water Management Committee.

Responsibilities Handed Over to Kshetra Panchayats:

- Functions and functionaries pertaining to Rural Development, Primary Health Centres, Veterinary hospitals, Seeds Stores and Marketing Godowns.
- Ten per cent share in the amount devolved to the local bodies out of the State's tax receipt provided to them.

- Six Subject Committees namely Planning and Development Committee, Education Committee, Construction Work Committee, Health and Welfare Committee, Administrative Committee and Water Management Committee will execute all works.

Empowerment of Zilla Panchayats

- Zilla Panchayat Chief in place of District Magistrate will be the Chairman of the District Rural Development Agency (DRDA).
- The governing body of DRDA will now comprises of Chairpersons of six Standing Committees of Zilla Panchayat and fifty per cent of the-Pramukhs.
- A separate officer designated as Chief Officer will be posted in place of District Magistrate for development works implemented by the DRDA/Zilla Panchayat.

The Government of Kerala has transferred Agriculture, Health, Veterinary and Primary Education Departments to the Panchayats. About 40,590 staff, moveable and immovable properties have also been transferred to the Panchayats. The Government of Kerala however continues to pay the salaries of the staff.

Box-3: Recent Initiatives taken by the Rajasthan Government

The Government of Rajasthan has also recently transferred nine schemes, were earlier being implemented by DRDAs, to the Zilla Parishad with effect from 1.4.1999. It has also set up a Village Level Standing Committee for each village under the Chairmanship of Sarpanch of the Gram Panchayat to act as "watch dog". It will keep watch an the absenteeism of grassroots functionaries of the departments, namely Patwari, Teachers, ANMS, MPW, VLW, Anganwadi workers and Compounder etc posted in rural areas. Primary and Upper Primary Education, Literacy and Continuing Education, Rajiv Gandhi Scheme for Restoration of Traditional Drinking Water Sources, Rajiv Gandhi Swam Jayanti Pathshalas will be implemented by the PRIs. Further, innovative projects like Lok Jumbish, Shiksha Karmi and District Primary Education Programme (DPEP) have also been brought under the umbrella of the Panchayati Raj Department.

In the case of Gujarat, Maharashtra and Karnataka, devolution of three Fs stops at district level; the devolution to the lower tiers is minimal. In State like Andhra Pradesh, the State Government is implementing even a decentralised programme like Janmabhoomi programme mainly through bureaucratic apparatus, which is against the spirit of 73rd Constitutional Amendment Act. It has a content of people's participation and social mobilization, but it bypasses the panchayati raj bodies and in fact this programme poses a serious challenge to the system of Panchayati Raj due to its poor involvement in this programme. The State Government of Haryana had set up Village Development Committees (VDCs), which negates the provisions of 73rd Constitutional Amendment Act regarding reservation of SC, women and seems to replace the elected gram panchayat. The detail of these VDCs is given at Annexure V.

Constitution of District Planning Committees (DPCs)

The State Governments are required to constitute District Planning Committees (DPCs) as envisaged under Article 243 (ZD) of 74th Constitutional Amendment Act to facilitate the process of decentralised planning. DPCs are to be set up in each district to prepare composite plans covering both urban and rural areas. Despite passage of more than seven years, many States are yet to constitute the DPCs. Only eleven States, namely, Haryana (only in 4 Districts), Karnataka (in 18 out of 27 districts), Kerala, Madhya Pradesh, Manipur (in 2 out of 4 districts), Rajasthan, Sikkim, Tamil Nadu, Tripura, Uttar Pradesh and West Bengal. Among Union Territories, only Andaman & Nicobar Islands, Lakshadweep have constituted DPCs. Chandigarh is not in favour of setting up of DPC as 90% of population is covered by municipality. However, this argument is not valid as DPCs are to cover both urban and rural areas. No information is available about the actual operationalisation of DPCs in the States. The formation of DPCs must receive top priority by the State Governments, as it is only then that planning would genuinely begin from the grassroots.

The review of the formation of DPCs in the State revealed some aberrations, For instance, in the State of Madhya Pradesh, Tripura, Uttar Pradesh Minister is the Chairman of the DPCs while in Tamil Nadu, the Collector heads the DPCs.

To facilitate the preparation of the Plans at the district level, a core planning team comprising of experts from various disciplines needs to be formed for each district which could help in the preparation of plans keeping in view the physical and natural resource endowments of the area, availability of funds and the priorities of the people. In addition, experts could be hired on a consultancy basis if expertise is required in a specific area. In Kerala, a Voluntary Technical Corps (VTC) has been created consisting of about 10,000 experts to vet and re-work projects prepared by the Panchayats. These include retired persons with technical expertise, bank personnel and officials of government departments. Similarly, in other States, voluntary groups and institutions need to be identified for providing services, training and support for effective implementation of programmes at the local level. The Kerala model for people's campaign for decentralised planning to empower the local bodies to prepare their plans in a transparent and participatory manner could be replicated in other States. The details of Kerala Model are given in Box-4.

Box-4: People's Planning Campaign in Kerala.

The People's Planning Campaign has succeeded in providing a concrete methodology for participatory planning for local level development. The roots of the methodology can be traced back to an experiment carried in Kalliassery Panchayat of Kannur District in the early 90s. In 1996, it was modified and adapted for large scale application. The salient features of this methodology are described below, stage-by-stage.

1. **Needs Identification:** Through a meeting of Gram Sabha i.e. the ward or the electoral constituency of a village panchayat member, the felt needs of the community are identified. There is a period of environment creation to mobilize maximum participation in the Gram Sabha. Statistics reveal that about 10-12% of the rural population has participated in the Gram Sabhas held as part of the People's Planning Campaign. The Gram Sabha meetings are held in a semi structured manner with plenary sessions and sub group sessions dealing with specific developmental issues. The decisions are minuted and forwarded to the Panchayats. Each Gram Sabha is chaired by the elected member and has an official as its Coordinator.

2. **Situation Analysis:** Based on the demands emanating from the first special Gram Sabha and based on developmental data, both primary and secondary exhaustive Development

Reports have been prepared and printed in the case of every PRI in the State. These reports describe the status in each sector of development with reference to available data, analyse the problems and point out the directors for further development. This is an one-time exercise and the Reports will be revised before the next five year plan.

3. **Strategy Setting:** Based on the Gram Sabha feed back and the Development Report, a one day seminar is held at the PRI level in which participation of experts, elected members, representatives nominated by Gram Sabhas, practitioners from among the public is ensured. The development seminars suggest the broad priorities and general strategies of development projects to be taken up for a particular year.

4. **Projectisation:** The ideas thrown up by the above three stages are translated in the form of projects by Task Forces at the PRI level. For each PRI, there are about 12 Task Forces dealing with different sectors of development. Each Task Force is headed by an elected member and is convened by the concerned Government official. The Vice Chairman of the Task Force is normally a non-government expert in the sector. The projects are prepared in the suggested format outlining the objectives, describing the benefits, explaining the funding and detailing the mode of execution and phasing of the project.

5. **Plan Finalisation:** From among the projects, based on the allocation communicated, the concerned PRI finalises its plan for the year and this plan is submitted to the DPCs through the Expert Committees. The Panchayat is free to take up any project, irrespective of its cost, subject of course to the resources actually available and within the sectoral limits.

6. **Plan Vetting:** The Expert Committee at the Block or the District level vet the projects for their technical viability and conformity with the mandatory government guidelines on planning and costing and forward them to the DPC. They cannot change priorities or projects; they can only ask for rectification.

7. **Plan Approval:** The DPC gives the formal approval to the plans after which the PRI can start implementation. It is to be noted that the DPC also cannot change the priority of a PRI. It can only ensure that government guidelines are followed. Administrative approval for implementation is given project wise by the PRI. Every PRI has unlimited powers of administrative sections subject only to the limits of its financial resources.

The Campaign is facilitated by about 650 Key Resource Persons at the State level, about 10,000 District Resource Persons and about 100,000 Local Resource Persons (100 per Village Panchayat)-all of them trained on the basics.

Provision of the Panchayat (Extension to Scheduled Areas), Act, 1996-Central Act 40, 1996

The Provisions of the Panchayats (Extension to the Scheduled Areas) Act, 1996 came into force on 24th December 1996. The Act extends Panchayats to the tribal areas of nine States, viz; Andhra Pradesh, Chhattisgarh, Gujarat, Himachal Pradesh, Jharkhand, Maharashtra, Madhya Pradesh, Orissa and Rajasthan. The Act strives to enable tribal society to shape their own development and to preserve & conserve their traditional rights over natural resources.

All States barring Jharkhand have enacted State Legislation to give effect to the provisions contained in Act 40, 1996 as mandated under the Central Act.

The Central Act 40, inter-alia, provides the definition of a 'Village', powers and functions of the Gram Sabha/Panchayat in the Scheduled Areas. It prohibits the Panchayats at the higher level to assume the powers and authority of Panchayats at lower level. As per the Act, the powers of the Gram Sabha/Panchayat at the appropriate level can be divided into following categories viz; (i) Mandatory Powers; (ii) Powers to be consulted; (iii) Powers to be devolved by the State Governments to the Gram Sabhas/Panchayats to enable them to function as institutions of selfgovernment.

The State wise (excluding Chhattisgarh and Jharkhand) position of operation of powers under the Central Act 40 is given at Annexure VI.

Status and Empowerment of Gram Sabha

Article 243 (b) of the Constitution defines Gram Sabha as consisting of all persons registered as voters in the electoral roll relating to the village within the area of the panchayat at the village level. Article 243 (A) states that the Gram Sabha may exercise such powers and perform such functions at the village level as the legislature of a State may, by law, provide.

A survey of various State Acts reveals certain common features. Most State Acts have vested in the gram sabha the responsibility of supervising and monitoring the functioning of the gram panchayats. For instance, the gram sabhas are enjoined to examine the statement of accounts and audit reports. The second (almost universal) set of functions is the approval of plans, selection of schemes, its location and beneficiaries under it. The other functions include-consideration of budget and tax proposals, administrative report regarding implementation of schemes/ programmes and other activities of panchayat. In most cases, these functions have been vested as a result of the insistence by the Central Government that all works and beneficiaries for the schemes sponsored by the Ministry of Rural Development be approved by the Gram Sabha. Many State laws also contain general exhortations which are in the nature of expectations that the Gram Sabha would mobilise voluntary labour contribution in cash or kind for community welfare programmes, render assistance in the implementation of development schemes and services in villages; undertake programmes in adult education and family welfare within the village and promote unity and harmony among all sections of society. However, in many States, gram sabhas have not been given the final decision making powers. They only recommend/give proforma approval.

The State Governments of Bihar, Kerala, Madhya Pradesh, Maharashtra, Orissa, Tamil Nadu and Uttar Pradesh, made mandatory to hold gram sabha meetings four times in a year. In Andhra Pradesh, Goa, Gujarat, Haryana, Himachal Pradesh, Karnataka, Manipur, Punjab, Rajasthan, Sikkim, West Bengal and Lakshadweep, gram sabhas meet twice in a year whereas in Tripura, gram sabha meeting is held only once in a year. Most State Governments/UTs have prescribed a quorum for the gram sabha meetings. For instance, Governments of Bihar, Goa, Karnataka, Manipur, Orissa, Rajasthan, Sikkim, Tamil Nadu and UTs of Daman & Diu and Lakshadweep have fixed quorum as one-tenth of members. The other States have imposed different percentages of quorum and certain other conditions for fixing quorum.

Under Central Act 40 of 1996 comprehensive powers have been vested in the gram sabhas/gram panchayats in the Scheduled Areas of the nine States. The scope of these powers is not dependent on any legislative action by the State Governments. Gram Sabhas in Scheduled V areas have clear cut role in managing natural and community resource in addition to development planning and its implementation. Ownership rights of Minor Forest Produce (MFP) have been vested in the gram sabha and panchayats. The gram sabha was also viewed as the body that would protect the traditions and customs of tribal societies. Although 'contours' of powers of gram sabha need not be defined afresh, State Governments are required to amend existing subject laws in consonance with the provisions of the Central Act 40 of 1996.

However, if one looks critically at legislative provisions across the country one will find that the gram sabha has, by and large, been given very little importance. For instance (i) Provisions doing away with the need for quorum for adjourned meetings of the Gram Sabha reinforce the tendency to view Gram Sabha meetings as a mere formality; (ii) State laws set out highly ritualistic functions to be exercised by gram sabhas. For example, gram sabhas are to recommend and suggest to consider annual accounts, administration reports, audit notes, etc. These suggestions and recommendations of the gram sabha can be ignored by the gram panchayat; (iii) There are, at the same time, heavy expectations from this weak and powerless gram sabha it is expected to promote harmony and unity in the village, to mobilise voluntary labour and contribution in kind, to promote programmes for adult education and family welfare; (iv) It must be acknowledged that some State Acts provide for powers to the gram sabhas to identify beneficiaries-for instance the Panchayati Raj Acts of Punjab, Rajasthan, Uttar Pradesh, Karnataka and Bihar do vest powers in the gram sabhas to select beneficiaries. But in some cases strange qualifications have been added. For instance, the Rajasthan law provides that in case the gram sabha is unable to select the beneficiaries in a reasonable time, the gram panchayat shall identify them. This provision expresses lack of faith in the gram sabha while at the same time it also permits to be undermined, Here, one must take note of the legal provisions in Madhya Pradesh and Kerala, which makes the advice of gram sabha binding on the gram panchayat. In the tiny UT of Andaman and Nicobar islands, the Gram Sabha has been made a body corporate having perpetual succession and a common seal. However, the powers and duties of the Gram Sabha are to be exercised by the gram panchayat, except as otherwise expressly provided; (vi) the membership of a gram sabha varies widely from State to State from 250 to 8,000. It may be confined to a single village or may span 2-3 villages. Where the gram sabha covers more than one village-the meetings of the gram sabha are qualitatively very poor. The provisions of the 73rd Constitutional Amendment Act do not recognize that the very size of a Panchayat may work to disempower a gram sabha.

However, despite all these shortcomings, there are several examples of how the dedicated/committed, enlightened Sarpanches have transformed their villages into selfreliant ones. Some illustrations of successful Gram Sarpanches are given in the Annexure-VII.

Of late, however, as a result of several initiatives of the Central Government in partnership with State Governments-a view has emerged which favours strengthening of Gram Sabhas as the bedrock of democracy at the grass roots level. This view found its expression in the declaration of the year 1999-2000 as the "Year of the Gram Sabha".

Gram Sabha is not only an institution articulating the needs and aspirations of the community but also a method of mobilizing community participation. While gram sabhas check against abuse of powers by the panchayat, they can assist the very same panchayats to implement development programmes. Gram sabhas are supposed to act as watchdog to protect community interests and common property resources.

To make Panchayati Raj Institutions effective bedrock of democracy, gram sabha should be given a greater role in managing financial resources given to panchayats in addition to the routine functions. Further, PRIs particularly gram sabhas can facilitate the governance structure in the country as gram sabha could be an effective forum where elected representatives of panchayats and higher tier of government can explain their plan of action/development strategies and get spontaneous feedback on implementation of the programmes. The higher tier of panchayats; as well as State Governments may depute an official to attend the gram sabha meeting, to record gram sabha's views and to report to appropriate level of government to take remedial measures wherever necessary. The gram sabha, if regularly held, can become an effective forum of accountability not only for elected gram panchayat members but also for the elected representatives of the higher tiers where they could be compelled to explain to the people their past performance and future action plan for development. The existence of gram sabha/panchayats help in the process of social audit. Gram Sabha can evaluate the work carried out by panchayats and judge their quality, effectiveness and conformity with accepted norms. PRIs can also ensure wide publicity for their activities among the people through the gram sabha. Activities of various NGOs/CBOs working at the village level can be effectively monitored by insisting on their close cooperation with the gram sabha.

Agenda of Gram Sabha meetings must transcend the presently limited jurisdiction of Gram Panchayats. At present, gam sabhas attract only the potential 'beneficiaries'. The Stales/UTs must devolve more powers upon panchayats, particularly gram panchayats and remove provisions which undermine gram panchayats/gram sabhas. Gram Sabhas also have to learn to define their own agenda and seek local solutions. Further, States could extend powers enjoyed by gram sabha in Scheduled areas to the gram sabha in non-scheduled areas to make them the real fulcrum of the panchayati raj system.

Accountability, transparency, in the functioning of panchayati raj bodies, is some of the requisite factors for the success of the panchayati raj system. Panchayats being closer to the people, peoples' right to information and accessibility to the panchayats must be ensured. To ensure transparency and accountability in operation of these bodies, the State Governments may issue orders highlighting following factors: (i) PRIs should display all vital information pertaining to development projects especially receipt of funds and how they are being spent, in the panchayats offices for the information of the public. (ii) All relevant records should be opened to inspection. (iii) Members of public should also, be able to obtain photocopies of documents pertaining to development projects as also matters of general public interest by paying a nominal charges.

The challenge before the different stakeholders is to make the PRIs true representatives of local self government. A strong and vibrant Gram Sabha is the only bullwork against corruption, embezzlement of funds and exclusion of the poor and marginalized from the decision making process. Concerted efforts, therefore, are required to make Gram Sabhas the hub of all activities in our villages.

Empowerment of PRIs/Gram Sabha

In Budget Speech 1999-2000, Finance Minister had announced that to ensure that funds under wage employment programmes are spent with active involvement of the elected PRIs, 80 percent of the funds would be released to implementing agencies as per normal procedure, the remaining 20 percent will be released as an incentive only if the State has put in place elected and empowered PRIs in the State.

Pursuant to this, the Ministry of Rural Development has evolved a Panchayati Raj Devolution Index which consist of five parameters viz:

(i) Constitutional and Political Devolution (PD)

(ii) Administrative Devolution (AD)

(iii) Financial Devolution (FID)

(iv) Functional Devolution (FLID)

(v) Devolution to Gram Sabhas (EGS)

The Devolution Index (DI) can be computed on the basis of following methodology:

DI = (PD+AD+FID+FUD+EGS)/5

The Devolution Index would help us to know the extent of devolution of three Fs, i.e., Functions, Functionaries and Funds and administrative devolution to the PRIs in the States.

International Organisations views about decentralisation in India

International organizations like the World Bank and the UNDP have also recognized the role of the decentralisation for good governance. The World Bank has realized that India is the only country where democratic decentralisation at grassroots level is going on in the true sense in light of 73rd and 74th Constitutional Amendment Acts. The World Bank, in its Report 2000 Attacking Poverty-Part 11 has reported (refer Box-5) that decentralisation is pro-poor and increases the efficiency in the implementation and effectiveness of the programmes meant for the poor. However, the Bank has still to incorporate the role of PRIs in the design of its project.

Box 5: Is Decentralisation Pro-Poor?

- Democracy is valuable for human well being, in that political rights and civil liberties have an intrinsic, instrumental, and constructive value for human well being. State institutions are often accused of being too remote from the daily realities of poor people's lives. One recommendation for making them more pro-poor is to bring them closer to these realities through decentralisation.

- Decentralisation does indeed have enormous potential to benefit the poor. Development programmes can be more effective in meeting local needs if they can draw on the advantages of local information, local accountability, and local monitoring. Decentralisation has a strong potential for increasing, and sometimes formalizing, popular participation in civic processes, including by the poor. Effectively implemented, decentralisation has the potential not only to improve immediate development outcomes but also to be the driver for broader institutional changes, which benefit and empower the poor.

- Political participation directly improves the lives of the poor by increasing distributional equity and reducing the potential for civic conflict. Case studies of the Indian State of Kerala and elsewhere have shown that participation and public debate on values may contribute to improved social outcomes in education and health.

- Greater local control can help funds to be used more effectively for meeting local needs. Fiscal devolution gives communities the flexibility to design and implement projects without the cumbersome procurement procedures of Central Government. Fiscal decentralisation has been shown as having positive outcomes for governance. Fiscal devolution needs to be accompanied by some form of redistribution from the Central budget, to avoid exacerbating inequalities between regions. Decentralisation needs to be accompanied by enough fiscal devolution to enable local authorities to plan their activities effectively.

- A better use of local information through decentralisation can be advantageous in several ways:-(i) Local information can help in identifying more effective and efficient ways of building infrastructure or providing public services and subsequently of organizing their operation and maintenance; (ii) It can increase the efficiency of regulatory functions that are more easily performed at the local level with the help of local information and peer monitoring: and (iii) The increased flow of information from the local area to government officials increases government awareness of local needs and early warning of emergencies.

- Further decentralisation can increase accountability and transparency:-(i) local monitoring can be very effective for ensuring that officials perform diligently. Sanctions can also be imposed on defaulting or free-riding community members. Community sanctions are hard to ignore because of the longstanding relationships involved. The close interactions and relations of trust within communities can help make development projects more sustainable. The combination of local information and ability to impose sanctions makes local monitoring and supervision more effective and cheaper for many types of projects and programmes than national level monitoring; (ii) decentralisation makes it easier for people to obtain information on budgets and on the use of funds, thus increasing the transparency of public actions and reducing corruption. In addition to increasing awareness of budget constraints and the need to shape political demands accordingly, this kind of decentralisation helps communities hold local leaders accountable for performance

- Greater accountability and community participation help improve programmes and service delivery like curbing absenteeism among school teachers in India. The decentralisation in West Bengal has improved participation representation of the poor and responsiveness of the state bureaucracy to the poor and have direct positive impact on growth, equity and human development.

Source: World Development Report 2000 Attacking Poverty Part-II-Empowerment.

Appendice-2

Extracts from the New Horizons for West Bengal's Panchayats; A Report for the Government of West Bengal, Government of West Bengal, Kolkata, Conceptual Dimensions

Self-Government as Policy

3.1 The fundamental question before the Panchayats everywhere in the country has, for long, been whether they are there for development functions only or for the wider purpose of self-government. Article 40 of the Constitution explicitly visualizes self-government for village panchayats. The relatively limited notion of development came in with the Balwantray Mehta Report, 1957. Going refreshingly beyond its terms of reference, the Mehta Team recommended democratic decentralisation to a three-tier panchayat structure, but this would handle development work only. Seen against the provisions of Article 40, panchayats were no longer to be confined to the village level, but their functions were to be restricted to less than self-government. The recommended pattern was, with some variations here and there, adopted by most of the states, including West Bengal. It was also persisted with in the Ashoke Mehta Report, 1978, although a nominal bow was made to self-government in an annexure containing a draft Constitution amendment bill.

3.2 In his dissenting note to the A. Mehta Report, E.M.S. Namboodiripad stated: "Democracy at the Central and State levels, but bureaucracy at all lower levels-this is the essence of Indian policy as spelt out in the Constitution...I cannot think of the Panchayati Raj Institutions as anything other than the integral parts of the country's administration with no difference between what are called the 'development' and 'regulatory' functions...I am afraid that the ghost of the earlier idea that Panchayati Raj Institutions should be completely divorced from all regulatory functions and made to confine themselves only to developmental functions is haunting my colleagues." He set the goal as follows: "What is required is that, while certain definite fields of administration like defence, foreign affairs, currency, communication, etc. should rest with the Centre, all the rest should be transferred to the States and from there to the district and lower levels of elected administrative bodies". It seems to us that this was a plea for going beyond development to self-government, although that expression was not used.

3.3 The Constitution (73rd Amendment) Act defines Panchayats to mean self-government to which State legislatures are required by law, to endow "powers and authority as are necessary to enable them to function as (such)". However, it also on to say that "such law may contain provisions for the devolution of powers and responsibilities upon Panchayats at the appropriate level" with respect to-

"(a) the preparation of plans for economic development and social justice;

(b) the implementation of schemes for economic development and social justice as may be entrusted to them including those in relation to the matters listed in the Eleventh Schedule."

The Eleventh Schedule contains 14 items,. all in the field of development. Does this later portion abridge the rights of the State legislatures down to development functions only? Or does the earlier portion have overriding force, enabling any power or authority to be endowed if it is considered necessary for self-government?

3.4 Our own view is that it is entirely within the competence of the State legislatures to decide what powers and authority the Panchayats should have in order that function as credible institutions of self-government. This was the Constitutional position all along; the Amendment has served to reaffirm it. The introduction of the development motif in the Amendment, perhaps, limits the competence of the legislatures only in the sense of indicating the minimum that each 'State legislature should transfer to the Panchayats. There is, in other words, a floor but no ceiling. How far above the floor a particular State may go is a question of policy for that State, bearing in mind that the Panchayats from now on are (1) Constitutional bodies and (2) institutions of self-government.

3.5 The West Bengal Panchayat Act, 1973 makes no mention of self-governance. Its preamble reads: "Whereas it is expedient to reorganize Panchayats in rural areas of West Bengal and to provide for matters connected therewith". This is a piece of meaningless legal jargon. The powers and duties of the Panchayats are elaborately set out in Chapter III, IX and XIV for the different levels. They are largely developmental, some municipal and a few absurdly trivial such as the destruction of rabbits and ownerless dogs. There is nothing to suggest that the concept of self-government has informed the listing of powers and duties at the three levels. The general perception among all the concerned parties, whether it is the Panchayats or the district bureaucracy or the people, is also far removed from self-government. All are locked in the belief that the Panchayats are meant primarily for development. Perhaps that holds true for many of the political and bureaucratic functionaries at the State level also.

3.6 It certainly does not hold true for the political leadership of the Left Front parties, for otherwise these parties would not have voted for he 73rd Amendment. But if self-governing Panchayats is what they have in mind, something has to be done to close the gap between that and the reality as embodied in the State legislation and as obtaining in ground level perceptions. First and foremost, that must mean a clear enunciation of policy that the fundamental objective of the Panchayats is self-government at each level. This must be followed up by seeing to it that the policy is effectively communicated to the Panchayats, the district bureaucracy and, above all, the people. A good deal of education will be called for within the State government also. Thirdly, there must be a comprehensive overhaul of the Panchayat law, not simply to bring it in line with the 73rd amendment, but more importantly to give centrality to the principle of self-government. West Bengal was first off the mark with political Panchayats. It is well placed now to do the same with self-governing Panchayats.

Self-Government and Autonomy

3.7 The implications of a policy favouring self-government for the Panchayats need to be gone into thoroughly so that the policy is correctly propagated and adequately incorporated in the law of the State. Before doing so, we have tried to clear our minds about terms like powers, authority, responsibilities, duties and functions when used with reference to levels of governance. The Constitution prefers the term 'power', and delimits the 'powers' of the Union and the States in the legislative and executive spheres. However, the 73rd Amendment requires the States to endow Panchayats 'powers and authority' for self-government. The same Amendment also suggests that the States devolve 'powers and responsibilities' for specified development items. The West Bengal Panchayat Act uses the term 'powers and duties'. Namboodiripad, quated above, found 'functions' good enough to express himself. We feel uncomfortable with the terms 'authority' and 'duties', both suggestive of command structures, like the authoritarian Emergencey which brought fundamental duties into the Constitution. The terms 'functions' is entirely acceptable; 'powers' and 'responsibilities' come with it anyway.

3.8 The literal meaning of self-government is autonomy or government without outside interference. But obviously the Panchayats cannot enjoy full autonomy, set as they are within the State of West Bengal. Nor can the State, placed as they are within the Indian Union. What the 73rd amendment has done is to Constitutionalise three strata of governance for the country: the Union, the States and the Panchayats. In the West Bengal, the Panchayats themselves are three-tiered-ZPs for districts, PSs for blocks and GPs for village clusters. Therefore, there is now a five-layered pyramid of governance rising from the village cluster at the base to the Union at the apex. At each level below the Union there has to be an appropriate measure of autonomy. Thus self-government at a particular level means such partial autonomy as is appropriate for the level.

3.9 How much partial autonomy is appropriate for a Panchayat level is for the State legislatures to determine, a position restated by the 73rd Amendment. The West Bengal legislature has already done so in the Panchayat Act of 1973. But since it did so when self-government was not explicitly recognized as the central principle, it is necessary to review what was settled then. We had neither the competence nor the time to undertake such a review. But it seems to us that the very idea of autonomy, partial though it must be, suggests that the review should be made on the basis of entitlement from below rather than endowment form above. Consequently, GPs should be entitled, by law, to do what they can best do at their level. From the rest, PSs should similarly be entitled to do whatever they can best do. And the same for ZPs. The State Government should, thereafter, confine itself to such functions as are left over and need to be attended to only at the State level.

3.10 The functions to be performed at a particular level below the Union have to be a blend of autonomy by right and entrustment by discretion. In the case of the States, autonomy stems from the legislative and executive powers written into the Constitution, while entrustment depends on what the Union chooses in its discretion to entrust from its own functions, under Article 258 or otherwise. A similar pattern is there, in law, in the case of the Panchayats in West Bengal, with the minor difference that certain functions are 'assigned' by the State, not 'entrusted', to the Panchayats. But, whereas the autonomous functions of the States far out weigh the entrusted, the reverse is the case with the Panchayats. Their preoccupation with a handed down scheme like JRY, mentioned earlier, is illustrative of this. So is their near-total dependence on funds from above. If the Panchayats are to be self-governing in a real sense, it is essential that their functional and financial autonomy should stand out and count far more than assigned functions and devolved funds.

Self-Government and Panchayat Functions

3.11 As observed earlier, the Panchayats have so far operated mainly in the field of development. There also, they have functioned more as implementing agencies of Union and State schemes than doing things on their own. Even as implementers of such schemes, they have had to depend on departmental staff outside their control. On the face of it the Panchayats have resigned themselves to the situation but below the surface there is a great deal of dissatisfaction. Happily, many Panchayats have involved themselves in trans-developmental activity. For instance they mediate in disputes and try to solve a variety of people's problems. We were told that, as a result, fewer FIRs are now field. Police officers frequently advise disputants to seek Panchayat mediation. A Sabhapati told us that lawyers feel unhappy about the decline in their work. According to him, the prevalence of peace in the countryside bears testimony to the quality of Panchayat interventions. Another and more significant instance is that, at the request of District Magistrates (DMs), Panchayat leaders join in defusing communal and other public order situations. It is significant that in the communal violence that erupted after the destruction at Ayodhya on 6 December, 1992, Calcutta witnessed trouble but no area under the jurisdiction of the Panchayats. These positive signals are indicative of the potential in the Panchayats waiting to be released.

3.12 In our discussions with Panchayat leaders at different levels, we found that the idea of self-government was new to them, so new that their eyes had a touch of disbelief as they avidly took in its implications. But after initial hesitation, there was invariably keen discussion in which difficulties encountered in the present dispensation were elaborated and clarifications sought on what self-government would mean in practice. The point eventually came out boldly and clearly that the time had come for the DM-centric bureaucratic administration, inherited from colonial rule, to give way to people democratic self-governance. There was eager acceptance of a proposal that, though for the present law and order and related matters may remain out, all other functions performed at or below the district level should come within the self-governing scope of the Panchayats. Even in the law and order sector, there should be close cooperation between the concerned authorities and the Panchayat leadership. How the totality of functions with the Panchayats should be spread over the three tiers or divided between autonomous and assigned may be determined in the light of the principles suggested in paragraphs 3.9 and 3.10.

Self-Government and Panchayat Staff

3.13 At present, quite simply, the Panchayats have the functions and the development departments the staff. We heard numerous complaints about the cavalier attitude of the staff towards the Panchayats. So long as ZPs received substantial untied grants, the district heads of the line departments swarmed around them to get supplementary funds for their pet schemes. With that source virtually gone, things have changed. Attendance now is irregular and willing cooperation wanting, especially from the engineering departments. While at ZP level the Sabhadhipati's political clout ensures a semblance of cooperation, the situation at PS and GP levels is bad. In the key sector of agriculture, for instance, the Agriculture Development Officer (ADO) keeps his distance from the PS, his cooperation being available only by chance. A PS Karmadhyaksha is unable to call meetings of the Krishi Sech O Samabaya Sthayee Samiti because the Cooperation Inspector, who is the secretary, is rarely available. Things are worse at GP level, where officials like the Agriculture Technical Assistant (KPS) and the Health Assistant largely stay away. Expect for the vanishing tribe of old faithfuls, the chowkidars, GPs have no field staff.

3.14 The business of government is vertically arranged, with departmental hierarchies stretching from the Minister in charge of a particular portfolio at the top to the lowest departmental functionary at ground level. The Panchayats are horizontal interventions in this vertical jungle. Any hope that they would be able to secure horizontal coordination was doomed because the vertical hierarchies were too well entrenched and the Panchayats did not have even minimal administrative weaponry to bring them within their coordinating discipline. Consequently, a time-honoured device was invoked in the shape of committees for every subject. We tried to ascertain the number of such committees and also how well they worked. Jalpaiguri prepared a list in August, 1989 of 77 functioning committees, 34 of which were chaired by the Sabhadhipati, another 36 by the DM and the rest by others (see annexure 6). There have been additions since then. Our estimate is that currently there are 90 to 100 committees in every district, with the Sabhadhipati heading roughly half of them and the DM the other half. The committee system has proved to be costly, time-consuming, ineffective and inefficient.

3.15 Everywhere we went, the Panchayat members (with the solitary exception of one Sabhadhipati) were of the view that the officers and staff of the line departments should be placed squarely under the Panchayats. Thereafter, the committee system could well be substantially disbanded. The West Bengal Panchayat Act. 1973 provides, in sections 120 and 167, for placing the services of State Government officers and other employees at the disposal of PSs and ZPs. In the case of the Darjeeling Gorkha Hill Council (DGHC), the services of Government officials are made available on deputation. Deputation is a well understood term and, therefore, if staff is to be transferred to the Panchayats it would be best to do so on deputation. As to whether this should be done, we have no doubt that it should. For one thing, the present arrangement is not working well. The committee system has been tried as a measure short of transfer and has failed. By now, the Panchayats have been on probation long enough and cannot be regarded as unfit to govern. Lastly, self-government is hollow and meaningless without control over implementing staff. Therefore, development staff should be transferred in any case. When the functions of the Panchayats are enlarged, as visualized is para 3.12, other staff should follow suit.

3.16 As a policy measure, DMs were appointed part-time Executive Officers (Eos) in all ZPs to ensure that there was harmony between the pre-existing bureaucratic system and the incoming democratic

Panchayats. In practice, most DMs spare little or no time for ZPs. In 24 Parganas (South), for instance, we never set eyes on the DM. It is our impression that DMs really do not have much to do, because most development work has gone to the Panchayats and revenue and magisterial responsibilities have shrunk. They will have even less to do when the functions of the Panchayats are enlarged, vide para 3.12. Thus when DMs complain about spending much of their time attending meetings of committees, most of which should be abolished (vide para 3.15), or monitoring programmes, which should be the business of ZPs, it looks like a case of Parkinson's law coming into play: work expands to fill available time, Self-governing Panchayats, with wider functions and almost the entire district bureaucracy to look after, will need strong administrative support. For this, ZPs must have the fullest possible assistance from DMs in their role as Eos. The ZPs are the district governments of the future and it is in their performance as Eos, therefore, that DMs should henceforth be primarily assessed.

3.17 The Panchayat Act allots the EO the limited function of exercising control over the ZP's staff. But, by virtue of his title, he is in fact the chief executive of the ZP. In this capacity, he has three roles. One is to assist the ZP in formulating policies and programmes, and then in seeing to their implementation. This role will expand when the ZP's functions are enlarged, vide para 3.12. The second is to exercise control, subject to the terms of deputation, over the large body of the district bureaucracy to be transferred to the ZP, vide para 3.15, for which he should have legal sanction, if necessary by suitably amending sections 167 and 168. The third is to assist the ZP in the exercise of its general powers, under section 63, to supervise the PSs and GPs in the district. The EO's assistance would be particularly useful in administrative supervision, an aspect not at present mentioned in the afore-mentioned section. These are going to be demanding roles. It is not for nothing, therefore, that we visualize the future DM to be primarily the EO of the ZP.

3.18 He will need competent assistance. On the administrative side, there is already an Additional Executive Officer (AEO) of the rank of an ADM. At present, the post receives casual treatment. There is a high turnover through frequent transfers; vacancies are not filled for months; and the incumbent is frequently called away for other tasks as ADM. These weaknesses need to be removed. The post of AEO should no longer be viewed as a stepping stone to more important appointments elsewhere. It standing should be next only to the DM-cum-EO.

3.19 On the financial side, there is presently a vacuum. ZPs have considerable assets which are managed poorly and fetch low returns. Furthermore, money is going into items like supermarkets, industrial estates and tourist resorts, but there is no proper project appraisal and no idea of likely returns. Schemes which are bankable are instead financed from JRY and other sources on the false premise that this is more economical. Such subsidy-packed investments could be better directed to poverty alleviation. ZPs handle Rs. 20 to 30 crores per year, figures which are likely to go up with enlarged functions. What every ZP sorely needs to look after all these matters is a whole-time trained financial manager. No fresh recruitment need be resorted to. State civil service officers with the necessary aptitude should be put through specially designed courses at, say, the Indian Institute of Management, Calcutta and made available to ZPs. Even a modest reorganization of the various departments could yield a sufficient number of officers to be redeployed in ZPs.

3.20 Self-government at and below the district calls for strengthening the machinery of governance at each of three tiers. The financial manger at ZP level will need to be backed up by qualified accountants at each level. Traditional accounting should gradually give way to management accounting. A management information system (MIS) needs to be developed, so that ZPs, PSs and GPs know at any point of time what is going on under their respective charges and apply timely correctives. The present system under which the Panchayats are wholly dependent on figures supplied at the whim of staff not under their control leaves them groping in the dark. The under-utilized computers with DMs should be harnessed for Panchayat work and qualified persons put in charge. Both the preparation and the monitoring of, for example, area-specific agriculture production plans would be greatly facilitated by a well conceived MIS. None of this need involve fresh recruitment, for there is more than enough staff to spare in the total machinery of the State Government to redeploy personnel in the Panchayats after suitable training.

Self-Government and Panchayat Finances

3.21 It is axiomatic that self-government needs at least partial autonomy. Equally, autonomy needs at least partial self-reliance. However, the fact is that the Panchayats are not at all concerned about acquiring even a modicum of financial self-reliance. For instance, in an otherwise active Panchayat that we visited in Medinipore district, the PS had raised only Rs. 26,000 against Rs. 26 lakhs handled by it during the year; a mere 1% of the developed money. This is fairly typical of the general situation. The Panchayats seem to be content to remain spending agencies of money received from above. Every Panchayat that we visited prepared a performance report for benefit. In each such report, spending achievements were proudly displayed, but resource raising was not even mentioned. Such lop-sided performance, negates the very idea underlying the Panchayats, for it shows that there is near-zero self-reliance, which means near-zero autonomy and correspondingly near-zero self-government. It also makes the Panchayats highly vulnerable in the event of a changed political ambience. Furthermore, by failing to mobilize resources the Panchayats have served to increase the cost of governance at and below the district level, because now their own cost has to be added to the continuing cost of the pre-existing bureaucracy.

3.22 Our discussions with the Panchayats convinced us that, while there are constraints, it is not the case that virtually no resources can be raised. The constraints are legal, administrative and political. The Panchayat law authorizes GPs to impose taxes on property and professions under section 46 and all three tiers to levy rates and fees under sections 47, 133 and 181. The tax provisions are limited in scope and the levy provisions overlap the three tiers. It is well recognized that tax administration improves in efficiency at higher levels, which implies that there is a built-in factor of inefficiency at Panchayat levels. Politically, the closer a self-governing level is to the people the more difficult. It is for it to tax them. Notwithstanding these constraints, our admittedly non-expert eyes could see possibilities for going above near-zero levels. For instance, several GPs have assessed property at an outdated value of Rs. 500 per bigha of paddy land, and even at this low level collections are unsatisfactory. Both assessments and collections can be markedly improved up to what is bearable. Similarly, PSs can earn more from tolls on ferries and fees in *hats* and markets. Market fees are a particularly promising mode of legitimately creaming the evident growth in agricultural prosperity, once agricultural marketing is well organized (see Chapter 4).

3.23 The non-tax field also offers considerable possibilities ZPs, for example, have valuable land and buildings inherited from the old District Boards which commercially managed, could yield rich crops of revenue. So could the new assets built up such as industrial estates and tourist complexes. Social forestry, sponsored by the Panchayats, has generated assets that will keep growing and can provide GPs with steadily rising revenues. Some GPs spoke to us of earning lakhs, even crores, once trees are ready for felling. But this will need professional management, so that forest acreages are precisely recorded, inventories of trees by number and species regularly maintained and felling operations accord with properly drawn up working plans. Fishery schemes, again sponsored by the Panchayats, have also created assets which, if professionally managed and exploited, could not only benefit the fishing community but yield good revenues. As the efforts of the Panchayats keep fructifying in the shape of remunerative assets, the potential for non-tax revenues will correspondingly rise, provided there is good management.

3.24 The possibilities in regard to raising resources through local contributions could provide surprises. It is not uncommon to find instances of the people having contributed voluntarily, in the shape of land, labour and even money, to put up community assets, especially school buildings. If, therefore, schemes are taken up to provide visible benefits which meet the felt needs of village communities at their doorsteps, or within walking distance therefore, there is reason to believe that the people will be motivated to contribute generously for the capital and labour components of such schemes. We came across a striking example of this in Medinipore district where a PS has built a truckable wooden bridge across a bridge with the help of people's contributions. It is a pity that there is no means of ascertaining the magnitude of the cash equivalent of all such contributions made across the State. If there was, a truer picture of local resource raising would be observable. The short point is that local contributions, largely of a capital nature, can become major resource providers.

3.25 The foregoing paragraphs indicate that it is entirely possible for the Panchayats to climb well above the near-zero level where they are now. But it will entail moving out of the mould of "spending only". The political parties and the people need to have a new orientation, namely that the Panchayats must earn their way to autonomy and self-governing is a matter of judgement, depending in part on nature's endowment in the area. But we would suggest the following rule of thumb: every Panchayat should aim to raise at least a rupee for every rupee it gets by way of devolution from above. This would double the resources of the Panchayats. What is more, such self-raised resources would be wholly untied and thus available to be spent in accordance with each Panchayat's own priorities. The performance reports of the Panchayats should, from now on, show achievements in resource raising as well as in spending.

Self-Government and Financial Devolution

3.26 As observed earlier, the 73rd Amendment has Constitutionalised three strata of governance. In regard to financial matters, it leaves Union-States relations unchanged, but provides for State-Panchayats relations to be established through the mechanism of a finance Commission in each State. West Bengal has already amended its Panchayat Act in 1992 to incorporate the idea of a Finance Commission, though one has still to be set up. But State-Panchayats relations in the financial field have been evolving ever since the Panchayats were set up in 1978. The present position is that funds are devolved for development purposes only and the Panchayats get only a fraction of these directly. An elaborate exercise first takes place to prepare a District Plan. Thereafter, funds flow from the State along three channels. For small and non-technical schemes, they are allotted to GPs, PSs on the basis of prescribed spending ceilings. For other schemes, they are put under various budget heads and released by the respective departments to their respective district level officers, who then batch them out for district and block level use. Untied funds under the District Plans Schemes flow to the District Planning Committees (DPCs). (See Annexure 7 for details).

3.27 We tried to see how well this was working in the districts. We were told that there was hardly any relationship between the District Plans and the allocations eventually made in the State budget. Secondly, the budget does not show at one place the total amount approved for a particular district. We could not find copies of the budget in any of the districts we visited. For schemes executed by the Panchayats, funds are received in numerous unpredictable installments throughout the year, making rational implementation difficult. Salbari GP in Dhupguri PS of Jalpaiguri district, for example, received Rs. 4,26,872 in all for JRY in 1991-92. The money came in seven installments of varying amounts between 12 April, 1991 and 20 March, 1992. The Pradhan never knew how much would come and when. For how much has been allocated for what. The third channel of untied funds has almost dried up, making the district heads even more inaccessibly since the Panchayats have nothing to give them now. All in all, in guard language, the Panchayat leaders conveyed their dissatisfaction over the present arrangements for financial devolution.

3.28 The main thrusts of the States' demand for reordering Union-States financial relations are that devolution should take into account the totality of resources in the public domain, that there should be statutory (implying assured) devolutions rather than discretionary transfers, and that tying devolutions to specific purposes as in centrally sponsored schemes should go. These points apply with equal force to State-Panchayats relations. Hopefully, therefore, the State Finance Commission when appointed will keep them in mind.

3.29 For the present, bearing in mind the extended functions for the Panchayats visualized in para 3.12 and the transfer of development staff to them as contemplated in para 3.15, we would suggest the following measures:

(1) The State budget should exhibit devolutions district-wise, so that each district knows well in advance what it may expect to get. This is already being done in the case of the DGHC, and the pattern needs to be extended to the Panchayats.

(2) The scope of devolutions to the Panchayats should extend beyond a few development schemes to, not only all development activity, but also such non-development functions as are implicit in the extended responsibilities in terms of functions and staff suggested in paras 3.12 and 3.15.

(3) Instead of the complicated three-channel flow of funds, all devolutions shown in the budget for a district should be transferred *en bloc* from the Finance Department to the ZP, with such conditionalities as are deemed necessary. Ways and means compulsions may, of course, necessitate phasing out the *en bloc* transfer over the year.

(4) So long as the Union continues to impose conditionalities for centrally sponsored schemes, there is no option but to pass these on. But, for the rest, there should be minimum conditionalities, such as making funds non-transferable in the case of schemes for the Scheduled Castes (SCs) and Scheduled Tribes (STs) as also for women and children.

(5) ZPs should have the freedom to reappropriate funds between heads of accounts, subject only to the minimum conditionalities imposed under (4) above and the usual

restriction on transferring funds from non-staff to staff sub-heads.

(6) Subject to availability of resources with the State, wholly untied devolutions should be steadily enhanced.

3.30 The above measures would help to give more meaning and content to Panchayat self-governance. We would, however, readily accept the logic of establishing some linkage between the package suggested in the foregoing para and the measures suggested earlier in regard to the Panchayats raising their own resources. What form the linkage should take is for the State Government and the Panchayats to consider jointly. Perhaps, the two sets of measures should be discussed in a conference of State and Panchayat representatives.

Self-Government and the Rural-Urban Divide

3.31 There is a firmly embedded concept that Panchayats are for the rural areas. It is rooted in the historic reality of *village* panchayats existed from ancient times. The Directive Principle of State Policy in Article 40 also requires the organization of *village* panchayats. The democratic decentralisation devised by the B. Mehta Report rested on village panchayats at the base. So, with some refinements, did the scheme of the A. Mehta Report. It is no surprise, therefore, that the preamble of the West Bengal Panchayat Act, 1973 refers to reorganizing Panchayats in the rural areas. The linking of Panchayats with the rural areas has now been Constitutionalised by the 73rd Amendment. Administrative arrangements reflect the linkage in that the Union has a Department of Rural Development looking after Panchayat matters and West Bengal has a Minister for Panchayat and Rural Development. The Panchayats are thus locked into a dual bind, 'development only' and 'rural only'. The 'development only' bind has been discussed earlier. The 'rural only' aspect requires going into.

3.32 As far back as 1963, a Rural Urban Relationship Committee was appointed by the Government of India to make "recommendations regarding the relationship between the urban local bodies and the Pancahyati Raj Institutions". The Committee observed that urbanization should be considered as a "continuous process of transition from rural to urban", that "a whole area should be treated as one unit for administrative purposes" and, further, that "rural and urban areas falling within it should be treated as integral parts of the area" for the purposes of planning and implementations. Recalling this, the A. Mehta Report remarked that the "evolution from rural to urban way of life is a continuous process with sequences from a tiny hamlet to a sizeable city." Instead of an urban-rural dichotomy it saw a rural-urban continum, which called for linking up the rural areas with urban focal points and for composite District Plans spanning both urban and rural areas. West Bengal accepted the latter idea. The District Planning Committees (DPCs) are umbrella bodies for composite planning. It is significant that they are headed by ZP Sabhadhipatis. But the DPCs have no executive functions and, therefore, fall short of self-governance.

3.33 During our district tours, we saw evidence of the transition from rural to urban in the shape of a number of urbanized villages. At present, these are growing in a haphazard manner with little or no civic amenities. If there is no proper town planning from now, these will become ugly urban spreads, the redevelopment of which will be enormously costly later. The Panchayats, whether GPs or PSs, are trying to look after them as best as their resources and competence permit, but the 'rural only' stamp constrains them. With the growth of agriculture and increasing prosperity in the countryside, more such centres are likely to come up as focal points of business, trade, marketing and servicing. Places like Dhupguri in Jalpaiguri district and Garbeta-Amlagora in Medinipore district have grown beyond recognition in the last decade or so, and are now bustling urban market centres for the agricultural produce of the neighbourhood as also supply and servicing points of agri-inputs. It seems to us that, notwithstanding their 'rural only' origin, the Panchayats must squarely should this rapidly growing urban responsibility in their respective areas. If this enlargement of their functions calls for suitable legislative, administrative and financial backing, that should be forthcoming

3.34 We were told that the DPCs were not much more than staging posts in the planning process, we could see no evidence of composite rural-urban planning. It is more a case of the DPCs aggregating the requirements projected by the two sides and subsequently disaggregating the allocations received. The 73rd and 74th Amendments have, unfortunately Constitutionalised what is in fact an artificial dichotomy between rural and urban self-government. If there is a continum stretching from hamlet to city, what is called for is an overarching institution of district self-governance which does away with dichotomy and underscores the reality of the continum. In West Bengal, serious thinking requires to be undertaken about moving in this direction, without offending the basics of the two Amendments, Integrative legislation will be needed to amend both the Panchayat and the Municipal Acts. While the megapolises of Calcutta and Howrah may continue to be governed in a manner suited to them, the municipalities in the districts should become component units of self-government within an overall set up for district self-governance. In that event, separate departments for Municipal Affairs and Panchayats would be rendered anachronisms.

Self-Government and Plantations

3.35 In Jalpaiguri district, we found that tea plantations and forest villages are outside the jurisdiction of the Panchayats. Plantation workers are entitled to services and facilities from plantation managements. But there are non-workers residing in plantation areas who are not so entitled. Nor, of course, are the residents of forest villages. All three categories are denied the tangible benefits of development as well as the intangible of being participants in self-governance that accrue to those under the jurisdiction of the Panchayats. The rationale of excluding these categories is not clear to us, except the possibility that the Panchayat law may conflict with legislation applicable to the plantations and to forests. We were told that neither plantations nor forests had been excluded from the ambit of the Panchayats in Karnataka. Perhaps the same is the case in the areas under the DGHC. The legal hurdle does not, therefore, appear to be insuperable.

3.36. During our discussions, the Jalpaiguri ZP expressed a consensus view in favour of bringing both plantations and forest villages within the fold of the Panchayats. A suggestion was made that the ZP might levy a nominal cess on the tea produced in the plantations, the proceeds of which could go towards development activities in plantation areas to complement what the managements do. In Malbazar PS, opinion was initially divided. A Pradhan who was also a trade union leader favoured status quo on the grounds that plantations administration was different to block governance, that outside interference would upset, the internal management of highly productive units and that, in the event of the Panchayats coming in, the management would have an alibi to do less for labour than they should. Eventually, the majority view was that the jurisdiction of the Panchayats should extend to plantations with the stipulation that the managements must continue to do what they are mandated to do, either under law or under collective bargaining agreements.

3.37. We agree with the general consensus that plantation workers and residents and forest villagers should not be denied their democratic right to participate in Panchayat self-government, nor should they be deprived of the benefit of development activities undertaken by the Panchayats, without any diminution of the benefits and services to which any of them are entitled under labour legislation or in pursuance of collective agreements.

Self-Government and Unit Sizes

3.38 Self-government for the Panchayats requires that districts, blocks and village clusters should be of governable sizes. Outstanding leadership can deliver reasonably good governance even in otherwise ungovernably large units. But if there is only moderately good leadership, as would ordinarily be the case, it becomes important that unit sizes are governable. The Asoka Mehta Report, in a section on smaller districts, pointed out that when districts are too large plan formulation as well as supervision of development work is rendered difficult. Also popular representation in ZPs based on population becomes too large. It visualized a population of a million with local variation as a 'reasonable target' for a district. What then is to be done with a district like Medinipore with a population of 8.5 million and 52 blocks? Or with the two halves into which the old 24 Parganas district has been split, both with populations of over 6 million? The answer is to divide each of them into governable districts.

3.39 Every district has its own history, physical features and even local sentiments and these do not yield to a mechanical formula for dividing them. Creating new districts also has cost implications, both recurring and capital On the other had, in mega-districts, good money is inefficiently spend on maintaining a machinery of governance which is simply unable to cope. It is not only districts that are of unwieldy size, but blocks and village clusters also. We came across GPs with as many as 25 to 30 mauzas, and blocks with around 4 lakh population. In oversized districts, blocks and village clusters, hierarchies tend to come into existence with those nearest to the system, geographically or socially, receiving prime attention, those further away left-over attention and those further away no attention at all. If these are to be reorganized into small units in which such hierarchies have less chance to develop, the additional cost for doing so will need to be treated as balancing investment to get more out of the investment already on the ground in the shape of better governance and great people's satisfaction. West Bengal is not doing itself or its people good by carrying on with its over-large districts and other units lower down. A major reorganization is long overdue and should be undertaken as a priority operation.

3.40 We did a rough exercise in this direction in regard to the district of 24 Parganas (South). The details are set out in Annexure 8. Briefly, the old 24 Parganas district was divided into two parts in 1986, North and South. The South district has a population of 6.52 million and has 30 blocks and 335 GPs. Our exercise divides the district into three new districts with headquarters at Alipore, Baruipur and Diamond Harbour. Each of the new districts will have a population of roughly 2 million. We found that the blocks needed to be reorganized to restrict the population of a block to around 1.5 lakh, as far as possible. After reorganization, each district will have 10 to 15 blocks and each block also 10 to 15 GPs, with a dip here or an excess there outside these ranges. The exercise convinces us that the reorganization of the districts and other units is entirely possible. Further, it has yielded the following tentative yard-sticks: districts to have population around 2 million; blocks around 1.5 lakh; districts to have blocks within a range of 10 to 15; and blocks to have GPs also in a range of 10 to 15. These could be borne in mind when the overall reorganization suggested in the preceding para is undertaken.

Self-Government and the Composition of Panchayats

3.41 As noted earlier, when the first Panchayat elections took place in 1978, the power structure in the rural areas had already undergone a change. The newcomer who displaced the traditionally dominant landowners belonged to a middle category of society. It was they who, therefore, came into the Panchayats and went on to occupy the key positions of heads of the GPs, PSs and ZPs as well as heads of the standing committees in PSs and ZPs. Mnay of these were school teachers. The dedicated work of this group over the years is responsible for the present standing of the Panchayats. The dislodgment of the 'uppers' by the 'middles' and its subsequent legitimation in the Panchayats have been events of great consequence.

3.42 It seems, however, that the downward movement of power that events represent has remained arrested. Power has yet to travel down to lower levels. SCs and STs have been elected to GPs in fair numbers, even approaching their share in the population in some cases. Their representation in PSs and ZPs is less. So far they seem not to have found representation in positions of effective power, such as Gram Pradhans, Sabhapatis or Karmadhyakshas at PS level and Sabadhipatis or Karmadhyakshas at ZP level. What is true of the SCs and STs is even more the case with the poor in general. In some GPs we visited, surveys conducted to identify IRDP beneficiaries show that the people below the poverty line constitute 45 to 55 per cent of the population in the Panchayats. But there is hardly any representation from this section at any level and none at all in key positions. The middle category, it looks, remains in firm control of the Panchayats.

3.43 It is not good enough to argue, as was said to us by a senior Panchayat functionary who is also a lecturer in a college, that caste or class composition is not as relevant as what those occupying important positions do for the people, and that by this test the present occupants have done well. We were taken aback to hear an argument reminiscent of the 'white man's burden' from an elected Panchayat functionary. Good governance is no substitute for self-governance, as Gandhiji once said. By the same logic, Panchayats packed with well-intentioned 'middles' are no substitute for Panchayats with fair representation from both 'middles' and 'lowers'. The 'lowers' will surely know what is good for them more accurately than any possible notion the 'middles' many entertain on their behalf. Therefore, conscious efforts need to be made by the political parties to ensure that the middle category does not become an impermeable layer preventing the percolation of power to lower levels. The poor generally, and the SCs and STs in particular, need to be inducted not only as members of the Panchayats but also as occupants of at least some of the key positions where power resides, so that they become shareholders in power.

3.44 The recently enacted reservation for women presents a problem as well as an opportunity. A problem in that, largely because of societal constraints, there are very few women in the Panchayats at present, and even few in key positions. Women's representation is less than one per cent of the total elected Panchayat members. In our tours, we came across only one lady Karmadhyaksha of a ZP and one lady elected member of a GP. From this almost 'nil' position to go up in one leap to 'not less than one third' will not be easy. But woman power is there waiting to come in and here lies the opportunity. The induction of women in substantial numbers could turn out to be as momentous a measure as land reform in that it would release a hitherto pent up force, much like what land reform did. The political parties will have to take determined steps to raise the level of political awareness among women. Also they will need to see that entry into Sthayee Samitis in fair numbers. Women's development programmes should be worked out at each level and vigorously implemented. It may be useful to have statutory Sthayee Samitis at ZP and PS levels of and for women.

3.45 Over the years, the Panchayats have achieved an important objective. They have recruited new people into political and given them on-the-job exposure to the art of self-governance from the grassroots level upwards. The Panchayats have thus served as nurseries for new entrants and have by now created a rich pool of experienced leaders. We were happy to observe the high rate of new intake. In some of the Panchayats, only two or three members are survivors from the previous five year spell, all the rest being newcomers. We were also impressed by the 'upward mobility' to be seen. Many Panchayat functionaries have, on the basis of their performance, moved up to higher levels. Two former Sabhadhipatis have become Ministers in the State Government. Political parties need to continue to follow a policy of recruiting new people into the Panchayats and grooming them for higher responsibilities.

Self-Government and Collegiate Functioning

3.46 If the 73rd Amendment has Constitutionlised the three strata of Union, States and Panchayats, there should, in theory, be a degree of compatibility in their forms of governance. There is compatibility as between the Union and the States in that the Constitution provides for Councils of Ministers at both strata, with the Prime Minister at the head in one case and Chief Ministers in the other. In the West Bengal Panchayat Act, however, the emphasis is on the head at each level. Whether it is the ZP Sabhadhipati, the PS Sabhapati or the GP Pradhan, the Act vests each of them, in identical terms, with functions as wide as general responsibility for financial and executive administration, administrative supervision over staff, and the transaction of business on behalf of the concerned Panchayat (see sections 165, 118 and 34). The quasi-presidential system this constitutes is moderate to an extent by the provisions at ZP and PS levels for subject-wise standing committees with Karmadhyakshas at the head. There is no such moderating factor at GP level. By law, therefore, power is concentrated in the hands of the respective Panchayat heads.

3.47 In practice, the Samanway Samitis statutorily set up ZP and PS levels to coordinate the work of the subject-wise Sthayee Samitis have introduced a measure of collegiate functioning between the heads and the Karmadhyakshas at these levels. At the GP level there are no Karmadhyakshas and concentration of power in the Pradhans' hands is complete. However, in a GP that we visited, the Pradhan has distributed a few subjects to four members for convenience of work and to ensure some amount of collective responsibility. These members are, in effect, members-in-charge (MIC). With the increase of work at all levels, especially the enlargement of functions and transfer of staff visualized in paras 3.12 and 3.15, the form of Panchayat governance needs to move in two directions. One, Karmadhyakshas should take fuller control over the subjects and staff relating to their Sthayee Samitis. The decentralisation implicit in this was urged upon us by many Sabhadhipatis, Sabhapatis and Karmadhyakshas. Along with this, all GPs should introduce the system of MICs, to whom responsibilities should be entrusted as if they are Karmadhyakshas. Two, at all three levels, there should be systematized collegiate functioning between the heads and those in charge of subjects, with collective responsibility for major decisions and decentralisation to subject chiefs for day-to-day tasks.

Self-Government and Inter level Links

3.48 Multi-level self-government requires the different layers do not operate in isolation from each other. The three tiers of the Panchayats are organically linked in that all Gram Pradhans are ex-officio members of PSs and all PS Sabhapatis ex-officio members of ZPs. The linkage needs to be made more of a reality than mere ex-officio membership. At present, we were told, ZP general meetings endorse the resolutions of the various standing committees by voice votes, virtually without any worthwhile discussion, even on substantial issues. The real business of the ZPs and PSs is transacted in their standing committees, but there is no organic link between the standing committee for a particular subject at ZP level with its counterpart committees in the PSs. There is a similar absence of links between PS standing committees and GPs. What is required is that the Karmadhyakshas of PS level Sthayee Samitis should be ex-officio members of the corresponding ZP level Sthayee Samitis, and GP level MICs (see para 3.48) ex-officio members of the relevant PS level Sthayee Samitis. If big districts or blocks complain of Sthayee Samitis becoming too large, the answer is to make such districts and blocks small (see para 3.39).

3.49 There is at present no organic link between the Panchayats and the State Government. Now that the Panchayats are to be a Constitutionalised third stratum of governance, they need to grow out of the tutelage of a Department of Panchayat or even a Minister of Panchayats. Their problems with the State Government should be discussed and resolved in a political forum comprising representative of the Panchayats and the State. Such a forum would also enable the Panchayats to exchange experiences and learn from each other. If there is a case for an Inter-State Council at the national level, this is equally a case for an Inter-Zilla Council at the State level. The decisions of such a Council, the setting up of which we recommend, should carry weight with the State Government and not lightly turned down.

3.50 An alternative and more far-reaching linkage, possibly at a later stage, would be to revive the Upper house under a new nomenclature and a new composition. Since the Constitution prescribes a uniform pattern for State level Upper Houses, any departure in the case of West Bengal would require a 'special provision' article in the '371 family'. The article could, notwithstanding anything in the Constitution, permit the State to have a Council of Districts as its Upper House. While the nomenclature would follow what exists at the centre, namely a Council of States, the composition of the council of Districts would need detailed consideration. A basic principle should be that the districts are equally represented.

Self-Government and Accountability

3.51 The maintenance of accounts at the GP level is governed by the West Bengal (Gram Panchayat Miscellaneous Accounts and Audit) Rules, 1990, which prescribe no less than 35 forms to be maintained by each of the 3304 GPs in the State. Pending finalisation of the PS and ZP accounts rules, the Local Self Government Accounts Rules, 1885, the ZP Rules 1964 and the District Board Manual are operating. The West Bengal Panchayat Act requires the State Government to prescribe the manner in which accounts should be kept at each tier (sections 50, 139 and 185). It is regrettable that this was not done for GPs till 1990 and has yet to be done for PSs and ZPs. It is also a matter fo concern that the compilation of accounts is in heavy arrears in many cases, as for example, the ZP of Howrah which has not finalized its accounts after 1985-86. Accounts of the Birbhum ZP are in arrears since 1988-89.

3.52 At a rough estimate, the funds handled annually at the GP level are of the order of 5 lakh rupee per GP, those at PS level between 25 and 30 lakhs per PS and at ZP level between 20 and 30 crores per ZP. With the enlargement of functions (para 3.12), the transfer of staff (para 3.15), the raising of more local resources and the Panchayats graduating into a new stratum of governance, the funds handled at each level are likely to increase substantially. Putting the maintenance of accounts at all three levels on a sound footing is, therefore, urgently necessary. The system should be as simple as possible, yet effective. Furthermore, it should incorporate the concept of management accounting. The GP rules need to be looked at afresh to see whether the system prescribed, involving 35 forms per GP, is simple enough to operate and, also, provides a management tool. Expert advice will be required to do this, as also to finalise the pending rules for PSs and ZPs. It would be useful to involve the Account General (AG) as well as qualified management accountants. The accountants to be appointed at each level will need to be properly trained in the new system of accounts maintenance that emerges.

3.53 For auditing the accounts at each level, the State Government is required to appoint an auditor (section 186 of the West Bengal Panchayat Act). The existing arrangement is that while GP accounts are audited by the Extension Officer (Panchayats) at the block level, PS and ZP accounts are audited by the AG through the Examiner of Local Account (ELA), an officer under his control. West Bengal is one of only two States in the country where the AG is entrusted with audit responsibility for Panchayat accounts, though limited to the two upper tiers. The arrangement has merit in that audit of PS and ZP accounts is in independent hands. The same cannot be said about the audit of GP accounts, since the block level Extension Officers are officials of the Panchayat Department and, further, work too closely with the Panchayat system to be viewed as independent enough auditors.

3.54 It would be desirable not only to continue the AG's audit of PS and ZP accounts but also to extend it to cover GPs. A large cadre of Panchayat and accounts officers exists principally for the internal audit of the Panchayats. All these officers could be transferred on deputation to the Audit Division of te Finance Department or brought under the AG's control. The move should be without detriment to their inter se seniority and promotion prospects in the parent cadre. After suitable training these officers could be utilized for the statutory audit of the Panchayats at all three levels. If for some reason the AG is unable to undertake hundred percent annual auditing of GPs, he could do 20 per cent test audit every year. With 20 per cent test audit by the AG, all the GPs will be so audited in a cycle of five years. The services of the Extension Officer (Panchayats) could be utilized by PSs in other ways, such as assisting GPs administratively.

3.55 The audit repors of GPs are required to be sent to the Director of Panchayat through the District Panchayat Officer. There is a huge back-log in the submission of these reports as is evident from the table below:

Table 1

No. of GPs in West Bengal	*Year*	*No. of Reports Received (as on 24-11-92)*
3304	1984-85	3156
	1985-86	3045
	1986-87	2877
	1987-88	3041
	1988-89	2770
	1990-91	1824
	1991-92	259

Source: Directorate of Panchayats, West Bengal.

3.56 The ELA is grossly under-staffed, as a result of which ZP and PS accounts have not been audited for years. Table 2 illustrates this for ZPs. The most recent cases are of Birbhum and Malda, where audit has been done only up to the year 1987-88. In other districts, audit is even further behind with Medinipore not having been audited after 1983-84. The situation is worse in PSs. Without updated audit, it is impossible to tell whether the Panchayats are in a good state of health in respect of financial management. Therefore it is essential that the ELA's requirements are met, first to meet her responsibility vis-à-vis PS and ZP accounts and next to meet the additional responsibility in respect of GP accounts. Considering that around half of the Plan funds of the State are devolved to the districts, the desirability of having a whole-time AG for the Panchayats needs to be gone into in consultation with the Comptroller and Auditor General (C&AG).

Table 2

	Name of ZPs	*Accounts Audit upto the year*	*Accounts compiled for Audit upto the Year*
1.	Hooghly	1985-86	1990-91
2.	Purulia	1986-87	1990-91
3.	Medinipore	183-84	1990-91
4.	Bankura	198687	1989-90
5.	Birbhum	1987-88	1988-89
6.	Burdhaman	1985-86	1990-91
7.	Howrah	1983-84	1985-86
8.	Nadia	1986-87	1989-90
9.	Murshidabad	1986-87	1990-91
10.	24 Parganas (S)	1985-86	1991-92
11.	24 Parganas (N)	No audit since inception 1986-87	1990-91
12.	Malda	1987-88	1990-91
13.	W. Dinajpore	1984-85	1991-92
14.	Cooch Bihar	1984-85	1991-92
15.	Jalpaiguri	1985-86	1989-90
16.	Siliguri Mahakuma Parishad	No Audit	1990-91

Source: Directorate of Panchayats, West Bengal

3.57 Although the AG audits the accounts of both ZPs and PSs, it is only in respect of the former that his observations find a mention in the C&AG's report for the State. The basis for excluding PSs, as verbally explained by the AG, is that the C&AG is only concerned with transactions ex-Consolidated Fund of the State and thee are limited to ZPs. Transactions lower down are ex-ZP or ex-PS funds and thus not within the C&AG's purview. As a result, only ZP's audit is reported to the State legislature. The reasoning seems illogical, because if the tiers below the ZP level are outside the C&AG's jurisdiction, how is it that the AG is auditing PS accounts? Besides, while money from the Consolidated Fund does flow to ZPs, some of its flows on to PSs and again to GPs. Therefore, public interest requires that the audit of all the tiers should be reflected in the C&AG's report.

3.58 The few paragraphs that do figure in the C&AG's reports at present are inadequate, not only because they are limited to ZPs only but also because they fail to bring out important points, such as the highly unsatisfactory state of arrears of both accounts and audit. With the Panchayats becoming a new stratum of governance at and bwlow distrct level, their audit needs to be done in greater depth and kept upto date. The C&AG's report should have a separate part entirely devoted to the Panchayats. Occasional supplementary audit reports dealing with important aspects or programmes would also be useful, such as resource raising by the Panchayats or the manner in which the JRY has been implemented or the progress made in new schemes like, for instance, the promotion of agricultural marketing.

3.59 We were unable to see the observations of the Public Accounts Committee (PAC) on the audit paragrapohs relating to ZPs. The Chairman was, however, good enough to inform us that the PAC had made useful points with regard to the Panchayats. Hard pressed for time as it is, the PAC may find it difficult to give due attention to Panchayat accounts in the event, firstly, of the AG's jurisdiction being extended to GPs and, secondly, the audit reports of the C&AG covering the accounts of PSs and GPs as well as those of ZPs. In that case the Vidhan Sabha could consider setting up a separate PAC wholly fro the Panchayats. The PAC (Panchayats) would then be assisted by the whole-time AG (Panchayats), should one be appointed. Its functions would be to consider the audit reports of the C&AG on the Panchayats, whether regular or supplementary.

Self-Government and Elections

3.60 As a Constitutional third stratum of governance, the Panchayats are now to provide self-government at and below the district level, largely replacing the bureaucratic administration that has so far occupied that space. Democracy needs reliable elections. To our knowledge, electoral reform for Panchayat elections has not been a major issue. The 73rd Amendment provides for "the suprintendance, direction and control of the preparation of electoral rolls for, and the conduct of, all elections to the Panchayats" to be vested in a State Election Commissioner who, through appointed by the State Government, "shall not be removed from his office except in like manner and on the like grounds as a Judge of High Court". The unstated but clear enough intent of the Amendment is that not only should Panchayat elections be free and fair but they should appear to be so. It is with this in mind that we have had a look at the legal provisiona, administrative practice and past experience in respect of Panchayat elections in West Bengal.

3.61 The West Bengal Panchayat Act deals with elections in two sections of a residual end chapter titled "Miscellaneous". Our first reaction is that the subject is important enough to deserve a separate chapter, as has been done for audit. Leaving that aside, the State Panchayat Election Officer (SPEO) appointed under section 203 has no tenurial protection. The Act, therefore, needs to be amended to bring it in line with the 73rd Amendment on this point. In practice, SPEOs have invariable been relatively junior officers of the Department of Panchayat. Instead of supervising the conduct of all Panchayat elections, as the Act intends, they have in all previous elections been regularly by-passed, with the State Government issuing orders direct to subordinate election authorities, even after the issue of an election notification. Now tht there will be a State Election Commissioner, his status as a Constitutional authority should be reflected in the very first appointment. Further, he should be enable to function independently not only of the Department of Panchayat but of the entire executive Government. He could be loosely attached to the Law Department, as the Chief Election Commissioner is to the Minister of Law at the centre.

3.62 Past experience indicates action on two points:

(3) Except on one occasion after 1978, no by-elections have been held to fill vacancies. In some cases, GPs have not been able to function as the number of members fell below the required quorum. The number of casual vacancies is likely to be large enough to organize bunched by-elections, possibly every half-year. Simple rules should be framed for holding by-elections regularly under the supervision of the State Election Commissioner.

(4) The counting of votes at polling stations creates problems, especially if the contest is close. Under pressure, irregularities tend to be committed in the counting of votes and in the declaration of results. Sometimes, wrong persons are declared elected results reported to returning officers. Whether matters would improve by shifting the venue of counting to the block headquarters needs to be discussed with all political parties.

Self-Governing Panchayats and State Government Machinery

3.63 If self-government means measured autonomy for the Panchayats, to that extent the functions of the State must diminish and its machinery of government contract. Conversely, if the machinery of the State Government remains intact, the meaning is clear that its functions have remained undiminished, from which it follows that the Panchayats have failed to attain even partial autonomy. Even though the expression 'self-government' has come in only with the 73rd Amendment and is not there in the West Bengal Panchayat Act, it is implicit in the situation that there has been some of autonomy, and hence self-government, in the Panchayats from the start in 1978. But has this resulted in any reduction in the machinery of the State Government?

3.64 The annual expenditure of the State is a fair indicator, for it reflects the basic cost of running the Government, a major part of which is accounted for by staff and related matters. The figures of the total revenue expenditure (TRE) from 1977-78 to 1991-92, as obtained from budget documents, are as below:

Table 3

Year	*TRE (in crores of Rupees)*
1977-78	701
1978-79	907
1979-80	977
1980-81	1115
1981-82	1312
1982-83	1622
1983-84	1739
1984-85	2151
1985-86	2260
1986-87	2697
1987-88	3027
1988-89	3475
1989-90	3971
1990-91	5128
1991-92	5181 (Pre-actual)

Source: Priyojit Das: Public Finance in West Bengal; Farma KLM (P) Ltd., Calcutta, 1992.

3.65 The table shows that TRE increased by 639 percent of the decade and a half in question, an average of 49.14 per cent per annum. The figures include the additional expenditure that had to be incurred on implementing the recommendations of the Second and Third Pay Commission of the State. But this does not, perhaps, wholly explain the phenomenal growth of TRE. From 1980 to 1991 (March), the number of employees of the State Government increased by 68,900, those of quasi-governmental organizations by 53,200 and of local bodies by 34,900. In all, this amounted to an increase of 1,57,000 employees. (Source: Economic Review 1991-92, Statistical Appendix, GOWB, Calcutta, 1992). It seems that the governmental machinery, far from diminishing, has expanded during the very period that the Panchayats have been in existence. The implication is that, whatever the rhetoric about the success of the Panchayats, the State Government has not felt under any compulsion to reduce either its functions or its staff, and consequently any claim that the Panchayats have a degree of autonomy is not sustainable.

3.67 The Administrative Reforms Committee of the State headed by an eminent former Finance Minister, did not deal with the Panchayats at all. Perhaps, in the early eighties when it reported, the Panchayats had not made their presence felt sufficiently. But if, even now, Calcutta carries on as an expanding version of the machinery inherited from the British times, all talk of Panchayat self-governance may as well, cease. A major reorganization of the machinery of government at the State level is, therefore, called for. The aim would have to be, say, to halve the number of Minister, secretaries, heads of departments, and other functionaries down the line The functions to be performed at the State level need to be derived from what the State itself has asked the Union to decentralize, on the one had, and, on the other, the remnant functions that would be left after the State divests itself of its overburden to the districts. An entirely new set of portfolios may emerge for the fewer Ministers then required, following which there could be an entirely new way of utilizing the reduced number of secretariat and departmental staff. Those rendered surplus should be redeployed, after such training as may be necessary, to meet the extended requirements of the Panchayats at and below the district level.

Appendix-3

West Bengal Act XXV of 1994

The West Bengal Metropolitan Planning Committee Act, 1994.

[Passed by the West Bengal Legislature]

[Assent of the Governor was first published in the Calcutta Gazette, Extraordinary, of the 27th June, 1994]

An Act to provide for the constitution of Metropolitan Planning Committee in every Metropolitan area in West Bengal for preparation of draft development plan for the Metropolitan area as a whole.

Whereas it is expedient to provide for the constitution of Metropolitan Planning Committee in every Metropolitan area in West Bengal for preparation of draft development plan for the Metropolitan area as a whole.

It is hereby enacted in the Forty-Fifth Year of the Republic of India, by the Legislature of West Bengal, as follows:

Chapter I
Preliminary

Short Title, Extent and Commencement

1. (1) This Act may be called the West Bengal Metropolitan Committee Act, 1994.

2. It extends to the whole of West Bengal, except the areas to which the provision of the Darjeeling Gorkha Hill Council Act, 1988, apply.

3. It shall come into force on such date as the State Government may, by notification, appoint, and different dates may be appointed for different areas.

Definitions

2. In this Act, unless there is anything repugnant the subject or context,-

(a) "Constitution" means the Constitution of India;

(b) "district" means a district of West Bengal;

(c) "Metropolitan area" means an area have a population of ten lakhs or more, comprised in one or more districts and consisting of two or more Municipalities or Panchayats or other contiguous areas, specified by the Governor by public notification to be a Metropolitan area for the purposes of this Act;

(d) "Municipal area" means the territorial area of a Municipality as is notified by the Governor;

(e) "Municipality" means an institution of self-government constituted under article 243Q of the Constitution;

(f) "notification" means a notification published in the *Official Gazette*;

(g) "Panchayat" means a Panchayat constituted under article 243B of the Constitution;

(h) "population" means the population as ascertained at the last preceding census of which the relevant figures have been published;

(i) "prescribed" means prescribed by rules made under this Act.

Chapter II

Constitution of Metropolitan Planning Committee, Its functions and Matters Related Thereto

Metropolitan Planning Committee

3. (1) There shall be constituted in every Metropolitan area a Metropolitan Planning Committee (hereinafter referred to in this Act as the Committee) consisting of such number of

members, including a Chairperson and a Vice-Chairperson, as the State Government may determine, to prepare a draft development plan for the Metropolitan area as a whole :

Provided that not less than two-thirds of the members of the Committee shall be elected by, and from amongst, the elected members of the Municipalities and Chairpersons of the Panchayats in the Metropolitan area in proportion to the ratio between the population of the Municipalities and of the Panchayats in that area.

(2) The representation in the Committee of the Government of India and the State Government and of such organizations and institutions as may be deemed necessary for carrying out the functions assigned to the Committee shall be such as may be notified by the State Government from time to time.

(3) The Committee shall perform such functions relating to planning and coordination for the Metropolitan area as the State Government may, by notification, assign to it.

(4) The Committee shall, in preparing the draft development plan,-

(a) have regard to–

(i) the plans prepared by the Municipalities and the Panchayats in the Metropolitan area;

(ii) matters of common interest between the Municipalities and the Panchayats, including co-ordinated spatial planning of the area, sharing of water and other physical natural resources, the integrated development of infrastructure and environmental conservation.

(iii) the overall objectives and priorities set by the Government of India and the State Government;

(iv) the extent and nature of investments likely to be made in the Metropolitan area by agencies of the Government of India and of the State Government and other available resources, whether financial or otherwise;

(b) consult such institutions and organizations as the Governor may, by order, specify.

(5) The Chairpersons of every Committee shall forward the development plan, as recommended by the Committee, to the State Government.

Chairperson, Vice-Chairperson, other members, not being elected members, term of office and filling up of vacancy

4. (1) The Chairperson, Vice-Chairperson and other members, not being elected members, of every Committee shall be appointed by the State Government.

(2) The terms of office and other conditions of service of the Chairperson, Vice-Chairperson, and other members, not being elected members, of the Committee shall be such as may be prescribed.

(3) Any vacancy in the office of the Chairpersons, Vice-Chairperson, or any other member, not being an elected member, of the Committee shall be filled by fresh appointment by the State Government.

Election of members of Committee

5. The manner of election of members of the Committee and all matters related thereto shall be such as may be prescribed.

Term of office of, and allowance for, elected members of Committee

6. The elected members of the Committee shall hold office for a term of five years from the date of their election, and shall receive such allowance for attending the meeting of the Committee or any sub-committee thereof as may be prescribed:

Provided that every such member shall, on his ceasing to be a elected membeer of a Municipality or Chairperson of a Panchayat, as the case may be, cease to be a member of the Committee notwithstanding that the term of five years has not expired, and the vacancy shall be filled by election in the manner prescribed.

Validation

7. No act or proceeding to the Committee shall be invalid or called in question by reason of any vacancy, initial or subsequent, in, or defect in the constitution of, the Committee.

Meeting of Committee

8. (1) The Committee shall meet at such places and at such times, and shall observe such rules of procedure in regard to the transaction of business at its meeting (including the quorum for a meeting), as may be prescribed.

(2) The Chairperson or, if, for any reason, he is unable to attend any meeting, the Vice-Chairperson or, if, for any reason, both are unable to attend any meeting, any other member elected by the members present, shall preside at the meeting.

Secretary of Committee

9. There shall be a Secretary of the Committee who shall be appointed by the State Government.

Sub-committee

10. (1) A Committee may constitute, for such purpose as it may think fit, as many sub-committees consisting wholly of members of the Committee or wholly of other persons or partly or other persons as it may consider necessary or expedient.

(2) The members of a sub-committee, not being members of the Committee, shall be paid such fees and allowances for attending the meetings thereof as may be prescribed.

Power to make Rules

11. (1) The State Government may make rules for carrying out the purposes of this Act.

(2) In particular and without prejudice to the generality of the foregoing power, such rules may provide for all or any of the matters which under any provision of this Act, are required to be prescribed or to be provided for by rules.

(3) All rules made under this Act shall be published in the *Official Gazette* and shall, unless some later date is appointed

by the State Government, come into force on the date of such publication.

(4) All rules made under this Act shall be laid for not less than fourteen days before the State Legislature as soon as possible after they are made and shall be subject to such modification as the State Legislature may make during the session in which they are so laid.

By order of the Governor,
S. Maitra
Special Officer & Ex-officio
Jt. Secy. to the Govt. of West Bengal

Appendix-4

Government of West Bengal Urban Development Department

No. 2257-UD/O/M/SB/A-1/98 Kolkata, the 12th June, 2001.

Notification

In exercise of the power conferred by sub-section (1), read with sub-section (2) and sub-section (3), or section 11 of the West Bengal Metropolitan Planning Committee Act, 1994 (West Bengal Act XXV of 1994), the Governor is pleased hereby to make the following rules:

The West Bengal Metropolitan Planning Committee Rules

1. Short Title and Commencement

(1) These rules may be called the West Bengal Metropolitan Planning Committee Rules, 2001.

(2) They shall come into force on such date as the State Government may, by notification in the *Official Gazette*, appoint.

2. Definitions

(1) these rules, unless the context otherwise requires-

(a) "the Act" means the West Bengal Metropolitan Planning Committee Act, 1994 (West Bengal Act XXV of 1994);

(b) "ballot box" includes any box, bag, or other receptacle, used for the insertion of ballot papers by voters;

(c) "Election Authority" means an officer appointed by the State Government for conduct of election for constitution of a Metropolitan Planning Committee under sub-section (1) of section 3;

(d) "Form" means a Form appended to the West Bengal District Planning Committee Rules, 1994, as may be adopted under rule 6 for the purposes of these rules, and includes a translation thereof in Bengali;

(e) "list of voters" means the list of (i) elected members of Municipalities and (ii) Chairpersons of Panchayats, by whatever name called, in a metropolitan area, as may be prepared by the Election Authority under sub-rule (2) of rule 6.

(f) "polling station", in relation to an election, means the place for taking poll of that election;

(g) "returning officer" includes any assistant returning office when performing the functions of a returning officer;

(h) "section" means a section of the Act.

(2) The expressions used in these rules and not otherwise defined shall have the same meaning as in the Act.

3. Metropolitan Planning Committee for every Metropolitan area

The State Government shall constitute a Metropolitan Planning Committee for every Metropolitan area as defined in clause (c) of section 2 of the Act.

4. Determination of number of members of Metropolitan Planning Committee

(1) The State Government shall, as soon as may be and within one month from the date of commencement of these rules, specify, by notification, the total number of members of a Metropolitan Planning Committee falling within the district or part of the district within the jurisdiction of the said Metropolitan Planning Committee.

(2) The State Government shall, while determining the number of elected members in each district within a

Metropolitan area, take into account the population of urban area and rural area, and keep a parity between them while fixing the number of members to be elected from urban area and rural area separately.

5. Appointment of Election Authority

The State Government shall, within 60 days of the notification referred to in sub-rule (1) of rule 4, appoint the District Magistrate of each district falling within the Metropolitan are as the Election Authority for conduct of election of the members notified under sub-rule (1) of rule 4:

Provided that the Director of Local Bodies, West Bengal, shall be appointed as the Election Authority for conduct of election for constitution of a Metropolitan Planning Committee in the area within the jurisdiction of the Calcutta Municipal Corporation.

6. Conduct of Election

(1) The Election Authority shall, as soon as possible and not later than 30 days from the date of appointment, proceed to conduct election of members to the Metropolitan Planning Committee in the manner not inconsistent with the provisions of these rules, prescribed for election of members of District Planning Committee in Chapter III of the West Bengal District Planning Committee Rules, 1994. The procedure laid down therein, and the forms thereunder, shall be followed *mutatis mutandis*, and to the extent they are not repugnant to any provision of these rules in conducting the election.

(2) For the purpose of sub-rule (1), the Election Authority shall also prepare a list of voters.

7. Constitution of Metropolitan Planning Committee

The State Government shall, on receipt of the results of election of members to the Metropolitan Planning Committee as may be received from the Election Authority and as soon as possible, but not later than 15 days form the date of election, constitute the Metropolitan Planning Committee after providing therein the representation of other members under sub-section (2) of section 3, and the Chairperson and the Vice-Chairperson as may be determined by the State Government.

8. Appointment of Secretary

The State Government shall appoint a Secretary of the Metropolitan Planning Committee under section 9.

9. Meeting of Metropolitan Planning Committee

(1) Every Metropolitan Planning Committee shall ordinarily meet at a place appointed by the State Government.

(2) The meeting shall be convinced by the Secretary on a date and time, and on the agenda, previously approved by the Chairperson or, in this absence, by the Vice-Chairperson:

Provided that the Chairperson or, in his absence, the Vice-Chairperson may, if he considers necessary, direct for convening an emergent meeting of the Metropolitan Planning Committee upon fixing the date, time and agenda thereof.

(3) The Chairperson or, in his absence, the Vice-Chairperson shall, on receipt of written requisition signed by at least one-third of the members of the Metropolitan Planning Committee, specifying the agenda, direct the Secretary to call a special meeting of the Metropolitan Planning Committee, fixing the place, date, time and agenda thereof.

(4) The quorum for an ordinary meeting shall be one-third of the total number of members of the Metropolitan Planning Committee. The quorum for a special meeting shall be at least 50% of the total number of members of the Metropolitan Planning Committee

(5) (a) The Secretary shall, under the direction of the Chairperson, give the members not less than 10 clear days' notice in writing of the agenda, data, time, and place of the proposed meeting:

provided that in the case of emergency, a meeting may be convened on giving not less than three days' notice.

(b) The notice shall be served upon every member, either personally or by registered post, addressed to such member:

Provided that no such notice shall be necessary in the case of a member, who is out of India at the relevant time.

(6) The Chairperson presiding at a meeting shall invite or initiate discussion on each item on the agenda for the meeting in such order or priority as he thinks fit, and shall guide the discussion to a fruitful conclusion with a view to enabling the members to arrive at a decision based on a consensus of the members present, and if there be no consensus amongst the members present, the matter shall be decided by the majority votes, the person presiding shall have a second or casting vote in the case of equality of votes.

(a) The decision arrived at one each item on the agenda, and any urgent matter of importance (not included in the agenda), which is discussed and considered at meeting, shall be recorded in a minutes book to be maintained for the Chairperson, which shall contain the necessary details including the names of the members present.

(b) The minutes of a meeting shall be-

(i) confirmed at the next meeting,

(ii) signed by the member presiding at such meeting after such confirmation, and

(iii) open to inspection by any member during the meeting.

(8) To complete the discussion and consideration of all the agenda and the urgent matters of importance raised by not included in the agenda, the Chairperson presiding at a meeting may, if he considers it necessary, continue the meeting for such day or days, or adjourn the meeting to such date, as he may think fit.

(9) No notice in writing to any adjourned meeting shall be given to the members, but an attempt shall be made to intimate the absentee members of the adjournment.

(10) The Chairperson or, in his absence, the Vice-Chairperson presiding over the meeting may, in his discretion, either himself raise, or permit any urgent matter of importance not included in the agenda for consideration at such meeting.

10. **Interpretation**–The power to interpret any provision of these rules is reserved to the State Government.

By order of the Governor,
N.L. Basak
Principal Secy. to the Govt. of West Bengal

West Bengal Municipal (Ward Committee) Rules, 2001 as Amended up to 2002

Part 1

1. Short Title, Application and Commencement

(1) these rules may be called the West Bengal Municipal (Ward Committee) Rules, 2001.

(2) They shall apply to all the Municipalities and Notified Area Authorities constituted under the West Bengal Municipal Act, 1993 (West Bengal Act XVII of 1993).

(3) They shall come into force from the date of their publication in the *Official Gazette*.

2. Definitions

(I) In these rules unless the context otherwise requires,

(1) "Act" means the West Bengal Municipal Act, 1993 (West Bengal Act XXII of 1993);

"1A. 'BPL family' means the family below the poverty line, as determined by the Ministry of Urban Affairs and Employment, Government of India, from time to time, for identification of beneficiaries in poverty alleviation schemes"

(2) "Chairman" means in Chairman of the Ward Committee;

(3) "Committee" means the Ward Committee constituted under these rules;

(4) "CDS" means the Community Development Society constituted in the municipal area for implementation of the Swarna Jayanti Sahari Rojgar Yogana";

(5) "Member" means a member of the Committee.

(II) The words and expressions used in these rules and not defined shall have the meaning respectively assigned to them in the Act.

Matter Missing

(5) While nominating the other members of the Committee the aspect of proper representation of engineers, physicians, educationists, social workers, cultural activists, sports-persons, women, persons form economically backward section of society or any other person form among the residents of the Ward, shall be made in such manner as may cover all sections of people of the Ward as aforesaid.

(6) Tenure of the Committee

(1) Tenure of the Committee shall be the same as that of the Board of Councillors of the Municipality/Notified Area Authority.

(2) In case of any causal vacancy in the membership of the Committee caused by the following reasons, it shall be filled up by the Councillor elected from the Ward or by the Municipality/notified Area Authority, as the case may be, by fresh nomination:

(a) death,

(b) resignation, duly accepted by the Councilor elected from the Ward or by the Municipality/Notified Area Authority, as the case may be,

(c) withdrawal of nomination by the Councilor elected from the Ward or by the Municipality/Notified Area Authority, as the case may be, or

(d) shift of residence by any member from the Ward to any other Ward or elsewhere.

Part III

Rules of Business of the Ward Committee

6. First meeting of Ward Committee

The first meeting of the Committee shall be convened by the Chairman of the Committee within fifteen days from the date of constitution of the Committee. Apart from normal business, the Committee shall, at its first meeting, select a Member-Secretary for the Committee from among the members who shall convene the subsequent meeting of the Committee in consultation with the Chairman and shall perform the secretarial functions of the Committee.

7. Ordinary meeting

(1) The Committee shall meet at least once in every month.

(2) The Chairman shall fix the date, place and time of the meeting.

(3) No meeting shall be held unless at least seven clear days, before the day of the meeting, notice specifying the date, place and time of such meeting and the business to be transacted there has been given to the members.

8. Annual General Meeting

(1) The Committee shall convene an Annual General Meeting of the residents of the Ward by intimating every resident of the Ward and also by public proclamation intimating the time and venue of the meeting, to be held within the 30th June of every year to apprise them the activities of the Municipality/ Notified Area Authority in general, and the Ward in particular, during the preceding year and to assess the popular needs of the ward for the current year.

(2) For the annual general meetings the Municipal/Notified Area Authority shall furnish the following documents to the Committee for public information and deliberation thereon:

(a) a detailed report about the activities of the Municipality/ Notified Area Authority in the Ward area during the preceding year.

(b) a copy of the Annual Administration Report along with the Annual Financial Statement of the Municipality/ Notified Area Authority for the preceding year.

(3) Annual General Meetings shall be arranged preferably in a public place within the Ward.

(4) Apart from the meeting is prescribed in sub-rule (1), the Committee shall convene an half-yearly General Meeting of the residents of the Ward by intimating every resident of the Ward and also by public proclamation intimating the time and venue of the meeting to be held in the month of October-November each year to apprise them the activities of the Municipality/Notified Area Authority in general, and the Ward in particular, during the period from the date of holding of the last preceding Annual General Meeting and to discuss the proposals for preparation of the development plan from the next year.

9. Minutes

(1) Minutes of the proceedings of the Ward Committee shall be entered in the 'Minute Book' specifying the names of the members who attended the meeting, the business transacted, the decision of the Committee on each item of business, the date of the meeting and the time of commencement and closing of the meeting.

(2) The minutes shall be written by the Member-Secretary of the Committee and signed by the Chairman, and a copy of the same shall be displayed in some conspicuous place of the concerned Ward.

Part IV

Powers and Functions

10. General Functions

(1) The Committee, subject to general supervision of the Borough Committee or the Municipality, as the case may be, shall, within the Ward, supervise and monitor:

(a) detection of violation of various provisions of the Act such as unlawful construction, encroachments on municipal and public properties, public nuisance, evasion of taxes, unlicensed activities, and the like;

(b) arresting wasteful uses of various municipal services like tap-water, street hydrant, street lights, parks and playgrounds, community centres and libraries, and the like;

(c) collection and removal of garbage;

(d) removal of accumulated water on streets, public places due to rain, and other causes;

(e) health immunization services;

(f) improvement of slums including its clearance wherever necessary;

(g) redressal of public grievances;

(h) maintenance of essential statistics;

(i) numbering of streets and premises;

(j) execution of various obligatory and discretionary functions and functions transferred by the State Government to the Municipality/Notified Area Authority as per provisions of the Act.

(2) The Committee, as per directions of the Borough Committee or the Municipality/Notified Area Authority, as the case may be, shall also monitor and supervise within the Ward:

(a) work of assessment, collection of property tax, other taxes, fees and other sums due to the Municipality/Notified Area Authority;

(b) maintenance and repair of roads and drains;

(c) execution of public works;

(d) maintenance of sanitation and public health;

(e) prevention and control of dangerous diseases;

(f) issue of birth and death certificates;

(g) all Urban Poverty Alleviation Programmes of the State and the Central Government;

(h) tree planting in the municipal properties;

(i) generation of internal resources;

(j) literacy expansion programmes.

(3) The Committee shall perform such other functions as may be entrusted to it by the Municipality or the Borough Committee or the Act or the rules made thereunder and supervise the implementation of decisions of the Municipality/Notified Area Authority and the other Committee constituted under the Act in respect of all matters relating to the Ward.

11. Planning

(1) Within three months from the date of constitution of the Committee, the Committee shall prepare a list of the schemes for development of the Ward during the next five years and also annual priority list of these schemes and submit the same to the Municipality/Notified Area Authority for incorporating them in the development plan of the Municipality/Notified Area Authority as per provisions of the Act.

(2) The priority list mentioned in sub-rule (1) shall be prepared after–

(a) identifying problem of the Ward, and

(b) fixation of priority of problems so identified.

12. Execution of Development Schemes

(1) When the Municipality/Notified Area Authority executes any development scheme in the Ward area, a beneficiary committee consisting of the citizens of the Ward, shall be constituted by the Committee, under its supervision, for looking after the work and making any suggestion related to the concerned work.

(2) The Committee shall make the work schedule of any development scheme available to the beneficiary committee constitute under sub-rule (1) for the purpose.

13. Powers of the Committee

(1) The chairman shall be entitled to–

(a) called for any information in so far as it relates to any matter within the Ward,

(b) call for any or all periodical statements relating to the receipts an disbursements.

(2) Any member may draw attention of the Chairman to any requirement of any locality or to any lapse in execution of the work or to any waste of the municipal fund or municipal property and may suggest any improvement which he considers desirable.

(3) The Committee may require, with the permission of the Municipality, any officer of the Municipality to attend any meeting of the Committee at which any matter dealt with by such officer in the course of his duties is being discussed. When any officer is thus required to attend any such meeting he may be called upon to make a statement of facts or furnish such information in his possession relating to any matter dealt with by him or produce any document or report as the Committee may require.

14. Duties of Municipality

(1) The Municipality shall make available to the Committee the following information:

(a) decisions of the Standing Committees;

(b) decisions or resolutions of the Municipality;

(c) Ward-wise budgetary allocation made by the Municipality;

(d) Copy of the Ward map;

(e) Details of municipal properties Ward-wise;

(f) Annual Financial Statement and Annual Administration Report;

(g) Demand and collection figures of tax and non-tax revenue of the Wards; and

(h) Such other information as required by the Committee.

(2) The Municipality, on a writer requisition form the chairman of the Committee, shall make available an advance amount required to meet the emergent needs of natural calamity, accident or any other reason, and the chairman of the Committee, within fifteen days from the date of receipt of such advance, shall submit a report of utilization of such sum and refund the unspent portion of such advance, if any, to the Municipality/Notified Area Authority.

(3) The Municipality shall provide an office for each Committee.

Part V

Creation of Internal Resources

15. Proposals for Creation of Internal Resources

(1) The Committee shall consider proposals for creation of internal resources to augment municipal income by way of,

(i) using land vested to the Government or Municipality/Notified Area Authority and land belonging to any Government department subject to permission of such department for:

(a) tree plantation on long term and short term basis; or

(b) constructing market complex, shops and buildings for commercial use; or

(c) integrating scattered small scale industries in industrial complexes; or

(d) constructing parking space for buses, trucks, car etc; or

(e) construction of housing complexes; or

(f) any other measure the committee considers feasible;

(ii) using private, public water bodies for promotion of pisciculture or entertainment purpose;

(iii) installing unconventional energy sources like solar electricity or biogas or any other alternative for commercial distribution;

(iv) using private land for commercial purpose on joint venture of Municipality/Notified Area Authority and the concerned owner;

(v) running municipal transport system on roadways and waterways for carrying good and passengers in such routes which are not covered by adequate public transport system and are financially viable; and

(vi) such other measures which the Committee considers feasible and viable.

(2) The Committee shall submit a detailed proposal for creation of internal resources, as specified in sub-rule (1), to the Municipality/Notified Area Authority:

provided that if it is felt by the Committee that involvement of other Ward/Wards is necessary for such creation of new resources, the Committee may interact with the Committee of such other Ward/Wards for finalisation of the proposal.

(3) It shall be obligatory on the part of the Municipality/Notified Area Authority to spend 60% of the income from the newly created internal resources, as per proposal of the Committee, in the Ward/Wards, where such new internal resources have been created, after deducting the cost for implementation of such project, if any.

16. Issue of General or Special Direction

The State Government may issue such general or special directions, not inconsistent with the provisions of the Act or these rules, as may, in its opinion, be necessary for the purpose of giving effect to these rules or for removing any difficulty in this regard.

Appendix-5

Extracts from the Relevant Sections of the West Bengal Panchayats (Amendment) Act, 1994

Gram Sabha means a body consisting of persons registered in the electoral rolls pertaining to a Gram declared as such under sub-section 1 of section 3.

Gram Sansad means a body consisting of persons registered at any time in the electoral rolls pertaining to a constituency of a Gram Panchayat delimited for the purpose of the last preceding general elections to the Gram Panchayat.

Amendment of section 16A

10. In section 16A of the principal Act–

(1) for the words Gram Sabha, wherever they occur, the words Gram Sansad shall be substituted;

(2) after sub-section (4), the following sub-section shall be inserted;-

"(4A) One-tenth of the total number of members shall form a quorum for a meeting of a Gram Sansad:

Provided that no quorum shall be necessary for an adjourned meeting which shall be held at the same time and place after seven days.";

(3) after sub-section (5), the following sub-section shall be inserted-

"(6) A Gram Sansad shall guide and advise the Gram Panchayat in regard to the schemes for economic development and social justice undertaken or proposed to be undertaken in its area and may, without prejudice to the generally of such guidance and advice-

(a) identify, or lay down principles for identification of the schemes which are required to be taken on priority basis for the economic development of the village,

(b) identify, or lay down principles for identification of the beneficiaries for various poverty alleviation programmes,

(c) constitute one or more beneficiary committees comprising nor more than nine persons, who are not members of the Gram Panchayat, for ensuring active participation of the people in the implementation, maintenance and equitable distribution of benefits of one or more schemes in its area,

(d) mobilize mass participation for community welfare programmes and programmes for adult education, family welfare and child welfare,

(e) promote solidarity and harmony among all sections of the people irrespective of religion, faith, caste, creed or race,

(f) record its objection to any action of the *Pradhan* or any other member of the Gram Panchayat for failure to implement any development scheme properly or without active participation of the people of that area."

The West Bengal Panchayats (Amendment) Act, 1994

Section 11-13

Insertion of new section 16B

"Public meeting of the Gram Sabha

11. After section 16A of the principal Act, the following section shall be inserted:

16B (1) Every Gram shall have a Gram Sabha consisting of persons registered in the electoral roll pertaining to the area of the Gram.

(2) Every Gram Panchayat shall hold within the local limits of the Gram an annual meeting, ordinarily in the month of December every year, of the Gram Sabha after completion of the half-yearly meeting of the Gram Sansads.

(3) One-twentieth of the total number of members shall form a quorum for a meeting of a Gram Sabha:

Provided that no quorum shall be necessary for an adjourned meeting which shall be held at the same time and place after seven days.

(4) The Gram Panchayat shall, at lest seven days before the date of holding the meeting referred to in sub-section (2), give public notice of such meetings by beat of drums as widely as possible, announcing the agenda, place, date and hour of the meeting. A notice of such meeting shall also be hung up in the office of the Gram Panchayat. Similar publicity shall also be given in the case of an adjourned meeting.

(5) A meeting of the Gram Sabha shall be presided over by the *Pradhan* of the concerned Gram Panchayat or, in his absence, bythe *Upa-Pradhan*.

(6) All questions coming before a Gram Sabha shall be discussed and points raised there shall be referred to the discussed and points raised there shall be referred to the Gram Panchayat for its consideration.

(7) The Gram Sabha shall deliberate upon, recommend for, and adopt resolution on, any matter referred to in sub-section (6) of section 16A and section 17A.

(8) The Gram Panchayat shall, on considering and collating the resolutions of the Gram Sansads, place before the Gram Sabha the resolutions of the Gram Sansads and the views of the Gram Panchayat together with its report on the actions taken and proposed to be taken on them for deliberating and recommendation by the Gram Sabha.

(9) The proceedings of the meetings of the Gram Sabha shall be recorded by such officer or employee of the Gram Panchayat or, in the absence of officers and employees of the Gram Panchayat, by such member of the Gram Panchayat as may be authorized by the presiding member in this behalf. Such proceedings shall be read out before the meeting is concluded and the presiding member shall then sign the proceedings."

Index

D

E

F

G